Reconciling Law and Legal Theory

This book is part of the Peter Lang Regional Studies list.
Every volume is peer reviewed and meets
the highest quality standards for content and production.

PETER LANG
New York • Bern • Berlin
Brussels • Vienna • Oxford • Warsaw

Reconciling Law and Legal Theory

A Translation of al-Tilmisānī's *Miftah al-Wusul*

Translated and Edited by
Mohammad S. Alrahawan

PETER LANG
New York • Bern • Berlin
Brussels • Vienna • Oxford • Warsaw

Library of Congress Cataloging-in-Publication Data

Names: Tilimsani, Muhammad ibn Ahmad, 710-771 AH/1310-1369 AD, author. | Alrahawan, Mohammad S.
Title: Reconciling law and legal theory: a translation of al-Tilmisānī's Miftah al-wusul/translated and edited by Mohammad S. Alrahawan.
Other titles: Miftah al-wuṣūl ilā binā᾿ al-furū῾ ῾ala al-uṣūl. English.
Description: New York: Peter Lang, 2020.
Includes bibliographical references and index.
Identifiers: LCCN 2019017562 | ISBN 978-1-4331-7017-1 (hardback: alk. paper)
ISBN 978-1-4331-7021-8 (ebook pdf) | ISBN 978-1-4331-7022-5 (epub)
ISBN 978-1-4331-7023-2 (mobi)
Subjects: LCSH: Islamic law—Interpretation and construction—Early works to 1800. | Evidence (Islamic law)—Early works to 1800. | Malikites—Early works to 1800.
Classification: LCC KBP440.55.T55 A3613 | DDC 340.5/9—dc23
LC record available at https://lccn.loc.gov/2019017562
DOI 10.3726/b15720

Bibliographic information published by **Die Deutsche Nationalbibliothek.**
Die Deutsche Nationalbibliothek lists this publication in the "Deutsche Nationalbibliografie"; detailed bibliographic data are available on the Internet at http://dnb.d-nb.de/.

The paper in this book meets the guidelines for permanence and durability of the Committee on Production Guidelines for Book Longevity of the Council of Library Resources.

Printed in the United States of America

With genuine humility, I acknowledge Your aid and Your endless support for me, my God. If this work is worth dedicating, please bless it with your acceptance.

Table of Contents

Transliteration of Arabic Words

Consonants:

ء	ʾ	ز	z	ق	q
ب	b	س	s	ك	k
ت	t	ش	sh	ل	l
ث	th	ص	ṣ	م	m
ج	j	ض	ḍ	ن	n
ح	ḥ	ط	ṭ	هـ	h
خ	kh	ظ	ẓ	و	w
د	d	ع	ʿ	ي	y
ذ	dh	غ	gh		
ر	r	ف	f		

Vowels:

Monographs		**Diphthongs**		**Geminate**	
ا	ā	لَو	*law*	تَبَعِيَّة	*taba'iyya*
و	ū	سيرٌ	*sayr*	سنيّ	*sanī*
ي	ī	طيٌّ	*ṭayy*	قوّة	*quwwa*
ى	ā	توّاً	*tawwan*	مرجوٌّ	*marjū*

Connected *Tā*ʾ:

ثقافةٌ	*Thaqāfa*
ثقافةٌ العصر	*Thaqāfat al-'aṣr*
الثقافة المعاصرة	*Al-thaqāfa al-mu'āṣira*

Initial glottal stop is not marked, for example *asbāb,* not *ʾasbāibn*
Initial long vowel is to be marked as follows: *ārā*ʾ
Ibn (son of) is replaced with ibn in the middle of a sentence but it written Ibn at the beginning.
Inflectional marks are only marked for the Quran and poetry.

Foreword by Translator

The main intent of *miftāḥ al-wuṣūl ilā binā' al-furū' 'alā al-uṣūl* is to provide a key for basing practical legal rulings on precepts of legal theory; a discipline that records and analyzes differences among legal theorists and demonstrates its impact on comparative law, which drove jurists of various intellectual backgrounds to draw variant rulings of legal issues. In the history of Muslim legal theory, six prominent authors attempted to answer this pivotal inquiry, that is, why do jurists differ? They all introduced genre on what was commonly known as *takhrīj al-furū' 'alā al-uṣūl,* or 'extracting a structural interrelation of theory and practice in Islamic law' (Ahmad, 2006, 1). Those six books are Dabbūsī's *Ta'sīs*, Zanjānī's *Takhrīj*, Isnawī's *Tamhīd*, Ibn al-Laḥḥām's *Qawā'id* and Timurtāshī's *Wuṣūl* in addition to Tilmsānī's *Miftāḥ*. Tilmsānī's work is the most influential of those six books. It postulates a basis for further interdisciplinary works in the realm of Islamic legal theory and its ramifications in modern *fiqh* issues. This translation assesses for revealing the contents of Tilmisānī's work and presenting it for English readers interested in Islamic law.

In addition to the book's being authored in the form of a fascinating hierarchy of high sense of coherence, the author rises high above bias and treats all the great schools of thought equally. He analyzes their methodology of reasoning and at many times he is critical to the Mālikī school to whom he belongs. This sets his book unique in the realm of Islamic legal literature and a powerful tool for the instruction of Islamic legal theory. Though being difficult to understand, it develops skills that enable a seeker of knowledge with crucial acumen to derive the law independently to pave his way in being a distinguished jurist.

The Author

Imam al-Sharīf abū ʿAbdullah Moḥammad b. Aḥmad al-Ḥasanī al-Tilmisānī al-Idrīsī was born in Tlemcen, a city in north-western Algeria, and the capital of the province of the same name, in 710 AH/1310 CE (Tunbaktī, 2000, 257; Ibn Maryam, n.d., 166). The eponym *al-sharīf* refers to his being one of the descendants of Prophet Moḥammad. Growing in a family of scholars and jurists, Tilmisānī could fully master Arabic syntax, Mālikī jurisprudence, polemics and scholastic theology. Al-Tilmiānī is a polymath independent legal theorist and jurist who belonged to the Mālikī school of law. Though being a Mālikī jurist of the highest caliber, Al-Tilmisānī proved his practice of independent personal reasoning by clearing himself of juristic emulation of Mālikīs (Wansharīsī, 1981, 126). Furthermore, he opted for juristic preferences contrary to predominant Ḥanafī, Mālikī, Shāfiʿ and Ḥanbalī approaches (Tilmisānī, 2013, 437; Farkūs, 2013, 135–8). Many of his contemporaries and followers described him as an encyclopedia, unique in knowledge and the head of Mālikī jurists in West Africa and Andalusia (Ibn Maryam, n.d., 167).

Due to dedicating his life for teaching and studying in Tlmisan, Fez and surrounding Moroccan provinces, Tilmisānī wrote a few works, yet they spanned the areas of Arabic grammar, Islamic theology, and Islamic law and legal theory. In addition of his *miftāḥ al-wuṣūl*, he wrote his *mathārāt al-ghalaṭ* (sources of erroneous argumentation), a short yet concise brief overview on fallacies that render a reasoning logically incorrect. The book was edited along with the *miftāḥ* in one critical and elaborate edition (Tilmisānī, 2013). He further wrote on ancillary sciences tailored to serve on the Islamic legal theory such as his commentary on Khawnajī's *Jumal* ([logical] statements) which elaborated on the science of logic (Wansharīsī, 1981, 126). He is further known for his book on *al-Qadar* (predestination) (Tunbaktī, 2000, 259), whose manuscript is lost, and for his juristic epistle on *muʿāwaḍāt* (financial transactions) (Ibn Maryam, n.d., 173). Tilmisānī was mentioned of authoring concise answers on juristic contemporary issues and on problems of Islamic legal theory.

Tilmisānī is the teacher of the great abū Isḥāq al-Shāṭibī (d.790/1388), the author of *al-I'tiṣām* (Holding Fast) and al-*Muwāfaqāt* (Congruities). Shāṭibī owes his knowledge of *ʿulūm ʿaqliyya* (rational sciences) to two great scholars.

First of them is Abū ʿAli Manṣūr al-Zawāwī, who lived in Granada between 753/1352 and 765/1363 until he was expelled. He had a great influence on Shāṭibī's knowledge of philosophy and theology. He was also benefited greatly from Abu ʿAbdullah al-Sharīf al-Tilmisani who was considered to be the most knowledgeable man of his time and to have attained the rank of *mujtahid* by his contemporaries.

Timisānī is further the teacher of Lisān al-Dīn al-Khaṭīb (d. 775/1374), who authored *al-Iḥāṭāh fī Akhbār Ghirnāṭah* (Compendium on the History of Granada) and ibn Khaldūn, the author of the *Prolegomena*. Tilmsānī had a great impact on ibn Khaldūn, who described his benign teacher by saying, "Nothing is absent from the mind of Tilmisānī of revelatory and rational sciences (Ibn Khaldūn, 1979, 57)."

Though being a target of their military adventures, Tilimsānī managed to be in the courts of political rulers of more than one dynasty. Tilimsān is known to have married the daughter of the Zayanid Sultan Abū Ḥammū Mūsa (d. 1359/760), who established a school for him (known as al-Madrasa al-Yabqʿbiyya or the Jacobean School), where Tilimsānī taught the religious sciences in which he excelled (Ahmad, 2014, 60). He had a strong relation with Abū ʿInān Fāris b. ʿAlī al-Muraynī who provided intellectual patronage for Tilmisānī. This is evident in Tilmisānī's acknowledgment of Abū ʿInān's efforts in his preface to the *miftāḥ*.

The Miftāḥ

The *miftāḥ* has been held a widely accepted textbook in the Muslim world for many year and has a great influence in scholarly circles in Africa and Andalusia. This is evident from the number of manuscripts still extant in Algeria, Morocco and Nigeria. Some of them were written in the ninth century by the well-known great jurist Wanshrīsī. Many of its manuscripts were written in the eleventh and twelfth Islamic centuries. Farkūs identified five manuscripts of the book which are still extant in different part of the world. (Farkūs, 2013, 179–183).

The book's title is *Miftāḥ al-Wuṣūl ilā Binā' al-Furū' 'alā al-Uṣūl*. It includes 189 principles of *fiqh* precepts which arose *uṣūlī* scholars' disagreement. It serves as an interdisciplinary textbook on how to relate *uṣūl* to *fiqh* and how to present *uṣūl* as an applied science with versatile examples that help a jurist in making decisions in practical legal questions. It provides a methodology for identifying reasons why scholars differ in providing various opinions on issues of *fiqh*.

According to Tilmisānī and the dominant approach of Muslim scholars of *uṣūl*, there is no legal determination without an evidence. An evidence may be a proof, in and of itself which includes Quran and Hadith, where a jurist refers to them directly or an evidence which is comprehensive of a proof such as *ijmā*ʿ and the report of uncollaborated view of a companion of the Prophet. Consensus is an evidence by virtue of the fact it must be based on a text from the Quran or Hadith and in its being based on overall infallibility of jurists' community; a concept which is inferred by jurists from Quran and Hadith. The view of a companion is an evidence due to a Companion's direct contact with the Prophet, his cognizance of the Arabic tongue, and versatile knowledge of *sharia* that qualify his view to be expressive of the intent and objective of the Lawgiver.

Based on his taxonomy of legal evidences, Tilmisāṣnī postulates four prerequisites for a revelatory proof to be authoritative. Personal reasoning practized by jurists in ascertaining the fulfillment of those conditions arose their disagreement in detailed *fiqh* problems. Tilmisānī observes that in order to be a valid legal source of law, a jurist must examine a revelatory proof by reference to its authenticity, meaning, efficacy in the sense of its continuity or being not abrogated and preponderance in case there is a conflict with other textual sources.

Tilmsānī presented a chapter for each criterion where he provided 16 principles on the question of authenticity of a transmitted text of the Quran or Hadith. Those principles discuss unquestionable admission of *mutawātir* reports and controversy over *aḥād* reports. On admission of *aḥād* he stipulates two major prerequisites mostly related to the verification of a reporter's integrity and exactitude in addition to the continuity and connectedness of the chain of transmission. He further discussed conflict between the text of a report and the view of its reporter; a controversial issue frequently raised in Ḥanafī-Shāfiʿī arguments.

On meaning, Tilmisānī provided 84 hermeneutical precepts which provoked disagreement among patrons and fellows of the early three schools of law. Those precepts discuss issues including the interpretation of commands and prohibitions, various inferences derived from a revelatory text, levels of ambiguity that may be present in these texts due to syntax, semantics, morphology and structure and how to clear them by reference to textual, contextual and paratextual clues. According to him a revelatory source may be a statement, an action or a tacit approval. The former's meaning may be imparted directly in the form of a pronounced meaning '*manṭūq*' or through logical and juridical construction in the form of an implied meaning '*mafhūm*'. Tilmisānī, therefore, discusses *manṭūq* by elaborating on the imperative form; an area where 'legal hermeneutics and the theory of practical legal determinations intersect, namely the area of interpreting commands and prohibitions (Ahmad, 2014, 84).' He further elaborates on Muslim approach of interpreting legal texts. According to Tilmsānī, a locution may be *naṣs* or *mjumal;* the former is a word which is linguistically appropriated to signify one specific meaning and *mujmal* refers to a term with multiple meanings. The latter is further classified into *mushtarak;* an equivocal text which imparts more than one meaning without discerning one as preponderant, *ẓāhir,* a text with a preponderant meaning and *mu'awwal;* a less preponderant meaning. Tilmsānī provided 8 major criteria where a location may retain its primary meaning or migrates to a secondary connotation based on contextual clues.

Tilmisānī's classification of implied meaning into convergent and divergent connotation clearly indicates his adoption of the Shāfiʿī theoretical approach of *uṣūl* which focuses on 'articulating the theoretical principles without necessarily attempting to relate them to the *fiqh* itself' (Kamali, 1991, 7). The controversy between Ḥanafīs and Shāfiʿīs over the validity of *mafhūm al-mukhālafa* or divergent meaning provided Tilmisānī with mines of examples which provoked juristic differences of subtle nuances. Timisānī's discussions on the Prophet's actions and tacit approvals were comparatively limited since 'all, these actions and tacit approvals have been reported as texts (can we read into this practice an anticipation of Derrida's *il n'est pas de text?*) (Ahmad, 2014, 107)'.

Questions on abrogation included 13 principles while those on conflicting texts included 20 precepts. Rational precepts related to *istiṣḥāb* included three precepts only while discussions of analogy, which is primarily based on a hybrid employment of both rational and revelatory evidence, included 48 principles. Sources of law are, according to Tilmisānī, revelation, reason and mix of both. This is the reason Tilmsānī did not assign a section of his book on *ḥukm,* as many earlier *uṣūlīs* like Ghazālī did.

Tilmisān's work is restricted to comparing the views of only three schools of law; Ḥanafī, Mālikī and the Shāfiʿī. Like Averroes; Tilmisānī did not provide discussions advocated by Ḥānābilī approach.

Other books on *ikhtlāf* or juristic differences such as Ibn Rushd's (Averroes') *Bidāyat al-mujtahid* is considered to be a book on *khilāf,* a discipline that records and analyzes the differences among Muslim jurists (ibn Rushd, *Distinguished:* xxviii). Ibn Rushd traces those differences to reasons he mentioned at the preface of his book. It is basically a book of comparative Islamic law. It tackles and records the views of different schools of law and compares them. The difference between the *Miftāḥ* and ibn Rushd's *Bidāya* is that the former attempts to recount the impact of theory on practice while the latter attempted a reverse process by relating detailed *fiqh* issues to their legal theoretical precepts. It shares Tilimsānī's goal of imparting skills that qualify a distinguished learner of law to become an independent *practitioner* by explaining reasons for juristic differences. Averroes' book goes from bottom to top while the book of Tilmisānī starts with theory and ends up with practice.

Miftāḥ is not purely like textbooks of *uṣūl* books which provide elucidation of the basic concepts and structures of *fiqh* methodology from a Hanafi or Shāfiʿī perspective or a hybrid of both. Tilmisānī's work differs in the sense that it solely discusses issues of difference among scholars of *uṣūl* and how could their difference in precepts influence their various prospective views on practical *fiqh* issues. It is more technically classified as 'applied *uṣūl.*'

According to Ahmad, "*the takhrīj al-furū' 'ala al-uṣūl* literature has neither weighed heavily in Muslim students' study of Islamic legal history nor been introduced as yet to English-speaking audiences" (Ahmad 2006: xxv). English readers completely miss a text on the genre to vision the significance of the field. In Arabic we have six main books embarking on the issue of *takhrīj* in addition to a Ph.D. Dissertation and two MA theses, all written in Arabic with the exception of the Ph.D. None of those Arabic works have been introduced to the English reader. A translation of Tilmisānī's work would contribute to an understanding of Islamic law for English readers.

The 14th century scholar Tilimsānī, while well-known in Muslim and Arabic-speaking contexts, has not received as much attention in Western scholarship, in part owing to a dearth of sources. As the project is a translation and not a monographic study, its primary and outstanding contribution to the field of Islamic Studies is to bring an essential work by an important figure in Islamic law to wider audiences. There are a number of commentaries on the *Miftāḥ* in Arabic, and it is still studied in Muslim educational contexts. This is evidence of the work's importance both to the Islamic legal tradition and to the history of legal systems in the Middle East today. Unfortunately, there is a general scarcity of reliable English translations of crucial works of Islamic legal theory such as the *Miftāḥ*. Those that do exist are often unwieldly for the classroom and not well-referenced enough for researchers.

The Arabic Original

The translation of Tilmisānī's *Miftāḥ* was based on manuscript no. 1167 of the *Real Bibliotheca del Monasterio San la Lorenzo del Escorial*, Spain. The manuscript was written by ʿAbdul-ʿAzīz ibn Ibrahīm ibn Hilāl Al-Sajlamāsī (d. 910 AH/1504 AD). I have also based the translation on other various edited and published copies of the book in addition to one of the modern published commentaries. They include the following references:

Tilmisānī, al-Sharīf abū ʿAbdullah Muḥammad b. Aḥmad al-Ḥasanī al-Tilmisānī al- (2013). *Miftāḥ al-Wuṣūl ila Binā' al-Furūʿ ʿala al-Uṣūl*. Ed. Muṣtafa Shaykh Muṣtafa. Beirut: Dār al-Reisāla.

Tilmisānī, al-Sharīf abū ʿAbdullah Muḥammad b. Aḥmad al-Ḥasanī al-Tilmisānī al- (2013). *Miftāḥ al-Wuṣūl ila Binā' al-Furūʿ ʿala al-Uṣūl*. Ed. Abū ʿAbdul-Muʿiz Muḥammad ʿAlī Farkūs. Algeria: Dār al-Mawqiʿ and Dār al-ʿAwāṣim.

Sarīrī, abū al-Ṭaiyyb Mawlūd al-Sūsī al- (2012). *Sharḥ Miftāḥ al-Wuṣūl ila Binā' al-Furūʿ ʿala al-Uṣūl*. Beirtu: Dār al-Kutub al-ʿIlmiyya.

Acknowledgements

This work would not have been possible without the support of my teacher shaykh professor Moustafa ibn Karmatullah Makhdoum; professor of Islamic legal theory at the University of Taiba, Medina, to whom I read the Arabic book during my writing of the translation. I am especially indebted to Heather Shaw, who edited a good part of my translation. I am grateful to all my students who read first drafts including Hafiza Aimaq. I would like to thank my parents, whose love and guidance are with me in whatever I pursue. They are the ultimate role models. Most importantly, I wish to thank my loving and supportive family.

Medina
Ramadan 12 th, 2040 AH/ May 17, 2019 AD.

Acknowledgements

The Author's Preface

In the name of Allah, the most Gracious, the most Merciful. May blessings and peace of Allah be upon our master and leader Moḥammad and on his family and companions. The doctor of religion, jurist and erudite, sole and all surprising in knowledge, the horseman of excogiated and discerned knowledge, the author of *fiqh* precepts and their derivatives, abū ʿAbdullah Moḥammad ibn Aḥmad ibn ʿAlī al-Sharīf al-Ḥasanī al-Tilimmisānī said:

Praise is due to Allah the One who created the creation as evidence of Him and sent Messengers from amongst themselves to guide them. Prayers are on them all in general and on Moḥammad and his family in particular. It is prayers that we will find [its outcome] before His Hands.

To proceed, knowledge is the best of all human traits and the greatest of all divine gifts, especially religious knowledge of *sharia*. It is the most lustrous in the sky and its august. The people of knowledge are the most dignified amongst those who occupy noble ranks. By virtue of its influence, the greatest terror of the severe torment will be averted. By the light of its guidance people will illumine in the abyss of resurrection and access gardens of bliss. Those who revive what was effaced of the sciences of religion and retain a greater share of them will [definitely] seize happiness along with high zeal.

It is him; [Abū ʿInān Fāris ibn ʿAlī al-Muraynī] the one who subdued knights of Arabs and non-Arabs, whose bountiful hands embark on arts of sword and pen, who united the words of [the people of] Islam after being scattered, who deterred the oppressive and the wicked and stopped their injustices until the ropes of his safety extended to all of his subjects, so that they have been dressed in its ample garments and in its surety they remain in peace. He rained them with clouds of his benevolence so that they rushed into taking his large bounties in ease, and lived under his mighty shelter in peace. He is the one who averted away whatever they feared of and showered upon them of whatever they wished, the master of people, the Caliph and commander of the faithful, the reliant on the Lord of worlds; abū ʿInān, may Allah keep him with the good omens that tell of his elevation and enjoy the times that add to his pleasures. He had full mastery of preserving legal evidences through his witted and shrewd mind. Through his right and triumphant opinion, he could easily grasp a grip of all inquiries and, thus, became conclusive of disclosed arguments among disputants. He could remove obscurities by revealing mysteries. I wanted to gain through this epitome a great fortune of closeness to him so that I attempted to compile these innovative dicta and subtle nuances of sciences. His bounty, may God support him, is to endow this work with a pleasant approval to let its author attain the end of his hope. I am going to start it by the mighty of the Almighty, the One sought for help and in Him we trust.

Evidence, which is the basis for any ruling pertaining to an issue of jurisprudence, falls under one of two classifications: (1) evidence that is proof, in and of itself [such as a Quranic passage or a hadith]; or (2) evidence which is comprehensive of a proof [such as consensus[1] or the uncorroborated opinion of a Companion[2]].

Evidence that is a proof in and of itself is further classified into two categories:

(a) That which is an independent legislative source [such as a Quranic passage or an authentic report from the Prophet, which are sufficient to substantiate a legal verdict without recourse to further substantiating evidence].
(b) That which is a corollary proven by a legislative source [whereby the legal ruling is determined by means of analogical reasoning, as in the case of *qiyās*].

Independent legislative sources are further classified into:

(i) That which is a transmitted source [such as Quran or Sunna]
(ii) That which is an inferred source [that is, *istiṣḥāb* (presumption of continuity)[3]].

Notes

1. *Ijmā'* is defined as the unanimous agreement of the *mujtahidūn* (jurists with high qualifications) of the Muslim community following the demise of the Prophet Muḥammad with regard to any matter (Āmidī, n.d., 1, 196; Shawkānī, 1999, 71). It is not the consensus of the *mujtahidūn* that constitutes the proof that is the essence of the evidence; rather, it is the Quranic phrase, the report, or the analogy upon which the consensus is based.
2. The opinion or *fatwa* of a single Companion is not considered legal proof, in and of itself. Instead, it is the Companion's direct contact with the Prophet, his cognizance of the Arabic tongue, and versatile knowledge of *sharia* that qualify his view to be expressive of the intent and objective of the Lawgiver.
3. According to the Shāfi'īs and Ḥanbalīs, *istiṣḥāb* denotes continuation of that which is established, and negation of that which is not. *Istiṣḥāb*, in other words, presumes the continuation of both the positive and the negative, until the contrary is established by evidence (Kamali, 1991, 338). In this sense it cannot be regarded as a transmitted source; rather, it is an inference drawn on the basis of a Quranic narration or hadith.

CHAPTER ONE

Transmitted Proof [Quran and Ḥadīth]

[To be authoritative,] a transmitted proof must: (1) have an authentic chain of transmission to the Prophet; (2) clearly indicating the intended ruling; (3) be continuously effective [in the sense that it has not been abrogated]; and (4) outweigh any other conflicting proofs.

Each of these four conditions shall be addressed in separate chapters [as follows:

1.1. The authenticity of a transmitted text
1.2. The meaning of a transmitted text
1.3. On the continuity of a transmitted proof
1.4. On the predominance of a transmitted proof].

1.1. The Authenticity of a Transmitted Proof

[The chain of transmission of a] revealed source [of legislation] is either *mutawātir* (consecutively recurrent) or *āḥād* (solitary). *Mutawātir* describes a narration by a group of people whose collusion to forge a lie is inconceivable. *Āḥād* is any report that does not attain the classification of *mutawātir*. Each of these shall be covered in a separate section.

1.1.1. *Tawātur*[1]

Legislative evidence is derived either from the Quran or from hadith. In the case of the Quran, the text must [necessarily] be *mutawātir*.[2] In the case that it is not, it cannot be considered [part of the] Quran.[3] Thus, an argument based on a source that is alleged to be Quran, but which is not *mutawātir*, is invalidated [simply] by proving that the source is not *mutawātir*.

An example of this is the Shāfiʿīs' position that prohibition [of marriage] is effected by five [separate] breast-feedings,[4] whereby anything less than this does not effect this prohibition. Their position is based on what was reported in *Ṣaḥīḥ Muslim*, on the authority of ʿĀʾisha (may Allah be pleased with her), who said:

> One of the revelations of the Quran was that prohibition of marriage is constituted by ten known breast-feedings. Later, this was abrogated to be "five known breast-feedings" and when the Messenger of Allah passed away, this was still being recited as part of the Quran.[5]

Our [Mālikī] companions would argue that this position is invalid, as such an injunction would have to be *mutawātir* to be part of the Quran. Being that it is not, it follows that it cannot be considered part of the Quran.

The Shāfiʿīs counter argue that *tawātur* is [only] a prerequisite for a narration to be recited as scripture; not [to establish] the ruling [it entails]. Thus, according to them, the intent of the narration, in this case, is to establish the ruling of five breast-feedings, rather than to establish the validity of its recitation.

Another example is the Ḥanafīs' position that the fasting of a person who is expiating for having broken a vow must be for three consecutive days. If his fasts are not consecutive, the expiation will be invalid, according to Ibn Masʿūd's reading of Q. 5: 89:

"Then a fast of three *consecutive* days [is required]."[6]

Our Mālikī companions, however, would argue that this addition is not a part of the Quran as it does not meet the condition of being *mutawātir*[7].

Likewise, the Ḥanafīs adopted the position that if a man swears not to have sexual relations with his wife, he may only return to normal spousal relations within four months of his oath, not after the expiry [of the four-month time limit]. They based their view on the reading variant of Ubayy ibn Kaʿb of (Q. 2: 226):

But if they return *within those* [months to normal relations]—then indeed, Allah is Forgiving and Merciful.

Our Mālikī companions argue that returning to normal relations should take place upon the expiry of the four months. The basis for their refutation of the Ḥanafī position lies in the fact that the additional wording in Ubayy's variant cannot be considered Quran because it was not transmitted by *tawātur*,[8] and to be a part of the Quran the narration must be *mutawātir*.

[The Ḥanafīs] counter argue that such an addition must [necessarily] have either been part of the Quran, or a statement [from the Prophet]. Were this not so, it would have been prohibited for the reciter to recite it [as part of the Quran], as doing so would be deceptive.

On the other hand, whether [this addition] is part of the Quran or a statement [of the Prophet], it is incumbent to act accordingly, as *tawātur* is a prerequisite for the validity of recitation, not a condition for the obligation of acting accordingly.

As for the Sunna, narrations that are cited as evidence are not required to be *mutawātir*, according to the foremost scholars of the foundations of *fiqh*, except when they must reach the definitive level [of a ruling indicated by a narration] of the Quran, in which case, the sunna narration must be *mutawātir*. An example of this is the evidence cited by the dominant majority of scholars and by Imam Mālik in what is viewed to be the stronger of his two opinions regarding the [legality] of wiping over leather boots [when performing ablution]. These scholars' evidence is based on the statements and practices of the Companions, to the extent that this practice was attributed to seventy of the Prophet's companions.

It could be argued that these reports are [merely] *āḥād* (solitary) narrations, and thus, they do not carry the authority to qualify the injunction in Allah's words "*and [wash] your feet*" Q. 5: 6.[9]

This is refuted by the fact that though each report is transmitted [solitarily], they collectively are *mutawātir* in expressing [the legality] of wiping over boots. [Technically] this is known as conceptual *tawātur*,[10] such as [what is known regarding] the courage of ʿAlī and the generosity of Ḥātim. Although no specific incidents were transmitted to us by *tawātur* indicating ʿAlī's courage or Ḥātim's generosity, many isolated incidents were transmitted by way of solitary narrations, all agreeing on a collective theme, that is, the courage [of ʿAlī] or the hospitality [of Ḥātim]. However, the [text of the] Glorious Quran is an example for verbatim *mutwātir*.

1.1.2. *Aḥād* Narrations

With regard to *āḥād* narrations, scholars have raised objections related to their chain of transmission from two perspectives:

- General objections on *aḥād* narrations
- Particular objections on certain reports

1.1.2.1. General Objections on *āḥād*

Scholars of *fiqh* methodology differ with regard to their acceptance of *āḥād* reports in general. When an *āḥād* report is cited to prove a legal ruling, one may raise the objection that he does not accept solitary reports as a whole.[11] The answer [to such an objection] is found in the established principles of *fiqh*.

An example of this is: when someone objects to [a legal ruling] by discrediting a specific report. For instance, to establish the requirement of [the consent of the bride's] guardian for validity of marriage [Mālikī] companions relied on the Prophet's saying "No marriage [is valid] without [the consent of] a guardian."[12] Similarly, they refer to the Prophet's saying, "He who touches his penis must perform ablution"[13] to prove that a man's state of ablution is invalidated if he touches his penis; and to the Prophet's saying, "Every intoxicant is unlawful"[14] to prove the prohibition of [drinking] *nabīdh*.[15] A Ḥanafī, however, being that he differs regarding these three rulings, will state that none of these reports is authentic based on the statement of Ibn Maʿīn, who said, "Three traditions are not authentically attributed to the Prophet (may God exalt his mention). They are: 'No marriage is valid without the permission of the guardian', 'He who touches his penis must perform ablution', and 'Each intoxicant is unlawful.'"

Our answer is that a statement, such as Ibn Maʿīn's, cannot discredit a hadith that fulfills the conditions of authenticity because he did not clarify the reason for rejecting these reports. It may be that these hadiths do not support his view.

Another objection [to *āḥād* narrations] is the objection of Abū Ḥanīfa's companions [who reject any narration pertaining to] a widespread situation that has not been reported with *tawātur*. It is their position that *tawātur* is a condition for [the authenticity of a report related to] a common incident.

Our [Mālikī] companions and the companions of al-Shāfiʿī have, however, proved the necessity of performing ablution upon touching one's penis according to the narration by Busra, who reported the Prophet (may God exalt his mention) saying, "He who touches his penis must perform ablution." The companions of Abū Ḥanīfa argue that this is an *āḥād* report concerning something that happens frequently, and that which relates to such a widespread occurrence that it should have been reported through multiple narrators due to the common need for it. Thus, if such a report is not transmitted by *tawātur*, it follows that the report must be null and void.

Likewise, al-Shāfiʿī's fellows and Ibn Ḥabīb of our [Mālikī] companions maintained that the purchaser and seller have the option to effect the transaction or cancel it, as long as they are [physically] at the same session, according to the Prophet's saying, "Both parties in a business transaction have the right of withdrawal so long as they have not separated, unless it is a sale subject to an option."

The fellows of Abū Ḥanīfa assert that this is an *āḥād* tradition related to an oft-occurring incident, which cannot, therefore, be accepted.

Our answer and that of al-Shāfiʿī's fellows is that an *āḥād* tradition is unrestrictedly accepted, as is established in *uṣūl*. We [that is, Malikīs] have not admitted the option to cancel a sale contract due to [our] preference of the practice of the people of Medina.

Another reason [for scholars' objections regarding the authority of an *āḥād* narration] is when the report has been criticized by one of our righteous ancestors, not on the basis of its transmission, but rather from a rational, analytical perspective. For example, the majority [of jurists] maintained the legal obligation of washing one's hands before immersing them in water to be used for ablution on the basis of the Prophet's words, "When one wakes up from sleep he should not put his hands in the ablution water until he has washed them three times."[16] An opponent may argue that ibn ʿAbbās objected to this hadith, therefore, when it reached him and he heard it he said, "What then should one do if he uses a *mihrās*[17] for ablution?"

Likewise, the Shāfiʿīs and our [Mālikī] fellows cited the report of Sahl ibn Abī Ḥathma, regarding the story of Ḥuwayyiṣa and Muḥayyiṣa. According to the report, the Prophet (may God exalt his mention), upon the Jews' denial of the claim, said, "Will you swear fifty oaths and thereby be entitled to take the blood money of your companion or the blood money from the murderer?[18]" Thus, the Prophet started by asking the plaintiffs to swear [to the truth of their accusation] before asking the defendants to swear. The companions of Abū Ḥanīfa answer this by saying that this hadith was rejected by ʿAmr ibn Shuʿayb, who said, "This is not the norm, nor did the Prophet asked them to swear on things they do not know."[19]

The answer, according to our [Mālikī] companions, is that hadith cannot be criticized due to its [apparent] conflict with common sense if it meets the conditions [of an authentic report]. This is because the Prophet (may God exalt his mention) is a lawgiver, and most probably, that which was believed to be illogical may be a misunderstanding or there may be a reason for it.

Thus we have covered what concerns [overall objections to] the chain of transmission of *āḥād* reports.

1.1.2.2. Particular Objections

[To be authoritative] the chain of narration of a hadith must consist of accredited narrators connecting all the way back to the Prophet (may God exalt his mention). These are two of the conditions.

1.1.2.2.1. Credibility of a Narrator

The narrator must be of good character and accurate. Let us discuss the integrity first, and then accuracy.

An accusation against a narrator's character may either be related to a specific hadith [he relates], or it may be related to his integrity in general.

Examples of accusations related to a specific hadith include [When a source denies the report of someone who transmitted it from him].

An example of this is our [Mālikī] companions' proof for the requirement [of the presence of the bride's] guardian [when contracting] marriage based on the Prophet's words "Any woman who marries without the permission of her guardian, her marriage is invalid, her marriage is invalid, her marriage is invalid. If he has intercourse with her, then the dowry is for her in lieu of his intimacy with her. If they dispute, then the ruler is the guardian for who has no guardian."[20] This narration is related by ibn Jurayj through Sulaymān ibn Mūsa from ibn Shihāb al-Zuhrī. Ibn Jurayj said, "When I met with ibn Shihāb I asked him [about this report] but he told me he did not know it." When a narrator denies what has been reported on his authority, it cannot be used as evidence, as in the case with testimony.

Our answer to this is that the source of the narration did not explicitly accuse the person who transmitted the hadith from him of being a liar. Thus, if a trustworthy narrator relates a hadith on that source's authority, the hadith should be followed, even if the source [later] forgets what he had previously reported. It is common among narrators of hadith that the source of a hadith may relate the same hadith from someone who transmitted it from him if he forgot the narration he previously transmitted. Al-Dāraquṭnī compiled a brief book on this [subject].[21]

In the case that a source explicitly belies someone who has transmitted from him, we ascertain that one of them must be lying. According to the principles of *fiqh*, however, this does not cast doubt on other reports transmitted by either of them, as it is impossible to definately ascertain which of them has lied.

A source's forgetfulness only affects the report of someone who transmits from him when bearing witness, due to the strictness [required] in testimonies. That is why other conditions are required for testimony to be considered, such as the number of witnesses and their being free and male; while such conditions are not required for the transmission of a hadith.

To further elucidate the matter, eye witnesses (the source of a report) may authorize others to deliver their testimony before the judge on their behalf. In the case that they forget their testimony, however, they cannot empower anyone else to deliver it in their place. This is contrary to the case of a transmitter of a report, who does not authorize anyone to deliver it on his behalf. A full discussion [of this issue] can be found in books of *fiqh*.

Furthermore, one of the causes that impairs a narrator's integrity is when he or she solely reports an addition [in the text of a *hadith*] while the report is being related by his colleagues without giving mention to such an addition. An example is our [Mālikī] fellows' proving that the minimum *zakat*-payable amount for crops is five *wasaqs*[22] according to what was related from the Messenger of Allah (may God exalt his mention): "There is one tenth [due] on land watered by rain. There is a twentieth [due] on land irrigated by wells, if it reaches five *wasaqs*."

The followers of Abū Ḥanīfa would argue that this addition is not verified to be a part of the hadith because the majority of those who related this report have not referred to it. It casts doubt on its narrator.

Our answer is that the addition [of a trustworthy narrator] cannot negate the [original] report, as long as it is not decisively revoked by the majority. We can decisively assure [conflict] if the session [in which the two reports were related] is one and the same and all were present to [assure] nothing has been accidently forgotten [of the report]. Therefore, one finds no suspicion with such a report.

An example of a general objection regarding [a narrator's] integrity[23] is when he is classified as a liar,[24] or when he quotes rejected reports.[25] For example, our [Mālikī] companions proved the inappropriateness of briefly sitting after the second prostration [of prayer], before standing, on the basis of the report that the Messenger of Allah (may God exalt his mention) would get up during his prayer on the tips of his feet.[26]

The companions of al-Shāfiʿī would argue *hadith* is related by Khālid ibn Ilyās through his chain of transmission, on the authority of Abū Hurayra. Khālid, according to the scholars of *hadith*, was known to quote rejected reports. The answer is that the report we used in our argument is not solely related by Khālid from Abū Hurayra, but it is also related by another [parallel] path of transmission, as it is related by al-Aʿmash through [various] paths of transmission, on the authority of ibn Masʿūd, ibn ʿUmar, ibn ʿAbbās and others.[27]

If a report is exclusively related by a single narrator, without [also] being transmitted through other [reliable] sources, it cannot be used as a legal proof. For example, Abū Ḥanīfa's followers have proved the obligation of rinsing the mouth and nose thrice when performing the ritual bath, according to the Prophet's saying, "Rinsing the mouth and sniffing water into the nose three times are obligatory constituents of a ritual bath."[28] Our [Mālikī] fellows would argue that the report is only related through Baraka ibn Muḥammad. Moreover, al-Daraquṭnī stated that he used to forge *hadiths*.[29]

Another [cause that may question a narrator's integrity] is when his religion is generally blemished, such as [in the case of] the report cited by our [Mālikī] companions to exempt a person following [the *imam* in prayer] from reciting *surat al-Fātiḥa* [in congregation]. It is reported that the Messenger of Allah (may God exalt his mention) said, "If one has an *imam* [leading him in *ṣala*], then the recitation of the *imam* serves the purpose of his recitation."[30] In other words, it is no longer incumbent upon him to recite *al-Fatiha* because the recitation of the *imam* suffices him.

The companions of al-Shāfiʿī may argue that this *hadith* is related by Jābir al-Juʿfi[31] who avowed reincarnation[32]. Our [Mālikī] companions would answer that they have received the same report through a different path of transmission attributed to Ḥanīfa ibn Mūsa ibn Abī ʿĀʾisha from ʿAbdullah ibn Shaddād from Jābir ibn ʿAbdullah.

Another [defect that impairs uprightness] is when a narrator's integrity is not verified. He is, then, called *majhūl al-ḥāl.*[33] According to one of the two variant views [of Mālik, as recorded in his] *al-Mudawwana*,[34] it is permissible to turn one's face towards the *kaʿaba* [while answering the call of nature] as long as one is screened, even if there is no necessity to do so. This is according to the report of Khālid ibn Abī al-Ṣalt through his chain of transmission on the authority of ʿĀʾisha who said, "A mention of a people, who disliked to turn their faces towards *qibla* with their private parts was made in the presence of the Messenger of Allah (may God exalt his mention). Thereupon, he said, 'I think that they indeed have acted thus'. Turn my seat towards *qibla.*" This [legal ruling] is specific to indoor toilets.

A proponent of this view amongst our [Mālikī] fellows and others may argue that Khālid ibn Abū al-Ṣalt is of unverified integrity. According to Abū Thawr, a report from someone of unverified character cannot be used as a proof.

Our fellows' answer is that he is recognized as an upright and trustworthy transmitter because reliable transmitters such as Mubārak ibn Fuḍāla and Wāṣil, the client of ibn ʿUyayna, and others who were known for exclusively quoting qualified narrators transmitted accounts on his authority.

However, if it is feasible to relate the same report through another narrator who is known for his trustworthiness, our fellows [among the Mālikīs] can effectively respond to this argument by introducing this point. It is important to note that scholars of *uṣūl* differed on accrediting a report transmitted from *majhūl al-ḥāl.* The issue is fully explained in the books of *uṣūl.*[35]

1.1.2.2.2. Accuracy of a Narrator

Discrepancy, in this regard, may be for two reasons:

First, a disputant may argue that a specific narrator is of excessive errors or he is inattentive.[36] Such is the case of our Western [Mālikī] fellows[37] who referred to the report of ibn al-Qāsim [from Mālik] to prove that raising hands in *ṣala* is [recommended] only on the commencement of prayer,[38] due to what is related that the Messenger (may God exalt his mention) used to raise his hands upon the commencement of prayer, but he did not repeat it [within prayers].[39]

An opponent among the shāfiʿīs and our Eastern [Mālikī] fellows may argue that this report is of Yazīd ibn abī Ziyād, on whom the scholars of Hadith said, "He was [classified as] chronic forgetful and became jumbled in his late age."[40] During his stay in Mecca, Sufyān ibn ʿUyayna reported him relating that the Messenger of Allah (may God exalt his mention) used to raise his hands on bowing down. Sufyān said, "When I reached Kufa I heard him saying, 'The Prophet (may God exalt his mention) used to raise his hands on the commencement of his *ṣala* and he did not repeat that [within prayers].' I made sure that his students instructed him to add [to the original]."[41]

The answer of our [Eastern Malikī] fellows is that they do not relate the report through Yazīd only, but they relate it through ʿĀṣim ibn Kulayb from his father on the authority of ʿAlī ibn abī Ṭālib.[42]

Second, a narrator may be of those who [frequently] interpolate their views [into texts] so that the Prophet's statements cannot be discerned.[43] An example is the argument of abū Ḥanīfa's companions who stated that the four supererogatory *rakʿas* prior to *ẓuhr* are to be offered continuously without a final salutation in between due to the Prophet's saying, "Offering four [supererogatory] *rakʿas* before *ẓuhr* without being separated by the final salutation gets the gates of heavens open."[44]

Our [Mālikī] and Shāfiʿī fellows may argue [by saying] that this hadith is related by ʿUbayda ibn al-Muʿattib al- Ḍabbī.[45] Yūsuf ibn Khālid al-Samtī[46] asked him, "Have you heard all what you narrate?" He said, "I heard some of it while some were analogically deducted." He said, "Relate to us [only] what you hear and leave what you analogically deduce because I am more aware of analogy than you." Therefore, such a narrator's report cannot be used as a proof since it is probable to be of his personal reasoning.

The Ḥanafīs answer that the report has explicitly indicated that it is of the Prophet's saying according to the version of abū Ayyūb al-Anṣārī, who asked the Messenger of Allah (may God exalt his mention) whether to pronounce the final salutation [in between the four *rakʿas*]. The Prophet said, "No".[47] This is an explicit clarification, which leaves no room to think it is [a personal reasoning].

1.1.2.2.3. Continuity of the Transmission Path

The second condition of [elaborate discussion on *sanad*] is the continuity of the transmission line [from a compiler] all the way back to the Prophet (may God exalt his mention). The continuity and connectivity of a report back to the Prophet may be impaired either due to *inqiṭāʿ*, where an interruption occurs in the chain of transmission because of a missing link between two narrators,[48] or due to *irsāl*, when one who has not accompanied the Prophet ascribes a report to the Prophet (may God exalt his mention) without identifying the Companion who [directly] received it [from the Prophet],[49] or due to *waqf*, where a report does not end with the Prophet (may God exalt his mention).[50] These are three defects:

i. *Inqiṭā*ʿ

The first defect is *Inqiṭā*ʿ.[51] An example is our [Mālikī] companions' proving that one who is certain of incurring a harm [to his life] or of being seriously ill may perform dry ablution due to the report of ʿAmr ibn al-ʿĀṣ in which he said, "I had a wet dream on a cold night in the battle of *Dhāt al-Salāsil.*[52] I was afraid, if I washed I would die. I, therefore, performed dry ablution and led my companions in the dawn prayer. They mentioned that to the Messenger of Allah (may God exalt his mention). He said, 'Have you led your companions in prayer while you were sexually defiled?' I informed him of the cause which impeded me from washing. And I said, 'I heard Allah say: "Do not kill yourselves; verily Allah is merciful to you."' The Messenger of Allah (may God exalt his mention) laughed and did not say anything."[53] The companions of al-Shāfiʿī argue that *Hadith* chain of transmission '*munqaṭi*ʿ' because it is related by ʿAbdur-Raḥmān ibn Jubayr who did not hear it from ʿAmr ibn al-ʿĀṣ. If a report is of an interrupted chain of narrators, it cannot be used as a [legal] proof.

The answer of our [Mālikī] companions is that the line of transmission is connected through abū Qays, the client of ʿAmr ibn al-ʿĀṣ. ʿAbdur-Raḥmān ibn Jubayr heard it from abu Qays. Abū Qays received it from ʿAmr ibn al-ʿĀṣ.[54] This may be relevant to the issue of a report related by a narrator of unproven integrity '*majhūl al-ʿadālah*'. It is not accepted by our [Mālikī] companions, but it is approved by the companions of Abū Ḥanīfa. The extent status of a missing narrator is to be of unverified identity '*majhūl al-ḥāl*'.

ii. *Irsāl*

The second defect is *irsāl.*[55] An example of it is our [Mālikī] companions' proving that a marriage contract must have a guardian due to the Prophet's saying, "No marriage is valid without the permission of the guardian."[56] However, the companions of Abū Ḥanīfa state that this report was related by Abū Isḥāq on the authority of Abū Burda[57] from the Prophet, while abū Burda did not hear it from the Prophet (may God exalt his mention).[58]

The answer of our [Mālikī] companions is that *mursal* traditions are accepted because the *tabiʿūn*[59] did not cease quoting *mursal* reports, and using them as [legal] proofs because it became well-known that they only quote trustworthy narrators.

Moḥammad ibn Isḥāq al-Imām said, "I asked Moḥammad ibn Yaḥya[60] on this issue and he informed me that the report of Isrā'īl from Abū Isḥāq on the authority of Abū Burda is authentic in my view." I said to him, "Is it related by Shu'ba and al-Thawrī from Abū Isḥāq on the authority of Abū Burda from the Prophet?" He said, "Yes, this is how we relate it, but it was [further] narrated from Isrā'īl from abū Burda on the authority of his father from the Prophet. They used to relate it as *mursal* [with a missing link between Abū Burda and the Prophet], but when they were inquired [about this missing link] they used to [name it and] trace the report back to the Prophet." Furthermore, there is a group of narrators [other than Isrā'īl] who related it through abū Mūsa [the father of abū Burda] from the Prophet.

iii. *Waqf*

The third defect [that impairs a report] is *waqf*.[61] An example is our [Mālikī] companions' proving that *i'tikāf*[62] is not valid except when it is accompanied by fasting, due to 'Āi'sha's report that the Prophet said, "*I'tikāf* is not valid without fasting."[63] The Shāfi'īs argue that it is a statement of 'Ā'isha. al-Bayhaqī said, "It cannot be elevated to the Prophet." The answer of our [Mālikī] companions is that the report was related by 'Aṭā' from 'Ā'isha as a statement of hers, but al-Zuhrī has further related it through 'Urwa from 'Ā'isha as a statement of the Prophet.[64] When a saying is being elevated to the Prophet according to one version, there is no problem of attributing it to a companion according to another version. It is possible that a Companion has issued [the text] as a religious verdict [without ascribing it to the Prophet].[65]

Similarly, [scholars] disagree on certain statements whether to attribute them to the Prophet or not. [They are]: (1) when a narrator says "The Prophet's precedent is such and such" or "It is *sunna* to do such and such,"[66] An example is our [Mālikī] companions' proving that *li'ān*'[67] immediately causes dissolution of marriage due to what is related on the authority of Sahl ibn Sa'd who said, "The *sunna* (normative precedent) has preceded that the two involved in public imprecation must [immediately] separate."[68]

Another example is our companions' proving that the supplication of *qunūt*[69] is legally permissible in the morning prayer due to Ibn Mas'ūd's statement, "Offering *qunūt* at the morning prayer is a *sunna* which has preceded."[70] An opponent of this view may argue that '*sunna*' may refer to a Prophetic normative precedent or it may be called for a practice of those who came after the Prophet. The answer of our [Mālikī] companions is that the Prophet's normative precedent is the origin of all precedents. When '*sunna*' is unrestrictedly mentioned [in a text] it is most probable that the narrator means the Prophet's practice.[71]

And of the controversial statements concerning *isnād* is (2) that a narrator may say, "The Prophet has commanded us to do such and such," or "The Prophet forbade us to do such and such," or "He decreed such and such," as, for instance, what is reported about the Prophet that he commanded the [words of] *adhān* to be in even number[72] and forbade the sales on which there is a chance or risk '*bay' al-gharar*'.[73] and decreed the establishment of preemption[74] *shuf'a*' for a neighbor.[75]

An opponent may argue that the narrator did not convey the exact wording of the Prophet, so it may not be authoritative if he transmits it. The answer is that the narrator's upright conduct and piety keep him from doing so. Moreover, probable interpretations cannot affect an explicit indication [of the text].

[And of controversial statements related to *isnād*] is (3) when a report conveys a meaning by a rational consequence such as the statement of 'Ammār ibn Yāsir, "He who fasts the day of doubt [30th of Sh'abān] has already disobeyed abū al-Qāsim."[76] It consequently implies that the Prophet has verbally forbade fasting the day of doubt because 'disobedience' is a consequence of acting upon something the Prophet forbade or a result of abandoning something he has already commanded.

1.1.3. Conclusion

A tradition may be objected because the narrator's view differed with the instructions included in his report such as our [Mālikī] companions' proving that washing a utensil licked by a dog is seven times because *hadith,* "If a dog licks at the utensil of anyone of you it is essential to wash it seven times.[77]" The companions of abū Ḥanīfa argue that this *hadith* by abū Ḥurayra who gave a religious verdict to wash a utensil [in this case] three times. If a narrator departs from the instructions included in a report he relates, it is an indication that the report is defective in his view. Had it been legally effective, he would not have violated it.

The answer of our [Mālikī] companions is that a legal proof derives from the report. It is not based on the narrator's verdict because he might have departed it due to his personal reasoning. We are not, then, obliged to follow it. This is the end of our discussion on *isnād.*

1.2. The Meaning of a Transmitted Text

The clarity of an indication may vary according to the type of text. It may be a saying, an act or a tacit approval [of the Prophet].

1.2.1. The Prophet's Sayings

A saying may refer to a legal ruling in one of two ways: (1) *manṭūq* (pronounced meaning) or (2) *mafhūm* (implied meaning).[78]

1.2.1.1. Manṭūq

An indication derived by a pronounced meaning may refer to a ruling or to its relevant circumstances. A ruling may refer to one to whom the *ḥukm* applies that is the human agent or to the action judged in the *ḥukm* as appropriate or inappropriate. The action consists of accessories [essential for its performance] such as water and clean earth which are necessary for the act of purification, and food and slaves [required for the act of expiating] for penances. An action may further be contingent to the time of its performance, such as the designated time for prescribed prayers and fasting or to the place of its observance such as the [boundaries] of [Meccan] sanctuary, ʿArafa and mosques.

Generally, these accessories are not closely relevant to a ruling. Therefore, we will only focus in our discussion on the reference [of a pronounced meaning] to a legal ruling and to its circumstances.

1.2.1.1.1. A Proof's Reference to a Legal Decision by Means of *Manṭūq*

A Locution which indicates a ruling by means of *manṭūq* consists of a command, a proscription or an option.

i. Commands

We will discuss this section in a preface and ten questions. The preface will be on the definition of command and its Arabic [syntactic] forms.
Definition and Form.
A command proper is defined as a verbal demand to do something issued from a position of superiority over one who is inferior. Its form is the Arabic imperative mood *ifʿal* 'do'. It is used in [Arabic] language for fifteen senses:

- Order such as Allah's saying, "and establish prayers" (Q. 2: 43).
- Permission as in Allah's saying, "But when you come out of *iḥrām*, then [you may] hunt." (Q. 5: 2).
- Direction as in Allah's saying "And take witnesses when you conclude a contract." (Q. 2: 282). This is a direction for a worldly affair.
- Instruction as in the Prophet's words, "Eat from what is in front of you.".[79] Instruction is different from direction in the sense it is of others' due rights.
- Threat as in Allah's saying, "Do whatever you will; indeed, He is seeing of what you do." (Q. 41: 40).

- Option as in Allah's saying, "Then be patient or impatient—it is all the same for you" (Q. 52: 16).
- Sacrum[80] as in Allah's saying, "Taste! Indeed, you are the honored, the noble!" (Q. 44: 49).
- Scorn as in Allah's saying, "So decree whatever you are to decree." (Q. 20: 72).
- Bestowment as in Allah's saying, "Eat from the good things with which We have provided you" (Q. 2: 57)
- Honoring as in Allah's saying, "Enter it in peace, safe [and secure]" (Q. 15: 46)
- Rendering unable as in Allah's saying, "then produce a sura the like thereof" (Q. 2: 23)
- Supplication as in Allah's saying, "so forgive us our sins" (Q. 3: 16).
- Bringing forth as in Allah's saying, "Be apes, despised" (Q. 2: 65).
- Wish as in Imrū᾽ al-Qays' poetic verse, "O long night I wish you will be [soon] removed."
- Warning as in Allah's saying, "then be informed of a war [against you] from Allah and His Messenger" (Q. 2: 279). Some [scholars] interpreted it to mean threat.

The imperative mood has been used figuratively in all these connotations, yet it is primarily used to convey command.

Scholars differed on [the meaning of] a command which has been preceded by a prohibition, whether to regard it as a clue to indicate permission without being imperative. The reason is that in many occasions orders have been issued after preceding prohibitions, but they indicate permission such as in Allah's saying "But when you come out of *iḥram*, then hunt." Q. 5: 2. [It permits hunting though it has been previously prohibited] in His saying "… hunting not being permitted while you are in the state of *iḥram*." Q. 5: 1. Furthermore, Allah's saying "And when the prayer has been concluded, disperse within the land and seek from the bounty of Allah." Q. 62: 10 indicates the permissibility of sale though it has been previously prohibited in Allah's saying "when [the *adhan*] is called for the prayer on the day of Jumuʿa [Friday], then proceed to the remembrance of Allah and leave trade." Q. 62: 9. Similarly, Allah's saying "And when they have purified themselves, then come to them from where Allah has ordained for you" (Q. 2: 222) allows intercourse after being prohibited in His saying "And do not approach them until they are pure" (Q. 2: 222). This is the case of the Prophet's saying, "I forbade you of storing sacrificial meat, but now you can store it. I forbade you of *intibādh*,[81] but now you can do it. I forbade you of visiting grave but now you can visit them."[82] All those forms [of commands] are intended to indicate permissibility.

An imperative form may follow a proscription but it is intended to mean obligation such as in Allah's saying, "then kill the polytheists wherever you find them" Q. 9: 5 which has been reveled after His saying, "Excepted are those with whom you made a treaty among the polytheists and then they have not been deficient toward you in anything or supported anyone against you; so complete for them their treaty until their term [has ended]." Q. 9: 4. Furthermore, Allah says, "O Prophet, fight against the disbelievers and the hypocrites" (Q. 9: 73). It has been revealed after His saying, "but do not harm them, and rely upon Allah" (Q. 33: 48). Similarly, the same meaning may be deduced from Allah's saying, "And do not shave your heads until the sacrificial animal has reached its place of slaughter." (Q. 2: 196). It prohibits shaving but it becomes obligatory upon the animal's reaching their place of slaughter. These are examples of commands with prior prohibitions.

Scholars differed on this issue as we mentioned before. Some of them maintain that a command following a prohibition is a clue to interpret it to mean permissibility. This is the view of the majority of scholars. Others hold that a command implies its primary meaning of obligation. This is the view of a minority among scholars. The view of the majority prevails because an imperative form is frequently used to convey permissibility [in almost all texts] while it is rarely interpreted to mean obligation. Interpreting a locution according to its frequent usage is preferred.[83] This is the conclusion of our preface.

[Questions which arose scholars' disagreement on a command]

We will discuss the [ten] questions as follows:

First, scholars differed on an absolute command[84] whether it entails obligation, recommendation or something else? Therefore, they differed on many practical rules of *fiqh*.

For example, scholars disagreed on [the ruling of] having witnesses on the revocation of divorce; is it obligatory or not? Those who supported obligation, that is, the Shāfiʿī scholars, base their view on Allah's saying "And when they have [nearly] fulfilled their term, either retain them according to acceptable terms or part with them according to acceptable terms. And bring to witness two just men from among you." (Q. 65: 2). They confirmed that retaining spouses means recourse for marriage. Therefore, witnessing is imperative. It entails obligation. A proponent of this view does not interpret command to mean obligation.[85]

Similarly, Shāfiʿīs proved the obligation of *takbīr* upon the commencement of prayers by the Prophet's saying to the Bedouin, "When you stand up for prayer glorify your lord", by stating that it is a command and it conveys obligation, but an opponent of this view disagrees with them.

Based on scholar's disagreement on whether a command means obligation or recommendation, our [Mālikī] fellows differed on [the ruling of] washing a utensil liked by a dog seven times, if it is obligatory or recommended according to the Prophet's (may God exalt his mention) saying, "If a dog licks in ones utensil let him wash it seven times.[86]"

Abū Bakr al-Abharī of our [Mālikī] companions maintained that all divine commands entail obligation while the Prophet's commands mean recommendation.[87] Erudite among *uṣūlīs* upheld that both are meant for obligation. They prove it by arguing that one who does not comply with a command is disobedient, while one who responds to orders is considered obedient. Allah says, "[Moses] said, "O Aaron, what prevented you, when you saw them going astray, from following me? Then have you disobeyed my order (Q. 20: 92,93) and said, "[Moses] said, "You will find me, if Allah wills, patient, and I will not disobey you in [any] order." (Q. 18: 68) and Allah [described the angels in] His saying, "they do not disobey Allah in what He commands them" (Q. 66: 6). A violator of a command deserves punishment when he neglects the commands of Allah or those of His Prophet (may God exalt his mention). Allah says, "And whoever disobeys Allah and His Messenger—then indeed, for him is the fire of Hell" (Q. 72: 23). He further said, "So let those beware who dissent from the Prophet's order, lest *fitna* strike them or a painful punishment" (Q. 24: 63). The Prophet (may God exalt his mention) did not issue an [obligatory] command to his nation to use *siwāk* due to [the expected] difficulty, so that he said, "If it was not for the fact that I might be overburdening my community, or the people, I would have ordered them to use the *siwāk* for every prayer,[88]" Had his command conveyed recommendation a priori, he would not have relinquished it.

Second, does a command require prompt execution or not? *Uṣūlīs* disagreed on [answering] this question. Therefore, jurists disagreed on some issues of *fiqh* based on this question. Shāfiʿī and Abū Ḥanīfa disagreed on the performance of *hajj*; whether to be executed promptly or it can be delayed. According to Abū Ḥanīfa, whoever delays *hajj* [after meeting all its prerequisites] is sinful. According to al-Shāfiʿī, whoever delays it while being able to do it is not sinful.[89]

Therefore, we have two differing views in our [Mālikī] school [both] based on Allah's saying, "And [due] to Allah from the people is a pilgrimage to the House—for whoever is able to find thereto a way" (Q. 3: 97). The verse postulates that *hajj* is obligatory [without defining whether its performance is immediate or not].

Similarly, they disagreed on the payment of expiations for penances; either to be immediate or delayed? They further differed on one whose minimum proportion of *zakat* vanishes after being able to pay it, is he still liable to pay or not. If it has to be paid immediately, he is disobedient by delaying its payment. Ḥanafis maintain that he is not liable to pay it because the command is not to pay zakat immediately. Therefore, he is not to be sinful by delay.

Each group of scholars violated the principle they set in the issue of *Hajj* for a reason which is better elaborated in the books of *fiqh*.

Erudite of *uṣūl* uphold that an absolute command requires neither immediate nor delayed execution, because it is sometimes qualified to be prompt as when a slave says to his master, 'travel now,' it requires that he must depart immediately. It is sometimes described to be delayed such as a master's saying 'travel by the first day of the month' which conveys delay. If an absolute command is issued without restricting it to be immediate or delayed, it, then, vacillates between both meanings. Whatever vacillates between two meanings cannot be specifically constrained to one meaning.

Third, does a command require repeated execution? When the lawgiver enacts the execution of an act [the question arises] whether acquiescence is fulfilled by a single compliance or does it require repeated and persistent observance? *Uṣūlīs* differed on this.[90] Based on their disagreement, ibn Khuwayzmandād of our [Mālīkī] companions referred to the question on whether dry ablution is necessary for each obligatory *ṣala* or it is sufficient to observe it once as long as one does not vitiate his state of ritual purity?

Those who believed that it is obligatory for each prayer maintain that the command in Allah's saying, "…, then seek clean earth and wipe over your faces and hands with it" (Q. 5: 6) requires repeated execution. They further confirm that [a single] ablution is adequate for many prayers due to another proof, that is, the report of Ya'lā ibn Umayya[91]: "The Prophet offered many prayers upon offering single ablution."

Erudite among scholars uphold that a command does not definitely mean repeated or single compliance in all contexts. It varies from text to another. The Lawgiver enacted constant adherence to the Islamic beliefs while He commanded us to observe *hajj* once? Since an absolute command can possibly require single or repeated execution, the audience's question to clear ambiguity [regarding the number of times one has to offer *hajj* during his lifetime] was plausible. According to a report, al-Aqra' ibn Ḥābis or Surāqa ibn Mālik[92] (I do not know who) asked the Prophet on the year of the farewell pilgrimage, "O Messenger of Allah! Is this pilgrimage for this year or for lifetime?", that is, is this *hajj* adequate for this year only so we have to repeat it per year or is adequate for lifetime? The Messenger of Allah (may God exalt his mention) said, "It is [once] a lifetime." Had the meaning of a command definitely required a single compliance or repeated execution, the questioner would not have appropriately asked this question.

Fourth, does a command of a time limit require strict execution at the beginning of its designated time or at the last segment of the prescribed time or a flexible compliance? *Uṣulīs* differed on the answer of this question as follows: Some Shāfiʿī scholars affirm that a command requires strict execution at the beginning of its designated time. If it is delayed to the end of its prescribed time, it is called *qaḍāʾ* (belated observance) but it legally stands for *ʾadāʾ* (prompt performance).[93] Some Ḥanafīs uphold that the execution of a command pertains to the last segment of its designated time. A prompt observance is additional but it suffices for fulfilling obligation.[94]

Erudite among scholars maintain that it is not obligatory to respond to a command at a certain point of its prescription. If it has to be offered at the beginning of its prescribed time, the one who postpones should be regarded as undutiful and should be then considered as making up a belated [act of worship]. Therefore, he must, then, intend to make up a belated [worship]. Such a presumption is, however, contrary to the unanimous consensus of Muslim scholars. In case we presume that a command has to be executed at the end of its prescribed time, the one who offers an act promptly is regarded as offering a supererogatory act. He has, therefore, to retain an intention of a supererogatory act of worship and his performance is not [legally] efficient since he offers an act prior to its designated time. Such a presumption is contrary to unanimous consensus of all scholars. Consequently, a command does not have to be executed in a definite point of its prescribed time.

Based on this principle, scholars differed on the ruling of a child who offered a prayer at the beginning of its prescribed time but he, then, reached puberty before the end of its time. Shāfiʿīs maintain that the prayer [the child offered before reaching puberty] is sufficient because obligation to offer prayer is pertinent to the first segment of time. A child became pubescent when the obligatory point of time has already elapsed. Therefore, he is not to make up prayer exactly like a person who has reached the age of puberty after a designated time for prayer has elapsed.[95]

Ḥanafīs uphold that prayer is not sufficient [in such a case] because obligation is pertinent to the last point of the designated time. He reached puberty at the time of obligation. So, he has to pray [again] like one who reached puberty before prayer time starts.

We have two variant views in our [Mālikī] *madhhab* which are based on *fiqh* and are present in *fiqh* compendiums.[96]

Similarly, they differed on when is it preferable to offer the morning prayer either during predawn darkness or at daybreak. Shāfiʿīs upheld the former since it is the time for obligation while Ḥanfīs affirm the latter because it, [according to them] is the time for obligation.

Fifth, if a communal obligation is legally dropped due to the observance of some *mukallafs* (human agents), can we hold it obligatory for all *mukallafs* at the outset and then it is dropped fromt those who did not observe it or can we hold it held obligatory for some indefinite *mukallafs* at the beginning of its enforcement? The majority of scholars maintained that it is held obligatory for all *mukallafs* at the outset while some scholars held that it is obligatory for an indefinite number. The proof of the majority is that if punishment is liable to occur, it will collectively incur all of those who are responsible if they neglect it aggregately. Punishment will prevail because of the collective obligation.[97]

One of the ramifications of this precept is the ruling of a non-traveler and bodily abled person lacking water to perform ablution. He can perform dry ablution for the observance of obligatory prayers. He cannot perform *tayammum* for the observance of supererogatory prayers. Scholars disagreed on the legality of this person's performance of *tayammum* before the observance of a funeral prayer. This is based on their disagreement on this precept. Those who uphold that he can offer dry ablution [before the funeral prayer] based their view on presumption that communal obligation is required of all *mukallafs* at the outset. For them, there is no distinction between individual and communal obligations. Those who uphold that he cannot offer dry ablution [before the funeral prayer] maintain that a communal obligation is not pertinent to all *mukallafs*. [Once, funeral congregation is made by some] it becomes a supererogatory act for others.

Sixth, does a command require all means necessary for its execution or not? This is the meaning of their statement "Whatever is indispensable for the execution of an obligatory act is it held obligatory or not?" *Uṣūlīs* disagreed on this [issue]. The majority of them maintain that a command entails execution of everything contingent to it, such as when a master commands his slave to ascend a roof. A slave in such a case is similarly commanded to set up a ladder in order to facilitate his ascent to the roof.

Some scholars maintain that a command to do an act does not extend to things necessary for its execution. The proof of the majority is that if a means to execute an obligatory act is not commanded, a *mukallaf* will be then free not to do it. If he is allowed to quit an obligation, it cannot be then held compulsory. Based on this principle, scholars have differed on the obligation of seeking water prior to the performance dry ablution. Shāfiʿīs held that seeking water is obligatory while Ḥanafīs did not. There is, however, a disagreement among our [Mālikī] scholars.

Those who uphold seeking water is obligatory state that ablution is obligatory. It cannot be offered without seeking water. Therefore, seeking for water is obligatory because whatever is indispensable for the execution of an obligatory act is held obligatory. Scholars have unanimously agreed that whoever is obliged to free a slave in the context of an obligatory penance and can only afford it by purchase he has to purchase it since the obligatory act of emancipating a slave can only be offered by purchase. The purchase of a slave becomes obligatory in this case. This is the reason we made it obligatory to purchase water during travel to offer ablution. An exception is made when water is too expensive.

Seventh, when a command necessitates doing one thing of multiple alternatives, is it directed to all things equally or to an indefinite item of them? *Uṣūlīs* upheld different views regarding this [issue]; the most well-known of them are two. For example, [a command is issued to do one of the three] items of penance '*kaffāra*', namely feeding, clothing [of needy persons] or emancipation [of a slave]. The result of scholars' disagreement is shown in the case of a slave or a traveler's leading Friday congregation. Can we hold the prayer of their followers as valid or not? Ibn al-Qāsim maintains that it is not valid while Ashhab views it as valid.

The reasoning of ibn al-Qāsim is that the obligatory prayer in the case of a slave is indefinite because he is given the option to either offer Friday or *ẓuhr* prayer. It is obligatory for him to offer one of the two things, but if he offers Friday prayer it is counted as a supererogatory act in his case; [since he is only required to offer *ẓuhr*]. If someone follows him in offering a Friday prayer, the prayer of that follower is invalid. However, the reasoning of Ashhab is that the particular case of a slave with regard to Friday prayer necessitates its obligation for him due to the rule that a command to do an indefinite act of two things alternatives that each one of them is obligatory.

The view of the majority of scholars is that the command [in this case] necessitates the execution of an indefinite act of the two without discerning one of them. Their reasoning is that one who does not respond to one of those items is punished like one who does not respond to them at all.

Eighth, does an execution of a command entail a mere compliance or a clearance of liability [so that he does not have to offer it again]? *Uṣūlīs* differed on a *mukallaf's* response to a command is he still demanded to respond [again] or not? If we consider this question a genuine case of controversy among scholars, jurists will base on it many legal determinations. [Among those decisions is] when one does not find water or clean earth accessible [to purify himself with] and the time of prayer has entered, he is required to offer prayers [without due purification] according to the views of ibn al-Qāsim and Ashhab, but when he prays [without due purification] is he still required to make up such a prayer when he later finds water or clean earth or not? According to ibn al-Qāsim, he is required to make it up again, but Ashhab disagrees on that. His reasoning is that since a *mukallaf* is commanded to offer prayer in such a state, a further demand to offer it again is dropped. This is due to the rule that a command entails full compliance which makes a human agent unbound to make it up.

Such is the case of one who does not find a cloth to cover his *ʿawra* during prayer, but he engages in prayer. If he finds a cloth to cover himself later, does it necessitate him to make up prayer? Disagreement is based on this precept. Similarly, a confused person who offers prayer to a direction which he thought to be the right *qibla* but later finds out he is incorrect. There are other similar examples.

Erudite among *uṣūlīs* maintain that responding to a command means that a human agent has already complied with it. It, therefore, drops a demand to reoffer it again. That is because a command may include a further demand beyond what one has already done. In this case one has to further respond to this demand. If a command does not include anything extra, human agent will be no more liable.

Ninth, when a command specifies a time limit for doing an act, does it cover belated performance if the act is not performed within its designated time? If a *mukallaf* misses an act of worship which is presumed to be offered within a limited scope of time is he still demanded to offer it as belated performance due to the first command or should he be addressed with a new command to prove performance after time? There are two views of *uṣūlīs*: The majority of them maintain that belated performance is not included in the first command and that it necessitates a new command. They prove that a command requires [compliance] within a limited time. Therefore, if a master commands his slave to stay at home all Thursday, his command does not extend to include Friday. In this case if he readdresses him later to stay on Thursday and not to stay on Friday, his commands are contradictory in case we admit the first command covers both Thursday and Friday.

Based on this question jurists belonging to our [Mālikī] school differed if one who nullifies or neglects fasting of a day that he vowed to fast is he still required to make up fasting after the lapse of the day [he designated] or not? Those who maintain that belated performance can only be offered by a new command exempt him of making up fasting, since there is no command to make up fasting. This is contrary to making up of obligatory fasting because it is proved through a new command, that is, Allah's saying, "[Fasting is prescribed for] a limited number of days. So whoever among you is ill or on a journey [during them]—then an equal number of days [are to be made up]" (Q. 2: 184). Those who maintain that belated performance is included in the first command require one who missed the fasting of a vow day to make up fasting of that day [later].

They further differed on the case of a deliberate negligent of prayer, and if he is still required to make it up? The majority of Mālīkī scholars necessitate belated performance [in this case] because it is included in the first command to offer prayer. Ibn Ḥabīb of our [Mālikī] companions maintain that such a person is not required to offer his duty later because the first command [to offer prayer in time] does not require him to make it up [if it is deliberately neglected]. We do not have a new command demanding him to offer it except in the case of a forgetful or one who was sleeping that is, the Prophet's saying, "Whoever forgets a prayer or sleeps [until its time elapses] must pray it when he remembers it".[98]

Tenth, whether a command to do something implies the prohibition of its opposite or not? According to the majority of *uṣūlīs* and jurists, a command to do something does imply the prohibition to do its opposite. According to some of them it does not imply the prohibition of its opposite. The proof of the majority is that the opposite of an obligatory act may either be obligatory, prohibited or permissible. It cannot be obligatory because it is not possible to do two opposite things simultaneously. Similarly, it is not possible to be permissible since the permissibility of doing something means that it is tolerable not do such an act which has been proved obligatory. As the abandonment of an obligatory act is not permitted, acting upon its opposite is, thus, not permissible.

The result of such disagreement would obviously have a bearing on an obligatory act of worship. Its performance does not imply a prohibition to do its opposite concurrently as long as it does not lead to its total loss. Standing up in prayer, for example, is commanded. If a person sits down and recites what is supposed to be said during his standing, his prayer cannot be rendered void since he is not prohibited to sit down. This is based on [the maxim that] a command to do something does not imply the prohibition of its opposite. The majority of scholars maintain that sitting down in this case is prohibited since it is the opposite of standing. Therefore, if a worshiper deliberately sits down during his prayer while being able to stand, he is regarded as perpetrating a prohibited act during prayer. It results in invalidating his prayer.

Such is the case of prostrating in an impure spot. According to the majority of scholars, *ṣala* is then null and void since a worshiper is commanded to prostate on a pure place while a command to do something implies the prohibition of its opposite. Since prostration in an impure place is prohibited, such a prayer should be rendered void. Abū Yūsuf concluded that he must only make up *sujūd* by prostrating in a pure place. In this case, the prayer becomes legally sufficient, since one is only commanded to prostrate in a pure place which is already observed. Prostration in an impure place [according to him] is not prohibited since a command to do something does not imply the prohibition of its opposite.

Shāfiʿī scholars disagreed on the one depositing an article with someone commanding him to keep it in a definite place. If he does not prohibit him to keep it in another place and it is lost, the keeper will not be liable to compensate the depositor in case the new place is similar to the assigned place in meeting normal specifications for safeguarding similar articles. In case the depositor prohibited him to keep it in any other place but the keeper transferred it to a similar place that meets the normal specifications for safeguarding, scholars are of two views on the keeper's liability for damage. Those who maintained that a command to do something implies the prohibition of its opposite did not make a difference of commanding a keeper to preserve it in a specific place or adding to this command a prohibition to keep it other places. He is not financially responsible in case a depositor commands him of a specific place or add to his command a prohibition to keep it in another site.

Whoever maintains that a command to do something does not imply the prohibition of its opposite proposes that a keeper is not financially liable in case a depositor does not explicitly prohibit him to preserve it in other places, since he has not gone beyond the command of the depositor. In case a depositor explicitly prohibits that and a keeper violates his prohibition, financial liability becomes binding.

You should know that ibn Khuway Mindād mentioned that the view of Mālik (may Allah bless him) is that a command to do something does imply the prohibition of its opposite. He deduced it from Mālik's acceptance of *mafūm al-mukhālafa* (divergent meaning).[99] We will discuss it below God willing. This is the conclusion of our statement on commands.

ii. Prohibitions

Our discussion of 'prohibition' will consist of an introduction and elaboration of two questions. They are the most significant questions under this topic.

For the introduction, we are going to discuss the definition [of prohibition] and its linguistic form. It is defined as a word or words which demand the avoidance of doing something addressed from a position of superiority [to one who is inferior]. The typical form of a prohibitory order in Arabic is that of a negative command prefaced with '*lā*' such as *lā taf*ʿ*al* (do not do). This form is used in Arabic language to convey six meanings [as follows]:

- Prohibition as in Allah's saying, "do not approach prayer while you are intoxicated until you know what you are saying" (Q. 4: 43).
- Supplication as in Allah's saying, "Our Lord, and lay not upon us a burden like that which You laid upon those before us. Our Lord, and burden us not with that which we have no ability to bear" (Q. 2: 286).
- Showing evil consequence as in Allah's saying, "And think not that Allah is unaware of what the wrongdoers do" (Q. 14: 42).
- Desperation as in Allah's saying "Make no excuse; you have disbelieved after your belief" (Q. 9: 66,96; Q. 66: 7).
- Instruction as in Allah's saying, "do not ask about things which, if they are shown to you, will distress you." (Q. 5: 101).

- Degradation as in Allah's saying, "And do not extend your eyes toward that by which We have given enjoyment to [some] categories of them, [its being but] the splendor of worldly life " (Q. 20: 131).

This form is used primarily to convey proscription according to the unanimous consensus of Muslim scholars but it may be used metaphorically to convey other meanings. It cannot be interpreted to mean other than prohibition except when there is a clue [to warrant this].

The *uṣūlīs,* who advocated that an imperative preceded by prohibition is a clue which changes the meaning of a command from obligation to mere permissibility, have differed on the meaning of a prohibition preceded by a command. Some of them maintained that a preceding obligation turns prohibition from its primary meaning. Others stated that a previous obligation does not change the meaning of prohibition [to reprehension]. Abū Isḥāq al-Isfrāyīnī[100] reported scholars' consensus that a prior obligation is not a clue to drive the meaning of a prohibition from proscription [to reprehension]. The matter is, however, controversial.

For example, Allah says, "But if they obey you [once more], seek no means against them" (Q. 4: 34). [it is a prohibition] which has been revealed after Allah's saying, "[first] advise them; [then if they persist], forsake them in bed; and [finally], strike them" (Q. 4: 34). The meaning of the former is unanimously interpreted to mean prohibition.

Similarly, prohibition is noticed after an obligation as in Allah's saying, "Fight those who do not believe in Allah or in the Last Day and who do not consider unlawful what Allah and His Messenger have made unlawful and who do not adopt the religion of truth from those who were given the Scripture—[fight] until they give the *jizya* willingly while they are humbled." Q. 9: 29. It is confirmed that fighting against them became prohibited after taking *Jiziya* (tribute), though it has been previously enacted as an obligation.

After this introduction, let us proceed to discuss the two questions [which arose scholars' disagreement]:

First, whether *nahy* entails the illegality of something or just its being reprehensible? This is a controversial issue among scholars. The majority of scholars interpret it to entail illegality because the Prophet's Companions and their Followers (may Allah be pleased with them) persistently prove that *nahy* entails the illegality of the act prohibited. Similarly, a doer of a prohibited act is deemed sinful by consensus because he has violated a [legal] command. A sinful person is worthy to be punished. An act, whose doer deserves punishment, is considered unlawful. Therefore, *nahy* entails illegality.

Many juristic rulings have been based on this precept including:

Scholars differed on the legal ruling of praying at a rubbish dump, a slaughterhouse, graveyard, in the middle of a path, in a bathhouse, in camel abiding places and on the top of the *ka ʿba*. Some of them regard it prohibited while others hold it is reprehensible. In our [Mālikī] school, we have a disagreement [on the legal ruling on prayers offered at those places]. The difference is based on the meaning of *nahy*; does it convey illegality or reprehension. The Prophet denounced praying at those seven places as related by Tirmidhī.[101]

Similarly, scholars differed on the [legal ruling of] turning face or back to *ka ʿba* while answering the call of nature; is it prohibited or reprehensible? This is based on the Prophet's saying, "When any of you goes to relieve himself, he should not face the *qibla* nor turn his back on it. He should face the east or west." "Does this prohibition imply illegality or reprehension?

Second, does prohibition entail the invalidity of a proscribed act or not? There is a disagreement among *uṣūlīs* [on this issue]. The majority of them maintain that if an act is prohibited [such as a specific contract of sale], it becomes null and void right away. An exception [to this rule] may be made to specific cases due to other evidences.[102] They argued that the Prophet's Companions and their Followers (may Allah be pleased with them) have persistently ruled out that all prohibited contracts of sale and marriage are held null and void. None of them argued regarding the indication of a prohibition but they [made exceptions by] reliance on further extraneous evidences.

Based on this precept, scholars differed on the [legal ruling] of the *shighār* marriage[103] after its conclusion; is it null and void or not? According to Mālikī and Shāfiʿī scholars, it has to be dissolved while the Ḥanāfīs do not require its termination. According to the Prophetic tradition, the Prophet prohibited *shighār*. Those who maintained that a prohibition conveys the invalidity of a forbidden act regarded the marriage contract null and void. Those who maintained that *nahy* does not require invalidation of an act have not regard the contract invalid.

Another example is the Prophet's prohibition of a sale with a condition.[104] Similarly, the prohibition of *bayʿ wa salaf* 'selling and lending'.[105] Likewise, it is prohibited to offer prayers in a usurped property, but scholars differed on the validity of prayer offered in such a property. Scholars also differed on the validity of prayers offered at times of proscription or at places where it is prohibited to pray.

To verify the [Mālikī] school, they maintain that if the object of prohibition is one of the rights of Allah, the act is rendered null and void, but if it includes a right of humans it is not nullified. The Prophet prohibited *taṣriya* 'retaining milk in an animal's udders to impress the buyer' by saying, "Do not retain milk in the udders of a she camel or goat so as to exaggerate its yield. Anyone who buys a *muṣarrāh* has the choice, for three days after having milked it, either to keep it, or to return it with a quantity [that is, *a ṣāʿ*] of dates."[106] [According to the report], the Prophet has not repealed the sale contract. Had the contract been canceled, the Prophet would not have given the buyer the right to confirm or rescind sale. When he gave the purchaser the right to retain [the she camel or the goat] it indicates that he did not annul the contact because it is of the rights of humans.

If the act is an object of prohibition due to a divine right, it is rendered null and void. Therefore, concluding sale at the time of Friday prayer must be annulled, because sale at this time is prohibited for a divine right. This is the reason most of the narrators [from Mālik] made a distinction between prohibited forms of marriage which are dissolved by the pronouncement of divorce and other forms which are annulled without human intervention. They stated that each contract of marriage which may be confirmed or dissolved by the consent of a spouse or a guardian can only be dissolved through divorce, because the prohibition is due to a right of those who have the consent. Marriage in this case is effective by itself. As for a [prohibited] form of marriage which has to be automatically dissolved without a prior consent of a spouse or a guardian, it must be annulled in all cases since none of them have the right to dissolve or confirm it. Had one of them been granted the consent to dissolve or confirm the contract, he may [voluntarily] drop this right. But when dissolution of this form of a contract is out of their hands, we recognize that it is a divine right. Therefore, such a prohibited contract is regarded null and ineffective. In order to dissolve such a contract, one does not recourse to divorce, since divorce is for the dissolution of an already effective contract. As the contract which is a priori ineffective, it cannot be dissolved. This is the principle of the [Mālikī] school. Exceptions of this rule should rely on extraneous evidence.

You should also know that *nahy* entails persistent and immediate avoidance of a prohibited act and that the opposite of a prohibited act is commanded as [it is stated before that] the opposite of a command is prohibition. The questions we mentioned are the most important issues related to *nahy* in Islamic law.

iii. *Takhiyīr* (Option)

An utterance that indicates option to do or not to do an act does not entail that both alternatives are equally at the same level. A traveler is free to fast or not but fasting is preferred according to the majority of our [Mālikī] companions. Breaking fast is preferred for a traveling person according to some [Mālikī] scholars. Similarly, a traveler is at liberty either to shorten or complete his prayers but shortening prayers is preferred.

Such is the case of a slave, a woman or a traveling person who are free either to offer Friday congregation or *ẓuhr* prayer, but offering Friday prayer is preferred.

Therefore, it is not valid to use a form that indicates option to prove that an individual is equally free either to do an act or not. Those who presume *mandūb* as a category of command and *makrūh* as a category of prohibition state that forms that indicate option are interpreted to mean permissibility.

They further differed on whether to classify permissibility as a legal ruling or logical necessity based on the fact that everything is originally presumed to be lawful and free from liability. Based on this disagreement, scholars differed on legal rulings of some issues. They will be discussed under *qiyās*, God willing. This is the end of our statement on option and the conclusion of discussing proof's reference to a legal ruling by means of pronounced meaning.

1.2.1.1.2. A Proof's Reference to the Particulars of a Legal Decision[107]

A locution may impart two meanings or be a univocal. If a word is linguistically appropriated to signify one specific meaning, it is called *naṣṣ* (univocal), but if it vacillates between two connotations, one of them may be preponderant or both are equivocal. A term with multiple meanings, none of which can be said to be preponderant is *mujmal* (ambiguous or equivocal). However, its indication to a legal ruling is ambiguous. In case a locution imparts more than one meaning and one of which can be said to be preponderant based on textual evidence, it is called *ẓāhir* (manifest). A term with multiple meanings, one of which can be said to be preponderant based on non-textual evidence is called *muʾawwal* (amenable to interpretation). To conclude, an utterance may be univocal, ambivalent, manifest or apt to interpretation. We should discuss each category in a [separate] section.

i. *Naṣṣ*

Its connotation is not debatable except for cases not related to its indication. An example is our [Mālikī] companions' position that a vessel licked by a dog has to be washed seven not three times due to the Prophet's saying, "If the dog licks one's vessel, wash it seven times." The Ḥanafīs make it obligatory to wash it thrice. They do not argue about the indication of the number 'seven,' but they quote abū Hurayrah's verdict that a vessel is to be washed thrice, particularly because he is the narrator of this tradition. [They further argue that] the report cannot be legally effective.

One may presume that when a [ruling is connected to a definite] number in a given [text] it is exclusive [of other things beyond that number which may further be added]. For example, the Prophet has been reported as saying, "Five types of animals are all vicious and can be killed in the sacred sanctuary of Mecca: crows, kites, scorpions, mice and vicious dogs." The report does not definitely exclude other animals beyond these five. It cannot be, then, interpreted by recourse to its pronounced meaning, but it is rather explained by reference to its implied meaning. A stated number may have *mafhūm*[108] as it will be discussed God willing.

Some *uṣūlīs* distinguished between using an exclusive number intended by a legal ruling such as the Prophet's saying, "wash it seven times" and a number pertinent to a reason which is maintained in the ruling such as the Prophet's saying, "Five animals are all vicious and can be killed".[109] Similarly, they forbade exceeding the period of three days as an option to cancel a sale contact based on the Prophet's saying, "When you purchase something inform the seller that there is no fraud and you have the right to cancel sale within three days." [Shafiʿīs] stated that [the number three in] this report is intended [to be exclusive] for this ruling. Therefore, it is not valid to exceed the limit of three days if an option is provisioned at the contract to cancel a sale contract.

What they have mentioned is indisputable but we maintain that the option which is limited to three days and provided in this text is assigned [only] in case of possible fraud. As for option to test a purchased item, it is restricted [to three days] and it differs due to various types of purchased items.

Another example of a *naṣṣ* is our [Mālikī] fellows' position that a military leader is at liberty either to ransom or free captives based on Allah's saying, "and either [confer] favor afterwards or ransom [them]" (Q. 47: 4). [The text] is explicit to the effect that the ruler has the choice. But the fellows of abū Ḥanīfa stated that the ruling is temporal for an unknown term which is provided in Allah's saying, "... until the war lays down its burdens." (Q. 47: 4). It is possible to mean that the ruling is applicable until no polytheist exists, that is, up to the Day of Judgment or until fighting comes to an end. Further interpretations are also possible. In conclusion, the ruling is assigned a period which might have already expired and therefore, option no longer exists or it may be still effective. Therefore, the text is *mujmal* (ambiguous) [according to the Ḥanafīs].

The answer of our fellows is that eminent exegetes report ibn ʿAbbās' saying, "the verse means until Jesus, son of Mary descends or until no infidel exists on earth."

A locution may provide a univocal meaning not by means of language but by virtue of textual clues and the context. An example is our [Mālikī] companions' argument that it is impermissible to sell fresh dates for dried dates because when the Prophet was asked about this transaction he said, "Do the dates diminish in size when they become dry?" When he was told that they diminish, he said, "No, then." The fellows of abū Ḥanīfa maintain that the phrase, 'No, then' must include an ellipsis. There is a possibility that the phrase reads, 'There is no problem, then [to conclude such a transaction]' or 'no it is not permissible then'. When a locution vacillates between two meanings, it cannot be used to exclusively mean one of them.

The answer of our [Mālikī] fellows is that the answer of the Prophet conforms to the question. The Prophet stated that it is impermissible because the questioner asked him on the permissibility [of such a transaction]. Furthermore, the reason of making it impermissible is the decrease of weight of dates due to dryness. Such a reason is an appropriate reason for prohibition. Therefore, it is proved that impermissibility is explicit and definitive in this text.

Sometimes a text may be interpreted in such a way that it cannot be accepted by reason. For example, the Shāf ʿīs hold that saying of *al-fātiḥa* is obligatory for a follower in congregation based on the Prophet's saying, "If you are behind me [in a congregation] do not recite but (*illā*) the Mother of the Quran, for there is no prayer for anyone who does not recite the Mother of the Book."

Their opponents would argue that *illā* is used to mean 'and/or'. Therefore, it should read, "If you are behind me [in a congregation] do not recite [anything] or the Mother of the Quran either." Such is the case of the Quranic verse, "… turn your faces toward it in order that the people will not have any argument against you, *illā* (neither) those of them who are wrong doers" Q. 2: 150.

It is, however, used for the same connotation in the poetic verse, "and every brother, his brother forsakes him, by the life of thy father, and the *farqdān.*[110]" It means that people and wrong doers will have no argument against the believers and everyone will forsake his brother even the two closely connected stars. Therefore, the meaning of the report is ambivalent. The answer is that such a remote interpretation which obscures the text is eliminated by the ending phrase of the *hadith*, "for there is no prayer for anyone who does not recite the Mother of the Book."

Conclusion: an opponent may, however, claim that a text is self-evident in order to preclude its possible qualification by another text, such as our [Mālikī] fellows who have specifically held that the recitation of *al-fātiḥa* is obligatory in prayer based on the Prophet's saying, "There is no prayer for anyone who does not recite the Mother of the Book."[111]

The fellows of abū Ḥanīfa advocate that Allah's saying, "So recite what is easy from it" (Q. 73: 20) is definitively explicit to mean that it is sufficient to recite whatever is feasible of the Quran. The report, however, provides an addition to the verse. Such an addition should abrogate [the verse]. But according to them, it is not possible to abrogate the Quran by virtue of solitary traditions.

Our companions argued by saying that the meaning of the verse is not self-evident. It is *ẓāhir* (manifest) in the sense that it is abominable to interpretation by virtue of a solitary tradition.

This is the conclusion of our discussion of *naṣṣ*.

ii. *Mujmal* (Ambivalent)

We have introduced earlier that *mujmal* (ambivalent) does not have a clear indication.[112] In case a word imparts a univocal meaning, it cannot be called *mujmal*. Discussion of *mujmal* will focus on three points:

Causes of Ambivalence

Ambivalence occurs when a locution [inherently] vacillates between two equal meanings. It exists in a single word or in a structure. Ambivalence of a single word exists because of semantic, morphological or orthographic ambiguity of a single word. Structural ambivalence occurs due to a structural ambiguity, structural reading of a literal implication or literal reading of a structure. These are six reasons [and will be explained below]:

Semantic Ambiguity[113]

For example, our [Mālikī] fellows count a woman's prescribed waiting period based on her purification periods. They based their view on Allah's saying, "Divorced women remain in waiting for three *qur'*s" (Q. 2: 228).[114] *Qur'* is lexically defined as the purification period between two menses as used in the poet's saying, "And every year you are vigorously undertaking a battle, journeying and mastering the end of your patience. But such an act breeds properties to inherit and a praise of your glory to hymn. It is for [the days] you missed when your women had *qurū'*."[115]

Ḥanafīs argue that the word *qur'* means a menstruation period. They proved it by reference to the Prophet's saying, "Leave prayer at days you have *aqrā'*."[116] [In this context] *aqrā'* (pl. of *qur'*) means menstruation periods. The reason the term has been used for both meanings is that the Companions of the Prophet disagreed on the interpretation of *qur'*. They are, however, natives of the Arabic tongue.[117] If any of our [Mālikī] companions use *qur'* to refer to the period of purity, they have to prove that it is used in this context to convey that meaning. Some of them quoted ibn al-Anbārī who stated that the term *qur'* in singular form is equivocally used to mean both menstruation and purification periods, but it's plural form is *aqrā'* which should be restricted to mean 'menstruation periods' as in the Prophet's saying, ""Leave prayers at days you have *aqrā'*."[118] But when its plural is *qurū'* it means purification periods as in the poet's saying, "All is a recompense of what you missed of days your women had *qurū'*." The plural form used in the verse [Q. 2: 228] is *qurū'* and it should, therefore, refer to periods of purity, not menses.

Ḥanafīs contend [this view] by stating that had it been interpreted in this sense, the Companions would not have differed in its meaning. They were natives of Arabic and most cognizant of it. By their disagreement on the meaning, equivocality remains in both the singular and the plural as in the poet's saying, "He is like few men of malice, old in guilefulness, culminates in rancor as a woman agitates in her *qurū'* (menstruations)."[119]

Morphological Ambiguity[120]

An example is our [Mālikī] fellows' argument that the husband has the right in a child custody. They based their view on Allah's saying, "No mother should be *tuḍārr* (harmed) through her child, and no father through his child" (Q. 2: 233). Allah prohibits a woman to be harmed because of her child. It indicates that the husband has the right [and she must not be harmed by a manipulation of this right]. Opponents of this view among our [Mālikī] companions would argue that the verb may be pronounced *'lā tuḍārir'* (no mother should inflict harm through the child). In such a case it is possible to prove that custody is the right of a mother. But if the verb reads *'lā tuḍārar* in the passive form, it cannot be used an evidence for granting custody to mothers.

Those who [assigned the right of custody to mothers] countered that the verb must read in the active voice since the address is directed to a definite human agent [that is, mothers who are forbidden to inflict harm on fathers as mentioned in the text]. Considering the other interpretation would, however, make the addressee indefinite while commands and prohibitions must be directed to definite addressees.

Orthographic Ambiguity

For example, our [Mālikī] fellows uphold that selling gold and another item such as jewels for gold alone is prohibited. They based their view on the report of Faḍāla ibn 'Ubayd who related that a man asked the Prophet on a gold necklace inlaid with jewels he purchased for a piece of gold. The Prophet said, "It must not be sold until jewels and gold are '*tuffṣal*' separated."[121] The Prophet commanded him to sort gold out from jewels. He prohibited selling it as a whole. It indicates that selling gold along with another item for gold alone is not permissible.[122]

The disciples of abū Ḥanīfa would argue that the report is related in a variant wording, "It must not be sold until the price is '*tufḍal*' (that is, excels in amount)."[123] It means that such a transaction is not valid until gold paid as a price is of a greater amount than the gold inlayed with jewels. They, further, maintained that since the report with variant readings has been related as one occasion, the two [opposing] words cannot be issued by the Prophet (may God exalt his mention) due to discrepancy of their meanings. The phrase the Prophet has originally articulated should be definite but it is unknown for us. Therefore, we cannot take the report as a proof [until its meaning is clarified].

The answer of our [Mālikī] fellows is that the reading '*ḥatta tufaṣṣala*' (until it is separated) with the letter *ṣād* is more authenticated by the scholars of Hadith. It is a *maḥfūẓ* tradition.[124] It is further substantiated by a variant version, which reads, "*ḥatta tumayyaza*" (until gold is sorted out). Therefore, a variant version may provide explanation for the other. The version which reads, '*ḥatta tafuḍula*' necessitates adding a dot to letter *ṣād* to read it as *ḍād*. The default rule is that there is no diacritic mark to be added to a letter [except when there is a positive evidence to prove that].[125]

Another example is when ambiguity arises from a variance of the use of diacritic marks. Shāfiʿīs, for instance, prove that it is impermissible to sell grains in ears due to the Prophet's prohibition to sell corn until it *yufrak*, that is, rubbed and divested of its husks'. Ḥanafī scholars relate a variant reading of [*yufrak* by stating that it is pronounced as] *yafrik* that is, it becomes edible. [They further maintain that] when the pronunciation of a word differs, both [variants] are equivocal. Therefore, we cannot use it as a proof [for either side]. The Shāfiʿīs argue that both texts are regarded as distinct reports. Therefore, we have to act upon both.

Structural Ambiguity[126]

For example, our [Mālikī] companions prove that a father has the right to drop half of the assigned dowry [for the woman under his guardianship] in case the husband divorces her prior to the consummation of marriage. They based their view on Allah's saying, "And if you divorce them before you have touched them and you have already specified for them an obligation, then [give] half of what you specified—unless they forego the right or the one in whose hand is the marriage contract foregoes it" (Q. 2: 237). They interpreted the 'one in whose hand is the marriage contract foregoes it' as the guardian.

Shāfiʿī scholars argue that the structure may refer to the guardian or the husband. But Mālikī scholars contend that the context of the verse should refer to the father because it is an exception of the original rule, that is, it is incumbent on husbands to pay half of the specified dowry and exception occurs only when the woman or her guardian foregoes their right.

Structural Reading of Two Literal Segments

Abū Ḥanīfa's companions, for instance, uphold that it is permissible to perform ablution through *nabīdh*[127] of dates by reference to the Prophet's saying, "Dates are wholesome and pure water." They maintained that the Prophet referred to *nabīdh* by calling it a pure water. Our [Mālikī] fellows maintain that the phrase is a complex sentence [which reads: it is a date of a wholesome substance and a pure water] that is, *nabīdh* is a composite of dates and water. After mixing both it cannot either be called dates or pure water. Similarly, the number five is a composite of an even and an odd number, that is, three plus two. Neither of them can be called five since five is not an even number. *Muzz* is applied to a beverage that has a taste between sweet and sour. It cannot be described as sweet alone or sour alone. It proves that a complex phrase conveys a meaning different from meanings derived from its separable parts. Therefore, it is possible that the Prophet's saying (*thamaratun ṭayyibatun wa mā ʾun ṭahūr*) means that "*nabīdh* is a composite of wholesome dates and pure water." The Ḥanfīs further contend by stating that the report intends to give two separate [unrelated] units of a structure[128] because the Prophet used *nabīdh* for ablution.

Literal Reading of a Structure

For example, our [Mālikī] companions uphold that wiping over forefront alone cannot replace the wiping of head in ablution but it must be wiped along with the turban. They referred to the Prophet's practice that he wiped over his forehead and the turban. Had it been sufficient to wipe over forehead alone, the Prophet would have wipe it alone.

But the companions of Aḥmad and the opponents of [Mālikīs] argue that it is possible that the Prophet wiped over both of them at the same ablution and is equally possible that he wiped over his forehead or the turban alone. According to the latter assumption, it is permissible to just wipe over either the forehead or the turban [as a replacement of wiping over the head]. The answer of our [Mālikī] fellows is that al-Mughīra, the narrator of the report confirmed that it he wiped both the turban and the head at the same ablution.

However, these are the six reasons that cause ambivalence in a locution.

Clues[129]

Those clues may be locutionary, contextual or paratextual.

Locutionary Clue

An example [of a locutionary clue] is what has been related from ibn al-Anbārī regarding Allah's saying, "Divorced women remain in waiting for three *qurū ʾ*" (Q. 2: 228). When the [Arabic word] *qur ʾ* is presented in plural form as *qurū ʾ* [viz *aqrā'*], it, thus, means period between two menses and it cannot be used to signify menses. A form of plural makes the word univocal, though its singular is equivocal. The singular word *ʿūd* is equivocally used to mean 'a piece of wood' and 'a flute.' When its plural is *a ʿwād* it is exclusively used to mean 'pieces of wood' but when it is pluralized as *ʿīdān* it means 'flutes.' Such is the case of *amr* which indicates a command if it is pluralized as *awāmir* while its plural becomes *umūr* in case the singular means 'affair'.

Similarly, our [Mālikī] companions state that the word *aṭhār;* plural for *ṭuhr* (purification period) is masculine and therefore, the number adjective that precedes must be feminine. The word *ḥayḍ* (menses) is a feminine and the number adjective that follows must be masculine. So, we say, '*thalathu ḥiyaḍ*' (three menstruations) where we delete *tā'* which indicates feminine in the number '*thalathu*'. So when the word *qur'* was qualified in Allah's saying "*thalathatu qūrū'* (Q.2: 228)" by the number adjective '*thalathatu*' [with a feminine suffix], we made sure that *qūrū'* implies *aṭhār (*purification periods) which is masculine.[130]

Ḥanafī scholars countered that view by stating that one meaning may be expressed in two distinct words, one masculine and the other feminine. In such a case treating one word of them as a feminine is only because it has a feminine suffix. It does not mean that the word is masculine by meaning. We say, for example, it is a *jasad* and at the same time we say it is a *juththa* to mean one thing [that is, dead body], but in plural we distinguish them by saying *thalthatu ajsād* and *thalthu juthath* by treating the former as masculine and the latter as feminine.[131] Such is the case with regard to *ḥayḍa* which is a [singular] feminine. When it is used in its plural form, the suffix *tā'* was deleted of its number adjective. Similarly, *qurū'* is a masculine and therefore, its number adjective bears the feminine suffix '*tā'*'. Therefore, we can extend this rule to other similar locutionary clues.

Contextual Clue

For example, Ḥanfī and some Mālikī scholars permit the conclusion of a marriage contract by using a woman's spoken form 'I give myself to you' due to Allah's saying, "and a believing woman if she gives herself to the Prophet [and] if the Prophet wishes to marry her." (Q. 33: 50). If it is permissible for the Prophet to conclude marriage in the spoken form of a gift, the rule is extended to all other Muslims by means of analogy. Shāfiʿī scholars contend that when the Quran states that "this is a privilege only for you" (Q. 33: 50,) it implies that the Prophet (may God exalt his mention) has been privileged with something peculiar for him alone, without being shared by other Muslims. It is probable that such a privilege is the Prophet's right to marry without a dowry or it may be his right to conclude marriage in the spoken form of a gift. When a locution vacillates between two [equivocal] meanings, analogy cannot be based on one of them until one is preferred to the other. The preferred meaning may be that the Prophet is allowed to take a woman in marriage without compensation or that he is allowed to marry by the spoken form of a gift.

Shāfiʿīs maintain that the context of this verse better refers to the conclusion of marriage without a dowry since the verse was revealed in the occasion of showing the Prophet's eminence to his followers and for lifting any expected discomfort from him. This is indicated in Allah's saying, "We certainly know what We have made obligatory upon them concerning their wives and those their right hands possess, [but this is for you] in order that there will be upon you no discomfort." (Q. 33: 50).

Undoubtedly, excellence of the Prophet over others cannot be realized by just permitting him to get married through a specific spoken form and restricting it to others. His distinction may be attained by wavering dowry due on him. Therefore, Allah maintains three ways of permitting women for the Prophet:

1. Permission by means of a dowry, which is maintained in Allah's saying, "O Prophet, indeed We have made lawful to you your wives to whom you have given their due compensation." (Q. 33: 50).
2. Permission by means of possession as mentioned in Allah's saying, "and those your right hand possesses from what Allah has returned to you [of captives." (Q. 33: 50).
3. Permission to get married without a dowry as it is mentioned in Allah's saying, "and a believing woman if she gives herself to the Prophet [and] if the Prophet wishes to marry her, [this is] only for you, excluding the [other] believers." (Q. 33: 50).

Discomfort negated in this verse refers to the obligation of a dowry on him. It cannot refer to the permissibility of exclusively using a spoken form in concluding a contract of marriage which can be held by much easier forms. Peculiarity of the Prophet according to the context refers to getting married without compensation. It cannot refer to exclusively using a specific spoken form.

Paratextual Clues

It is when one of the two equivocal meanings is substantiated by virtue of an extraneous proof. This substantiating proof may be:

1. A partext
2. An analogy
3. A precedent of a *Ṣaḥābī*.

1. Paratext: For example, our [Mālikī] fellows maintain that *qurūʾ* implies purification periods due to Allah's saying, "O Prophet, when you [Muslims] divorce women, divorce them for [the commencement of] their waiting period," (Q. 65: 1), where Allah commanded women, upon divorce, to commence on their waiting period. According to ibn Masʿūd's variant reading, "divorce them for *the* *commencement of* their waiting period." This is only possible when a woman is in her purification period, since divorce is prohibited during a woman's menses.

Ḥanafīs substantiate their view by another external clue, that is, Allah's saying, "And those who no longer expect menstruation among your women—if you doubt, then their period is three months, and [also for] those who have not menstruated." (Q. 65: 4). According to this verse, months have been made as a substitute for menstruations, not for purification periods. Therefore, menses is the basis to determine a woman's waiting period. Such is the case of clean earth substitutes water according to the verse, "And if you are ill or on a journey or one of you comes from the place of relieving himself or you have contacted women and find no water, then seek clean earth." (Q. 4: 43).

2. Analogy: For example, our [Mālikī] fellows and Shāfiʿīs maintained that enjoining a waiting period upon divorce is an obligatory ordainment. It is an act of worship. Menstruation is an impediment of a number of rituals such as prayers, fasting and circumambulation around *kaʿba.* Analogy necessitates that postmarital waiting period is better measured by women's purification intervals. Therefore, the word *qurūʾ* is better interpreted to mean 'purification periods'.

3. Precedents of the Prophet's *Ṣaḥābī*. An example is the scholars' argument on the obligation of washing feet [in ablution] due to Allah's saying, "O you who have believed, when you rise to [perform] prayer, wash your faces and your forearms to the elbows and wipe over your heads and [wash] your feet to the ankles" Q. 5: 6, where the word '*arjulakum*' is of the accusative case in conjunction with face and hand and must therefore be washed like them.

An opponent may argue that the feet may be in conjunction with head [which is to be wiped]. In this case it cannot be used as a proof to prove the obligation of washing the feet. But scholars counter argue that all the *ṣaḥāba* and *tabiʾūn* (may Allah be pleased with them) have washed their feet and none of them wiped over them. Therefore, the meaning of *wa arjulakum* is "and wash your feet to the ankles" as being in conjunction with limbs which must be washed.

Uṣīlīs, however, differed on whether to regard the following texts ambivalent or self-evident:

First, when the subject matter of a legal decision is a human agent, does it, then, entail ambivalence[132]? An example is Allah's saying, "Prohibited to you are your mothers." (Q. 4: 23) and His saying, "Prohibited to you are dead animals." (Q. 5: 3), where He related prohibition to mothers and dead animals. Prohibition is a legal decision which describes an action [not a human agent]. [Scholars] differed on whether to regard this text ambivalent or not.

Those who state that it is an ambivalent text maintain that when it is unreasonable to apply a prohibition to a human agent, there must be a conceived meaning [without which the text would remain incomplete]

If we conclude that a necessary and logical meaning is conceived through the text, we may postulate all possible readings but this is void. The reason is that detecting a missing element in a phrase is an exception [to the default rule]. It is only read when it is deemed necessary to fulfill the proper objective of speech. Therefore, one possible reading must be conceived.

The missing part of the text may be definite or indefinite. If it is definite, it is invalid, since it is tantamount to the acceptance of a definite textual implication from variant possible readings of the text [without valid justification]. It would thus entail unjustified preference. This is the reason the text must be held ambivalent.

The majority of scholars uphold that the missing text cannot be ambivalent since it is determined by reference to custom or the context. For mothers, the missing intended meaning of prohibition is marriage while it is consumption in the case of dead carcass.

Second, a text does necessitate an ellipsis in order to become true, can we regard such a text *mujmal*? For example, the Prophet (may God exalt his mention) has been reported as saying, "Allah has rid my nation of inadvertence, forgetfulness." Those who necessitate a missing element in the text read it as follows, "Allah has rid my nation *of the burden of a sin done out of* inadvertence or forgetfulness."

Third, when the text negates the existence of something [which exists in reality], can we regard this text *mujmal*? For example, the Prophet (may God exalt his mention) has been reported as saying, "There is no marriage without a guardian," "There is no prayer without the recitation of *al-Fātiḥa*," and "There is no fasting for one who does not form his intention to fast before *fajr*." Scholars differed on this. Those who hold these texts ambivalent state that the existence of a marriage without a guardian, prayers without the recitation of *al-fātiḥa* and fasting without intention cannot be negated in reality. So that we have to add words to the text to seem intelligible. For example, we should make it: "There is no *valid* marriage without a guardian," "There is no *valid* prayer without the recitation of *al-fātiḥa*," and "There is no *valid* fasting without intention." It similarly possible to add the word 'complete' instead of 'valid' to make the text read as follows, "There is no *complete* marriage without a guardian," "There is no *complete* prayer without a recitation of *al-fātiḥa*," and "There is no *complete* fasting without intention." In this case of vacillation, the text proves to be ambivalent and we cannot, thus, [decisively] regard the missing of any of those elements as a base for invalidity [of those ritual acts].

Those who do not presume those texts ambivalent [are of two groups:] Some of them do not see a need for adding text to complement the meaning, because [marriage, prayer and fasting] are legal rites and they can be possibly negated [from a legal perspective]. Therefore, any ritual act which is devoid of its legal prerequisites cannot be named [for instance] a legal marriage or a legal fasting.

Others make it necessary to add a word to the text to regard those acts invalid [in case their conditions are absent]. Those acts are, thus, held invalid, since validity is the fruit [and benefit] of a legal act. Custom, moreover, supports this presupposition. They say, "There is no knowledge but that which avails a benefit." They further support their view by maintaining that when the literal meaning of the phrase is not intelligible, a recourse is due to the closest metaphorical interpretation. To add a word to the text to make such an act invalid is preferred to assuming the whole phrase untrue. That is why we negate the validity of such act instead of negating their occurrence in reality.

Fourth, when a locution is equivocal in the sense it vacillates between two meanings, is it *mujmal*?. In case we interpret it according to a certain meaning, one definite legal determination is deduced but when we interpret it according to the other meaning, two distinct legal rulings may be deduced.

For example, the Prophet is reported as saying, "*Wa-man istajmara fa-lūtir*" which may be interpreted to mean "If you use stones to clean your private parts do it in odd number" or "If you use stones to clean your private parts use an odd number [stones]." The odd number may be a requisite for the number of times one has to clean his private. It does not therefore require using an odd number of pebbles because one may clean himself three times by using two pebbles only [if he uses one pebble twice]. But if odd number is a requisite in pebbles, one has to use three pebbles and consequently repeat the action three times. Scholars differed on this text whether to regard it ambivalent or interpreting it according to the meaning which procures greater number of legal decisions. The erudite among *uṣūlīs* maintain it is ambivalent because eliciting legal rulings of a text comes after determining which meaning the text is interpreted accordingly. We cannot base our determination on the number of rulings deduced since it may lead to vicious circular argument.

Fifth, when a locution vacillates between a juristic and a literal meaning, [do scholars regard it a *mujmal*?] For example, the Prophet has been reported as saying, "Two or more are *jamāʿah* (*congregation*)" and "Circumambulation around the sacred house is a *salat.*" It is possible that he means that two or more are the least amount of plural and that circumambulation is literally defined as *salat.* It is similarly possible to interpret it to mean that the lawgiver made *ṭawāf* a form of prayer and assigned two as the minimum number for a congregation. Some scholars uphold these texts as ambivalent. They based their view on the fact that each word vacillates between two meanings. Others maintain that the Prophet has been sent to show legal concepts of words not to define them linguistically.

Sixth, when a word has a literal and a legal meaning. For example, the Prophet has been reported as saying, "Perform *wuḍūʾ* upon [eating] that which has been touched by fire." It is possible for *wuḍūʾ* to mean ritual ablution or washing. Some scholars presumed the word as ambivalent because it vacillates between two meanings. Others maintain it is self-evident by restricting the word to its legal meaning only.

iii. *Ẓāhir* (Manifest Meaning)

Ẓāhir is a locution that while it may be used to indicate two meanings is preponderantly used for one as opposed to the other with respect to its primary meaning. As such its indication is clear.[133] There are eight means by which the primary meaning of a word may be identified:

Literal vs. Allegorical

Ḥaqīqa is to use of a word in in its primary meaning such as using the word 'lion' to refer to the ferocious beast. *Majāz* is the use of a word to indicate something other than the literal meaning. This transference of meaning is based on a relationship between the metaphorical and the literal meanings such as using the word 'lion' to indicate a courageous person.[134] When it is possible to understand a word in both a literal as well as a metaphorical sense, the literal meaning takes precedence. The literal meaning is broken down into three subcategories:

(a) Linguistic meaning as opposed to metaphorical connotation.
(b) Legal meaning as opposed to metaphorical connotation.
(c) Customary meaning as opposed to metaphorical connotation.

An example of linguistic meaning is found in the argument put forth by the Shāfiʿīs and Ibn Ḥabīb, which purports that the option to cancel [a contract of sale] through *khiyār al-majlis*[135] is permitted [until the two parts take leave of each other] on the basis of the Prophet's words, "The two parties contracting a sale have the option of cancelling the contract as long as they have not separated.[136]" The Mālikīs and Ḥanafīs, however, interpret the word *al-mutabāyiʿān* to mean the two parties who are negotiating with each other [over the price of a sale]. They further interpret the separation [in this context] to be verbal [by verbally expressing their mutual consent]. Therefore, [according to their position] the option of cancelling a contract is [only] valid so long as the two parties are involved in negotiation. Upon concluding the contract [by expressing verbal consent], they have separated and thus the contract becomes binding.

[In support of their position, they assert that] the name for something may be used to refer to something which leads to it, as in the Prophet's words, "None of you should make [an offer of] sale against his brother's [offer of] sale, or a [proposal of] marriage against his brother's [proposal of] marriage.[137]" Here, the word *bay*ʿ [which originally means sale or purchase] is used to mean an offer of sale, and *nikāḥ* [which primarily means marriage] is used to refer to a proposal of marriage. [This transference of meaning is possible] because making an offer is a means to contracting a sale, just as proposing is a means to marriage. Moreover, this meaning is confirmed by another version of the *hadith*, wherein the Prophet is reported as saying, "A Muslim should not make an offer of sale against that of his brother, and he should not make a proposal of marriage against a proposal already made by his brother.[138]"

The Shāfiʿīs counter that using the word *al-mutabāyiʿān* to refer to the two negotiating parties to a sale is metaphorical, as is the use of *al-tafarruq* (separation) to refer to closing the sale. [Thus they refute the Ḥanafī and Mālikī interpretation as it contradicts] the basic principle that speech is to be interpreted literally [unless there is supporting evidence that clearly indicates that it should be interpreted otherwise].

With regard to legal meaning, scholars of *uṣūl* differed concerning the possibility of its occurrence. The majority of scholars of *uṣūl* uphold that this usage is possible. They based their view on citing a survey of religious texts as an evidence. Upon examination of words like *salat, zakat, sawm* and *hajj*, it is evident that the Lawgiver used these terms [primarily] in their legal connotations to refer to [well-known] acts of worship, which proves the existence of legal usage [of words].

An example of this is the Mālikīs' assertion that it is prohibited for one who is in state of *iḥrām*[139] to marry, according to the Prophet's words, "A *muḥrim* should neither marry himself, nor should he solemnize the marriage of anyone else.[140]"

The Ḥanafīs argue that *nikāḥ* is used in this *hadith* to mean intercourse, as the poet said, "Like a virgin, longing for the sweetness of *nikāḥ* (intercourse), yet dreading the aggression of her lover's passion." According to this interpretation, the report indicates that it is prohibited [for a *muḥrim*] to have intercourse; not to conclude a contract of marriage.

The answer of our [Mālikī] companions is that interpreting *nikāḥ* as conjugal relations is a metaphorical connotation, while using it for the marriage contract is the legal denotation. Moreover, interpreting the term according to the legal denotation takes precedence over interpreting it according to the metaphorical.

A customary meaning may also prevail when a spouse addresses his wife saying, "*antī ṭāliq*," (you are released) claiming that he meant that she is released from fetters. It is true that he used the word in its literal sense, that is, to be released from chains, etc., however, this word is used in its customary sense to refer to the dissolution of marriage, and in metaphorical sense to refer to being released from fetters. Interpreting it according to the customary meaning takes precedence over interpreting it according to the metaphorical meaning.

This is further exemplified by the Prophetic statement that was taken as evidence by our Mālikī companions that a virgin's father can force her to get married, "A *yatīma* should not be given in marriage except after consulting her.[141]" Being that a *yatīma* is a girl who is fatherless, it is thus understood that a girl who is not a *yatīma,* that is, a girl who has a father, may be given in marriage without being consulted.[142]

Our Mālikī fellows counter by saying that the customary meaning of *yatīma* is a fatherless woman. It is used in this context in Allah's Words, "And test the *orphans* [in their abilities] until they reach marriageable age" (Q. 4: 6), and His saying "And know that anything you obtain of war booty—then indeed, for Allah is one fifth of it and for the Messenger and for [his] near relatives and the orphans" (Q. 8: 41). This is the most common meaning according to the prevailing custom. According to this interpretation, interpreting this word according to its customary meaning is preferable to interpreting it according to its metaphorical connotation.

An opponent of this view argues that *'yatīm'* literally means 'one who is singled out or isolated'. Thus, when a poet issues a single verse of poetry it is called *'yatīm'*. It is similarly used to mean a matchless. Therefore, *'yatīma'* in the context of [the Prophet's statement] refers to a spouseless woman. The Arab poet says: Indeed, graves encompass the unmarried, such are the widowed and *yatāma* (lonely women). Since the word *'yatīma'* [literally] refers to an unmarried woman, the report cannot be used as a proof [for this ruling].

Our Mālikī fellows counter back by saying that the customary meaning of *yatīma* is a fatherless woman. It is used in the context of Allah's saying, "And test the orphans [in their abilities] until they reach marriageable age." (Q. 4: 6) and in His saying, "And know that anything you obtain of war booty—then indeed, for Allah is one fifth of it and for the Messenger and for [his] near relatives and the orphans." (Q. 8: 41). [Using it to refer to orphans] is the most popular meaning according to dominant custom. Therefore, interpreting a word according to its customary meaning is preferable to using it in other meanings.

Monosyemous vs. Polysemous

[The assumption that a word is] polysemous contradicts the default rule [that each word has only one primary meaning]. For example, the majority of scholars of *uṣūl* hold that the Arabic word, *'amr'* (lit. order) entails obligation when used in the context "*amr* of the Prophet" as in Allah's Words, "So let those beware who dissent from the Prophet's order, lest trial strike them or a painful punishment." (Q. 24: 63).

It could be argued, however, that while it is possible that the word '*amr*' in this text indicates a verbal order, it could also be interpreted to mean an affair and action, as in the context of Allah's words, "And the *amr (*affair) of Pharaoh was not [at all] right" (Q. 11: 97). If, in fact, the word *amr* can be used for something other than a specific statement, considering that the default rule is that words are used literally, then we must assume that the word *amr* is polysemous, denoting both meanings, [a command and an affair.] Polysemy, however, would render the text an inadequate source of evidence.

According to majority of scholars, the basic principle is that words are [by default] monosemous; not polysemous. Therefore, one of the two definitions must be the primary meaning of the word *amr,* while the other is metaphorical. We have reached consensus that *amr* literally means order. Therefore, using it to mean "an affair" is a metaphorical transference from the original meaning, according to what we mentioned previously, that a word should be interpreted literally, rather than metaphorically. Therefore, if there is a disagreement as to whether a word is being used metaphorically or equivocally, the former presumption takes precedence over the latter.

Mononymous vs. Synonymous

In the Arabic language, [words mentioned within a single text] are [presumed by default to] being unique in giving one intended meaning, rather than being synonymous. For example, our Malikī fellows argue that *tayammum* may be performed using whatever comprises the surface of land, as indicated by Allah's Words, "Then seek clean *ṣaʿīd* and wipe over your faces and your hands [with it]. Indeed, Allah is ever Pardoning and Forgiving." (Q. 4: 43).

The word *ṣaʿīd* is derived from *ṣuʿūd,* which means rising. Thus, it is used to signify everything which rises to the surface of the earth. The Shāfiʿīs maintain that *ṣaʿīd* is a synonym for *turāb* (dust). The author of *al-Ṣaḥḥāḥ* dictionary says, "*ṣaʿīd* means dust." Shāfiʿī, who is an authority in Arabic, sates that *ṣaʿīd* is a mononym for dust.

Our [Mālikī fellows] rebut this argument by maintaining that if *ṣaʿīd* is used to mean dust, the reason is that it is one of the elements which rises to the surface of the earth [thus it is derived from the verb *ṣaʿada*]. It may be also called dust disregarding its derivation. If it is used to mean dust without being derived from *ṣaʿada,* the word *ṣaʿīd* [in this case should be regarded as] a synonym for *turāb,* but this is not the norm. Therefore, *ṣaʿīd* must be regarded as distinct from *turāib* Therefore, *ṣaʿīd* is used for everything that rises up to the surface of the earth [including dust].

Straight vs. Elliptical

The consistent norm of Arabic speech is to be straight, that is, no word(s) are left out of a sentence. For example, some of our [Mālikī] fellows argued that it is prohibited to eat beasts of prey. They based their view on the Prophet's words, "Eating [the flesh of] beasts of prey is prohibited." Opponents of this view among Mālikīs contest that the Prophet (may God exalt his mention) only prohibited the remains of what is left by beasts of prey, not the flesh of beasts, since they are inedible. According to this interpretation, the report concurs with the [verse of the] Quran, "Prohibited to you are …., and those from which a wild animal has eaten." (Q. 5: 3).

The first view counter that if we interpret the report according to the Quranic verse, we must admit that something has been left out of the sentence by acknowledging that there is an ellipsis. Therefore, the report should read, "Eating [the flesh of] animals from which a wild beast has eaten is prohibited." As such, the style of the report is not straight, whereas, the default rule is to presume that all texts are straight [and do not have ellipsis, unless there is certain evidence to prove the contrary].

To Inform, Rather Than Convince

For example our [Mālikī] fellows argue that *mutʿa* (divorce compensation)[143] is not incumbent upon one who divorces his wife. They based their view on Allah's words, "But give them [a gift of] compensation—the wealthy according to his capability and the poor according to his capability—a provision according to what is acceptable, a duty upon the doers of good." (Q. 2: 236) and His saying, "And for divorced women is a provision according to what is acceptable—a duty upon the righteous." (Q. 2: 242).

Presumably, this obligation is not addressed solely to doers of good or righteous people. In fact, it is due on them in addition to others as well. It could be argued, however, that the divorce compensation is incumbent –[only] upon the doers of right and the righteous, in a style to lay emphasis. It is an incentive for other men who divorce their wives to act like those who are righteous and doers of good [but it is not obligatory on others]. In this case, the style is interpreted to be persuasive and [therefore] cannot be used as an evidence for obligation.

Our [Mālikī] fellows counter that the default rule is to a presume a text emphatic, not inceptive.

Syntagmatic vs. Ansastrophic

For example, the Mālikīs and their proponents hold that going back on *ẓihār*[144] is a proviso for the obligation of a penance due to Allah's saying, "And those who swear *ẓihār* to their wives and then [wish to] go back on what they said—then [there must be] the freeing of a slave before they touch one another." (Q. 58: 3).

An opponent argues that such a verse should [logically] read as follows: "And those who swear *ẓihār* to their wives [there must be] the freeing of a slave before they touch one another, and then if they wish they can go back to [to their spouses]", that is, those who rendered their wives unlawful by vowing an oath of *ẓihār* must pay a penance, then he can go back to conjugal relation with his wife without bearing a sin. This is because pronouncing *ẓihār* is both iniquitous and false. So, a mere pronouncement of *ẓihār* necessitates a penance.

But our [Mālikī] fellows counter that [reading by baseding themselves on] the existing order of sentence whis is supposed to to prevail over [other] interpretation which is based on [presumed] *hysteron proteron.*[145]

ʿAmm *vis* Khāṣṣ

ʿĀmm is a word which includes everything to which it is applicable[146]; being an antonym for *khāṣṣ* (specific). It refers to a word or a phrase, which is applied to a limited number of things. [The scope of] *ʿāmm* may be determined by reference to language, custom or reasoning.

ʿAmm *Determined by Language*

Know that a general word may indicate generality by its inherent [grammatical] pattern or by virtue of another grammatical form [added to the word such as a prefix or a suffix]. We are going to discuss the former type in the following three points:

Conditional Particles

They indicate generality at any context, provided that it grammatically befits them; one of those particles is the Arabic particle *man* (whosoever).

Our [Mālikī] fellows argue that a *dhimmī* (a non-Muslim living under the auspice of a Muslim state) can possess a waste[147] land by reviving it. They based their view on the Prophet's saying "Whoever cultivates waste lands does thereby acquire the property thereof."[148] A *dhimmī* is included within the general terms of the report.

They further argue for the execution of a female apostate[149] by the Prophet's (may God exalt his mention) saying, "Whoever changes his religion kill him[150]."

Furthermore, Ḥanafīs prove that whoever takes possession of his [slave] paternal or maternal uncles must immediately emancipate them by the Prophet's saying, "Whoever possesses a relative who is within the prohibited degree, that person becomes free".[151]

Furthermore, *mā* (whatever) is one of the particles of condition [which is used to indicate generality]. Our [Mālikī] fellows and the majority of jurists maintained that whatever is left of a deceased's estate after fulfilling entitled shares of inheritance is given for the male line of relationship. This is due to the Prophet's (may God exalt his mention) saying, "Give the shares of inheritance as prescribed in the

Quran to those entitled to receive them; and whatever is left should be given to the nearest male relative of the deceased."[152]

Likewise, some of our [Mālikī] scholars argue that whoever misses acts or invocations of a congregational prayer must make them up[153] due to the Prophet's (may God exalt his mention) saying, "and whatever you catch up with, pray, and whatever you miss, make it up." There are, however, other examples for what we have mentioned.

Interrogative Pronouns

Our [Mālikī] scholars argue that it is prohibited to take sexual enjoyment of what is between naval and knees of a wife [during menses]. They based their view on the report of a man who asked the Prophet's (may God exalt his mention) saying, "What is permissible for me to do with my wife during her menses." The Prophet said, "Let her wrap her waist-wrapper round herself tightly, and then what is above that is your concern."[154] There are further examples for this.

Relative Pronouns

Shāfiʿīs argue that a *dhimmī* has to afford the penance for *ẓihār* (injurious dissimulation) due to the general terms of Allah's saying, "And those who swear *ẓihār* to their wives ..." (Q. 58: 3).

Similarly, some of our [Mālikī] jurists recommended to exactly repeat all phrases of a prayer call due to the [generality] of the Prophet's (may God exalt his mention) saying, "When you hear the call to prayer, you should repeat the same words as the *muʾadhin* pronounces."

Some of the [Mālikī] jurists argued that whoever commits adultery with a woman, her descendants and ancestors are permissible to get in marriage, due to the [the general terms of] Allah's saying, "marry those that please you of [other] women." (Q. 4: 3). They further permitted to offer prayer led by a sinful person based on the Prophet's (may God exalt his mention) saying, "Offer prayer behind whoever proclaims that there is no deity but Allah.[155]" There are other examples like those which have been mentioned.

The second type of patterns that indicate generality is when another grammatical form [is added to the word as a prefix or a suffix]. It is further sub-classified into two types: (a) words or phrases, which indicate generality by use of prefixes and (b) those, which indicate generality by use of suffixes. The former includes particles of condition, interrogative pronouns, and negative forms preceding an indefinite phrase, the definite article for generic use, and words like *kull* (every, each) and *jamīʿ* (all, entire). All these particles indicate generality. We are going to discuss them in the following five points:

Ayy (Any, Whoever, Whichever) When Used in a Conditional Sentence

Our [Mālikī] jurists argue that if a free sane and puberulent woman concludes a marriage contract on behalf of herself, it must be rendered null and void. They based their view on the Prophet's (may God exalt his mention) saying, "Whichever woman marries without the permission of her *walī* (gurdian) her marriage is invalid, her marriage is invalid, her marriage is invalid.[156]" They further maintain that the hide of inedible animals can be purified through tanning. They based their view on the Prophet's (may God exalt his mention) saying, "Any skin that is tanned becomes purified.[157]"

Interrogative ayy 'which' [or kayf 'however']

It indicates the generality of any phrase it prefixes. Moreover, an answer following a question [which uses this particle] is general. Ibn al-Qāsim, the Mālikī jurist, argues that emancipating a non-Muslim slave is better rewarded than freeing a Muslim slave of a lower price.[158] He based his view on the report of the Prophet (may God exalt his mention) who was asked, "Which best slave to free?" he said, "The most expensive.[159]"

Such is the case of proving that a deceased's cognates have no share in the estate due to the report of Jābir who said, "My case of inheritance is that of a *kalāla* [where one leaves neither ascendants nor descendants]. So, how will be my inheritance?" Then Allah revealed the verse indicating prescribed distribution of inheritance (Q. 4: 12).[160] Because the verse assigning shares of inheritance was revealed in response to a question, it exclusively indicated who should inherit. It did not give any mention for cognates.

Indefinite Noun After Negative

Our [Mālikī] fellows argue that an increase of [*zakattable*] wealth which is procured during the year cannot be added to capital. They based their view on the Prophet's (may God exalt his mention) saying, "*Zakat* does not have to be paid on property until a year has elapsed over it."[161]

They further quoted the Prophet's (may God exalt his mention) saying, "Whoever does not form his intention to fast before *fajr* his fasting is not accepted.[162]" to prove that intending to fast before dawn is obligatory even in supererogatory fasting.[163]

Definite Articles Before Generic Nouns

The definite article *'al'* indicates generality if it precedes a noun either singular or plural. Some scholars maintained that it does not indicate generality in both cases. A third group uphold that it indicates generality when it comes before a plural noun only.

For example, our [Mālikī] jurists argue that selling a hound is impermissible due to the Prophet's (may God exalt his mention) saying, "The price of a dog is prohibited."[164] The word *al-kalb* (a dog) is a general word since it is a generic noun prefixed by the definite article *al.*

An example of the definite *al* prefixing a plural noun is our [Mālikī] jurists' argument that the leftover of a dog is pure. They based their argument on the report of the Prophet (may God exalt his mention) when he was asked, "Should we perform ablution of a donkey's leftover?" He said, "Yes and also of the leftover of beasts."[165]

Words Like Kull (Every, Each) and Jamī' (All, Entire).

If those words prefix a noun, they indicate generality. For example, our [Mālikī] fellows maintain that *nabīdh*[166] is prohibited. They based their view on the Prophet's (may God exalt his mention) saying "Every intoxicant is prohibited.[167]"

Similarly, Shāfi'ī jurists do not allow a husband to be a guardian for the woman whom he marries. They based their view on the Prophet's (may God exalt his mention) saying, "All marriages not attended by four are but fornication: a suitor, a guardian and two upright witnesses.[168]"

Generality may also be demonstrated by suffixes such when a word is related to genitive which is a proper noun, a definite noun, a pronoun, a relative pronoun or a demonstrative pronoun. For example, our [Mālikī] jurists argued that a congregation is graded according to the number of worshipers involved. They based their view on the Prophet's (may God exalt his mention) saying, "The prayer in congregation is twenty seven times superior to the prayer offered by a person alone."[169] They maintained that every congregation is 27 times superior to any prayer offered by anyone alone. Therefore, all congregations are equal in reward.

Another example is our [Mālikī] scholars' argument that when one engages in a ritual act which has a beginning and an end as prayer or fasting, he cannot cut it. They based their view on Allah's saying, "and do not invalidate your deeds." (Q. 47: 33). A supererogatory act is covered by the scope of the general terms [of this verse].

Another example is al-Shāfi'ī's argument that a penance is obligatory for one who indulged a *yamīn ghamūs.*[170] They based their argument on Allah's saying, "That is the expiation for oaths when you have sworn." Q5:89. A dipping oath is included in the general scope of oaths.

'Amm Determined by Custom

A text may have an ellipsis where it seems essential to complement it. The scope of a text in this case is presumed to be general by reference to custom. An example is Allah's saying, "Prohibited to you are your mothers." (Q. 4: 23). When custom determined the meaning on which the text is silent to be sexual enjoyment, it further maintained that prohibition is extended to include all types of sexual enjoyment with one's mother. When custom fails to determine a specific meaning, some scholars state that the text is general and it should be interpreted to include all possible meanings. The reason is that the text in this case should not be considered general and a specific meaning may be conceived. It is void to prefer a specific meaning to be conceived from a text without a justifiable reason. Moreover, presuming that the text is equivocal cannot be the default case.

Some scholars maintained that the text is equivocal. They hold that because it is necessary to presume an ellipsis in the text, the text cannot be meaningful without it. This ellipsis must be conceived within the limits of necessity. All possible meanings of an elliptic part cannot be conceived [simultaneously].

For example, our [Mālikī] companions held that it is prohibited to benefit from anything of a dead animal. They based their view on Allah's saying, "Prohibited to you are dead animals." (Q. 5: 3). When it became hardly possible to describe dead animals as prohibited, an absent meaning must be assumed. As there is no definite or specific meaning to presume, the text is deemed *mujmal* (ambivalent). Therefore, prohibition is generally extended to include all types of benefit [from a dead animal]. Some [scholars] may prefer to regard the text *mujmal* but can determine an assumed meaning by custom, that is, prohibition of eating dead animals.

Similarly, Shāfiʿīs held that whoever eats or drinks something unintentionally while fasting is exempted from making up that day. They based their view on the Prophet's saying, "Allah has rid my nation of inadvertence and forgetfulness.[171]" Since an absence of inadvertence and forgetfulness is not possible [in reality], the truthfulness of the lawgiver's statement necessitates that an absent meaning is assumed. Such a meaning is not [decisively] determined. Therefore, we can assume all possible meanings. The meaning is that my nation will not be held accountable for inadvertence or forgetfulness.

ʿAmm Conceived by Common Sense

It is classified into two types: (A) a ruling is deemed to be *ʿāmm* because its rationale is general. This is stated in the context of *qiyās*.[172] (B) when a verb is expressed in a negative form such as [the case of one who makes an oath by] saying, "By Allah, I have never eaten." His oath is breached by eating anything.[173] If he does not mention an object [in his oath by saying by Allah I have not eaten, scholars disagreed:] according to our [Mālikī] jurists, if he intends that he has not eaten something specific, his intention will benfit him. It would be like *ʿamm* determined by language [which is open for specification].[174] But, according to Ḥanfīs, his intention will not benefit since [the phrase] is regarded as *ʿamm* which is determined by reasoning. It is, thus, not apt for specification.

Conclusion of ʿAmm

We are going to conclude [our discussion on] *ʿamm* by elaborating two further issues:

The first issue is when a general word is equivocally used for two [equal] meanings or when one meaning is the primary meaning and the other is metaphorical and there is no clue to indicate whether one should be preferred to the other. In such a case, the question remains that is it possible to regard both meanings intended [by the lawgiver?]

The majority of *uṣūlīs* hold that such a word cannot be of general application to both meanings simply because if the two meanings do not have something in common, a single word cannot be interpreted to mean both.

An example of an equivocal word is the Shāfiʿīs' proving that divorce under coercion is not effective.[175] They based their view on the Prophet's saying, "There is no divorce [to be effective] when one is in a state of *ighlāq*[176] 'straitness'."[177] Literally, *ighlāq* means coercion.

The Ḥanafīs maintain that *ighlāq* is an equivocal term, which implies both madness[178] and coercion. It cannot be restricted to mean coercion without an indication [in the text] to support this meaning. The Shāfiʿīs counter them by stating that *ighlāq* is equivocally used to mean madness and coercion. Therefore, it is used to generally imply both madness and coercion.

An example of [a word having] a real and a metaphorical meaning[179] is some scholars' proving that whoever is invited to bear witness must accept invitation like the one who is invited to deliver a testimony.[180] This is based on Allah's saying, "And let not the witnesses refuse when they are called upon." (Q. 2: 282). Therefore, it is generally incumbent upon one who is invited to witness to go and bear testimony as it is obligatory for one who has already witnessed to [deliver the testimony].

The majority of scholars state that the word *shāhid* (witness) is originally used to mean 'a person who is going to see' and allegorically for 'the one who has already witnessed'.[181] Such is the case of understanding the word *ʿaṣīr* 'juice' to mean wine, though it has not been pressed to be called wine.[182]

The second case is when the textual implication of a general locution is speculative to include all its underlying members but it is definitive with regard to the least number of a plural.

Scholars differed on the minimum number of a plural. Some of them maintained that it is three[183] while others stated that it is only composed of two.[184] Therefore, ibn ʿAbbās differed with Zayd ibn Thābit on whether a mother's share of inheritance should be reduced to be a sixth instead of a third in the presence of two brothers or not. Zayd maintained that her share must be reduced in the presence of two while ibn ʿAbbas only reduces her share in the presence of [at least] three.

The fellows of our [Mālikī] school of law have differed on the one who acknowledges *darāhim* [pl. of *dirham*[185]] he owes to someone [without giving mention to their exact number]. Mālik states that he has to pay his creditor 3 *dirhams*. Ibn al-Mājishūn states that he owes him only two. This is based on their disagreement on the minimum number of a plural [in Arabic]. The majority of *uṣūlīs* maintain that primarily, the minimum number of a plural is three while it is allegorically used for two only. Based on this disagreement, scholars differed on the maximum number that may be exempted of a plural [to be either two or one].

Absolute vs. Qualified

When a word is in the form of a generic noun it is called *muṭlaq*.[186] *Muṭlaq*[187] remains absolute in application unless there is a limitation is found to qualify it. For example, the Ḥanafīs argued that a non-Muslim slave is legally efficient to expiate a futile oath due to Allah's saying, "or the freeing of a slave." (Q. 5: 89) and for expiating *ẓihār* (injurious dissimulation) due to Allah's saying, "then [there must be] the freeing of a slave." (Q. 58: 3).

But the Mālikīs and Shāfiʿīs argue that the slave intended in both verses refers to a Muslim slave as it is explicitly mentioned in the context of expiation for murder [in Q. 4: 93]. The Ḥanafīs counter argue that it is a restriction of an absolute word, which is supposed to remain unqualified. Due to the fact that *takhṣīṣ* (specifying the scope of a general) and *taqyīd* (limiting the scope of an absolute) are both related to *muʾawwal*. We are going to elaborate them when we discuss it later.

iv. Muʾawwal (Susceptible to Interpretation)

M*uʾawwal*[188] is a word or a phrase which vacillates between two or more meanings one of them predominates others due to an external proof, as opposed to *ẓāhir*.[189] The causes of endorsing a meaning as *ẓāhir* were eight and such is the case of endorsing a meaning to be *muʾawwal*. They are as follows:

Allegorical vs. Literal

We have proceeded that a word may have a literal, legal or customary meaning and each one these has its allegorical alternative. An example for a literal vs. allegorical meaning is our [Mālikī] jurists' argument that when a seller finds his commodities still intact in the possession of a bankrupt he can regain them without sharing other creditors in a bankrupt's [suspended] wealth.[190] They based their view on the Prophet's saying, "Anyone who dies or goes bankrupt, an owner of a property is more entitled with it, if he finds his very property.[191]" The Ḥanafīs maintain that 'an owner of a property' literally refers to the one who has the right of seizing. It literally refers to the bankrupt. It allegorically refers to the [previous] owner who is no longer a possessor of the property. When a word is derived to express a specific meaning and such a meaning no longer exists it becomes allegorical.[192] [Though it is possible in some instances,] it is not consistent in all cases. [Therefore], can you call an infidel who has already embraced Islam a *kāfir* [due to his previous state of disbelief]? It means that using a word to express a previous state [which no longer exists] is a migration [from literal to allegorical usage].

Our [Mālikī] fellows counter that [a textual] clue indicates that the allegorical meaning is intended. If it refers to the bankrupt, there will be no need to make insolvency a condition [for an owner's right to regain his property]. [Similarly, if he intends to mean the bankrupt] it would be more appropriate to say, "If one dies or goes bankrupt, he is more entitled with his property." When he uses a noun instead of a pronoun it indicates that he does that for a reason.[193]

An example for using a word in its jurisitc meaning is the argument of Ḥanafīs and their proponents who maintained that fornication entails prohibition of marriage [to those whom a father had illegal intercourse with]. They based their view on Allah's saying, "And do not have *nikāḥ* with those [women] whom your fathers had *nikāḥ*, except what has already occurred." (Q. 4: 22). The intended meaning of this verse is 'do not have intercourse with whom your father has cohibited'. [Acoording to Ḥanfīs,] a woman with whom a father had illegal intercourse is prohibited for the son to cohabit [either through marriage or fornication].

But Shāfiʿīs and their proponents would say that prohibition is intended [only when a father had concluded] a contract of marriage. The word *nikāḥ* is primarily used in *sharia* to mean a marriage contract while it is allegorically used to mean intercourse.

Proponents of the first view state that intercourse should be intended in this verse because Allah says, "except what has already occurred in the past." (Q. 4: 22). It refers to the Arabs' earlier practice of succeeding their fathers by [inheriting their] widows. They used to succeed their fathers by having intercourse with their step mothers without a contract of marriage. They used to take them by inheritance. This is the reason Allah says, "O you who have believed, it is not lawful for you to inherit women by compulsion." (Q. 4: 19), and He also said, "Indeed, it was an immorality and hateful [to Allah] and was evil as a way." (Q. 4: 22). Immorality is called for intercourse not for the legal contract of marriage.

An example for the customary usage of a word is the Mālīkīs' proving that expiation of *ẓihār*[194] is binding on a master with regard to his slave girl [if he swears she is as prohibited to enjoy as his mother], due to Allah's saying, "And those who swear *ẓihār* to their women." (Q. 58: 3). [However,] a slave girl is one of the master's women. But Shāfiʿīs and Ḥanafīs maintain that this word [your women] is particularly used in custom for spouses. That is why Allah says, "Tell your wives and your daughters and the women of the believers to bring down over themselves [part] of their outer garments." (Q. 33: 59). 'The women of the believers' unanimously refer to free spouses of the believers. Similarly, the woman of such a man refers particularly to his wife according to custom. It does not refer to his concubine. The expression *nisā*ʾ (women) is a plural of the word '*marʾa*' though it is not derived of its root.

The Mālikīs counter argue that *ẓihār* used to be a form of divorce in pre Islam heathendom. It was particular for wives. When [such a practice] was annulled [by Islam], it referred to [an oath for] the prohibition of enjoyment, which included both wives and concubines. Therefore, a slave girl may be prohibited by means of *ẓihār* exactly like a wife. Therefore, prohibition extends to both free women and slave girls.

Polysemous vs. Monosyemous

[Equivocality] is not a type of interpretation, because it is more appropriate to be a form of ambivalence. When one confirms that a locution is equivocally used for two meanings, he can, then, prefer one of those two meanings through the least preference measure possible. But if a word is used to express an allegorical [and, yet another literal] meaning, he has then to prove, through a stronger proof, that it is used to mean the allegorical.

For example, our [Mālikī] fellows prove that a woman's waiting period is calculated by purification periods not through menstruation cycles due to Allah's saying, "Divorced women remain in waiting for three *qurūʾs*." Q. 2: 228. *Qur*ʾ is an equivocal word which linguistically vacillates between purification and menstruation periods, but it is more preferable to interpret it to mean 'a period of purity' because it is the appropriate time for issuing divorce. Therefore, the waiting period must immediately start after the issuance of divorce in order to [realize] a prompt response to [divine] command. When Allah attributes the observance of a waiting period to passive participle [derived from the verb divorce], it implies that divorce is the reason for the ordinance of a waiting period. If we interpret the word *qur*ʾ to mean 'purity', an effective cause [that is, divorece] is immediately correlated to its effect [that is, observene of waiting period]. If it is explained as menstruation, a cause is not connected to its effect, but a gap exists in between. Making an effect immediately consequent to its cause is preferable.

The Ḥanafīs would argue that what Mālikīs have mentioned should not contradict with interpreting the word *qur*ʾ to mean 'menstruation'. The word *qur*ʾ originally means 'menses'. It is allegorically used for a period of purity. The reason is that *qur*ʾ is literally derived from *qarʾa* which means 'collected.' The Arabs, for example say, '*qaraʾtu al-māʾ fī al-ḥawḍ*' (I collected water in a basin). This is the reason the Quran is called so [since it is a collection of verses and chapters]. This is the same meaning used in the poet's verse, *'hijānu al-lawni lam taqr' janīnan'* (*A she camel a pick in its color, has not cast forth a young fetus.*[195])

It is similarly derived form *qar'a*, (to transfer from a state to another). The Arabs, for example, say, *'qara'a al-najm'* (the star transformed to the state of appearance or disappearance). Therefore, if *qur'* is originally derived from *qar'a*, which means 'to collect', it is more appropriate to be used for the menstruation period since it is the time when menses are colligated. It is not appropriate [to use it] for 'purity' which is a time a woman is free of menses. If the word is derived from *qar'* which means 'to transfer' it is still better to use it to express the starting point of transference from purity to menstruation not the opposite. Similarly, a woman is supposed to first transfer to menstruation [after passing through a period of purity]. Therefore, it is preferable to use the word *qur'* to mean menses. As for [our opponents'] argument that a women has to remain in waiting immediately upon divorce, we can say she does not have to, because we can say to a man at noon time, *'tarabbaṣ thlātha lyāl'* (remain waiting for three nights).[196] We cannot say that it is contrary to the original or manifest meaning [because he should wait up to the beginning of night to respond to the command].

Our [Mālikī] fellows counter that the Companions, who were native speakers of the Arabic tongue, dispute on this issue. It is an indication that the locution is equivocally used for both meanings. As for your saying that the time of menstruation is more worthy to be used for the time of menses colligation, it is void. Purity time is more worthy of that state since it is the time of colligating blood until it increases and [finally] discharges.

Such is the answer for [the claim that] *qur'* is [primarily] derived to mean 'transference', since a woman starts in her waiting period immediately after divorce by transferring from her status *quo* of purity into her state of menstruation. It is, thus, a transference from her original state [of purity] to an incidental state [of menstruation]. This marks the first transference which must be followed by a second and a third period. Then, she becomes permitted to marry by the commencement of the third cycle which marks the third transference.

When the two meanings are equivocal, it is sufficient to prefer one of them due to the least preference possible. We have already shown this.

Elliptical vs. Straight

For example, our [Mālikī] fellows prove that the one in a state of major ritual impurity is not allowed to enter mosques· They based their view on Allah's saying, "O you who have believed, do not approach prayer while you are intoxicated until you know what you are saying or in a state of *janāba*, except those passing through [a place of prayer." (Q. 4: 43). The sentence is presumed to read 'do not approach places made for prayers'.

An opponent would say this is based on the presumption of an ellipsis which it is contrary to the default rule. Our [Mālikī] companions counter back that the exemption of passers-by indicates that mosques are meant [for prohibition] since it is inconceivable to pass through prayers. If it is claimed that those 'who pass through' refers to travelers, we can say 'passing through' is used for crossing short distances such as passing over a vault. You cannot say 'I passed from Africa through Kuhrāsn.'

Synonymous vs. Mononymous

For example, our [Mālikī] fellows argue that it is impermissible to benefit from the skin of a dead animal[197] even if it is tanned due to the Prophet's saying, "Do not make use of *ihāb* and sinew of dead animals.[198]"

A proponent may argue that '*ihāb*' refers to untanned hide as stated by al-Jawharī. There is no other Arabic word to stand for untanned hides. Therefore, we have to either modify the word *jild* (skin) [by adding an adjective to identify it such as *jild ghayru madbūgh* (skin which is not tanned)] or use *ihāb* for untanned skin. If we regard *ihāb* a synonym for *jild*, it is contrary to the default rule.[199] Therefore, using *ihāb* [as a mononym] to mean untanned kin is preferable.

An opponent would counter that al-Khalīl ibn Aḥmad reported the use of *jild* to generally stand for skin either tanned or not and he is more authoritative in Arabic than al-Jawharī.

Emphatic vs. Informative

For example, our [Mālikī] companions hold that wiping over the whole head in incumbent. They based their view on Allah's saying, [and wipe *bā* (over) your heads." (Q. 5: 6). Had He said, 'wipe your head' [without *bā*], wiping the whole head would have become obligatory. Even when using the *bā* [which is used for emphasis, the meaning is wipe over the whole of your heads]. *Bā*ʾ cannot be used to preclude wiping the whole head. If it is used to rule out the wiping of the whole head, face should not be wiped wholly in *tayamum* since it is [prefixed by *bā*ʾ in] Allah's saying, "and wipe *bā* (over) your faces" (Q. 5: 6). As *bā* cannot be used to preclude the inclusion of the whole face, it must be wiped wholly.

But Shāfiʿīs and their proponents would say if the inclusion of the whole head is obligatory the *bā* would be of no use. Its existence and absence are, then, equal. If you, however, say that it is added for emphasis we would counter back that assuming that a phrase is emphatic [not informative] is not the default.[200]

The answer of our [Mālikī] companions is that it is used to indicate emphasis because the Arabs have been reported as adding it for [just] emphasis as it is used in Allah's saying, "And [also] whoever intends [a deed] therein *bā* (of) deviation [in religion] or wrongdoing—We will make him taste of a painful punishment," (Q. 22: 25) that is, whoever intends therein any deviation in religion or wrongdoing. Such is the case of Allah's saying, "And shake toward you *bā* the trunk of the palm tree," (Q. 19: 25) that is, shake toward you the trunk of the palm tree. Al-Farrāq has also related that the Arabs equally say 'shake it' or 'shake over it', 'take the rein' or 'take by the rein', 'take it' or 'take hold of it', 'shake his hand' or 'shake with his hand' and 'I touched his chest' or 'touched on his chest' and 'I wiped his head' or 'wiped over his head'. As the whole face has to be unanimously wiped in *taymmum*, [head] must be wiped in whole [in this context].

Hysteron Proteron[201] *vs. Syntagma*

For example, the Ḥanafīs interpreted the Prophet's statement to ʿAbdur-Raḥmān ibn Samura, "O ʿAbdur-Raḥmān! when you take an oath and find something else better than that, expiate for [breaking] your oath, and do that which is better," as having a reversal of the rational order [of its structure].

But our [Mālikī] companions and others used the [same] report to prove the permissibility of expiating an oath before breaking it. They confirm that the text is of its normal order.

The Ḥanafīs counter argue that if we assume that the existing order is real, we have to bring expiation ahead of braking an oath, which is advocated by nobody. This is due to the implication of the '*thumm*' which indicates doing things in order and due to the command which implies obligation.

Khaṣṣ vs. ʿAmm

A general text may be specified through a dependent or an independent [clause]. A dependent specifying text may be an exception, a condition, a *ghāyah*[202] (extent) or a qualifier.

Exception.

It is discussed in two questions:

First, scholars differed on [the implication of] an exception. Some of our [Mālikī] companions and Shāfiʿīs state that the excepted bears the opposite ruling of the general term.[203] So, if one says, 'I owe him ten except seven,' the ten are intended in total but he exempted the seven because the 'seven' takes opposite ruling of the ten.[204]

The companions of abū Ḥanīfa maintain that exception is intended to express the conclusion. So, if one says 'I owe him ten except three,' it is as if he admits that he owes him seven.

Based on this disagreement, scholars differed on [the ruling of] selling a handful [of barely] in exchange of two handfuls [of barely]. Our [Mālikī] fellows maintain that it is prohibited due to the Prophet's (may God exalt his mention) saying, "Do not sell food for food unless equal for equal.[205]" According to the first clause, it is prohibited to sell [usurious types of] food for [usurious types of] food either of measurable or unmeasurable quantities if there is excess in one side. Exception implies that the ruling of the exempted is in opposition for the first clause, that is, it is permissible sell if both are equal. The first clause entails prohibition with regard to unequal quantities either big or small.

The companions of abū Ḥanīfa argue that the text reads, 'unless equal for equal,' and according to custom, this equality is only achieved through measurement. The text should, thus, read, "Do not sell food for food when it is measured unequally." A handful [of barely] can be sold for two handfuls [since they are counted, not measured.]

Based on this precept, our [followers of Mālikī] school differed on one's addressing his wife by saying, 'You are divorced three times except three except one'. It is said that she is liable to one divorce, since the meaning of his statement is that three divorces are effective with the exception of two. [The two exempted are not effective, and] therefore, she is divorced only once.

According to the popular view of Mālikīs, it is counted as two divorces, because when he exempted three out of three, exception became void but when he further exempted one of three the result is two as if he says that three divorces are effective with the exception of one ineffective.

Second, when an exception follows a number of clauses conjugated by the conjunctive 'and' it unanimously refers to the last clause but scholars disagree on whether it refers to all other preceding clauses?

Based on this have the Shāfiʿīs and Ḥanfīs differed on the admittance of the testimony of someone penalized due to slanderous accusation of a chaste Muslim upon declaring his repentance. The Shāfiʿīs admit his testimony while the Ḥanafīs do not. The reason of their disagreement is Allah's saying, "…and do not accept from them testimony ever after. And those are the definitely disobedient, except for those who repent thereafter." (Q. 24: 4,5). The Shāfiʿīs extend exception [in this verse] to include [the acceptance of their testimonies and their incurring a sin] while Ḥanfīs restrict it to the last phrase only. They maintain that the phrase 'and do not accept from them testimony ever after' remains general [and is not subject to exception].

The truth is that the text is ambivalent and none of those interpretations should override the other except through an external clue.

As for specification by means of conditionals, *ghāya* and qualifiers, which are the remaining means of specification, we are going to elaborate on them when we discuss *mafhūm* (implied meaning).

As far as specification by independent texts we are going to discuss it in three questions:

First, it is possible to specify a part of the Quran by a part thereof, a prophetic tradition by another tradition, a prophetic tradition by a clause of the Quran and the Quran by virtue of *mutwātir* tradition. There is no disagreement among scholars on that. Only the majority of scholars admit the specification of Quranic passage by means of solitary reports because it is possible to act upon both types of evidences.

In order to be qualified for specification by means of a solitary hadith, the majority of Ḥanfīs necessitate that the text of the Quran must have been specified by another text of the Quran to weaken its indication. For example, our [Mālikī] companions hold that dead sea animals are permissible to eat. They based their view on the Prophet's saying, "It's water is purifying and its dead [animals] are lawful [to eat][206]." But the companions of abū Ḥanīfa maintain that this [report] conflicts with Allah's saying, "Prohibited to you are dead animals." (Q. 4: 3). As it has not been specified by any text, it cannot be specified by virtue of the aforementioned report. We cannot regard Allah's saying, "But whoever is forced [by necessity], neither desiring [it] nor transgressing [its limit], there is no sin upon him," (Q. 2: 173) as specifying the general terms of Q. 4: 3 because it explains the meaning of the pronoun in the phrase 'Prohibited to you,' not the phrase, 'dead animals'. Our answer [to the Ḥanfīs' argument] is that a solitary hadith can specify the general meaning of a Quran text because [the implication of a general word] is a type of *ẓāhir* (manifest indication) [which is apt to interpretation and specification]. Its indication is definitive. When it is specified by a solitary report it means that we act upon both evidences.

Second, the general meaning of a solitary hadith can be specified by analogy according to the majority of *uṣūlīs.* For example our [Mālikī] companions claim that the general meaning of the Prophet's saying, "When a dog licks one's utensil, it should be washed seven times,[207]" has been specified by means of analogy, where dogs which are permitted to grow may be compared to cats in the sense that both are animals which intermingle with humans.[208] Similarly, according to the majority of scholars, the general meaning of Quran may be specified by means of analogy. The majority of Ḥanfīs, however, stipulate that another specifying text should be in effect [to weaken its indication] as they did with regard to the issue of specifying a text of the Quran by means of a solitary hadith.

Third, it is possible to specify the general terms of a text by means of the *mafhūm* 'implied meaning' of another text according to the majority of scholars who admitted *mafhūm* as a legal proof. For example, our [Mālikī] companions maintain that it is prohibited for a free man to marry a slave girl even if he can afford financial means. They based their view on the implied meaning of Allah's saying, "And whoever among you cannot [find] the means to marry free, believing women, then [he may marry] from those whom your right hands possess of believing slave girls." (Q. 4: 25). The implied meaning of the verse is that marrying a slave girl is impermissible for those who can afford means [to marry a free woman]. But the Ḥanfīs and their proponents maintain that it conflicts with the general meaning of Allah's saying, "...then marry those that please you of [other] women." (Q. 4: 3). The answer of our [Mālikī] fellows is that it is possible to specify the general terms of a text by the implied meaning of another because it would result in acting upon both proofs.

According to the majority of *uṣūlīs*, when a text of a general meaning is revealed or issued for a specific occasion, its meaning cannot be confined to that specific occasion. For example, the Shāfiʿīs maintain that the washing of limbs required in ablution has to be performed according to a set order. They based their view on the Prophet's saying, "Begin with what Allah had begun with.[209]" The relative pronoun 'what' is used to indicate generalization. Ablution is, thus, included. Therefore, we have to begin [ablution] by the washing of our faces and then [washing] what follows.

The opponents of this view including Mālikīs and Ḥanafīs maintain that this [hadith] has been issued with regard to a specific occasion when the Companions asked the Prophet (may God exalt his mention) upon the revelation of Allah's saying, "Indeed, al-Ṣafa and al-Marwa are among the symbols of Allah." (Q. 2: 158), which hill they are supposed to start with. The Prophet (may God exalt his mention) said, "Begin with what Allah had begun with." They maintain that when a general text is revealed for a specific occasion, it has been confined to apply to this incident.

Shāfiʿīs counter back that a general text, according to the correct view of *uṣūlīs,* cannot be confined to the specific occasion in which it has been revealed. It must remain general because the reason for regarding it as an *ʿamm* is still extant. A specific occasion is not an impediment to regard it so. It is possible that a general text may specifically address a particular occasion on which it has been revealed but its general terms remain applicable to the rest [of other cases].

Qualified vs. Absolute

An absolute text may have the same cause and ruling of its qualifying text. They may have been issued in explanation of the same cause but they discuss different rulings or vice versa. They may also be different in both cause and rulings. If a text of absolute terms is qualified by another text while both are related to the same cause and speak about the same ruling, it has been unanimously agreed that *muqayyad* qualifies the *muṭlaq* such as the Prophet's saying, "There is no marriage without a guardian, a dowry and two witnesses.[210]" According to another version, "There is no marriage without a guardian, a dowry and two upright witnesses[211]." Accordingly, witness have been qualified to be upright. Abū Ḥanīfa has not restricted them to be upright but permitted the conclusion of marriage by a profligate person because the [quoted] report is not authentic according to him.[212] An absolute clause of the Quran may be qualified by a solitary report according to us [Mālikīs, Shāfiʿīs and Ḥanbalīs] but it cannot be qualified according to abū Ḥanīfa because he regards [this restriction] as an addition to the text which is deemed to be abrogating the earlier text. A solitary report, according to him, cannot repel a ruling enacted by the Quran.

For example, the Quranic verse, "And mentions the name of his Lord and prays," (Q. 87: 15) has been qualified by the Prophet's (may God exalt his mention) saying, "The key to prayer is purification, its opening is to say '*Allahu akbar*' and its closing is to say '*As-ṣalamu ʿalaykum*'[213]." According to the absolute terms of the former, it is permissible to enter into prayer by pronouncing any invocation.

When the cause and ruling of an absolute and its qualifying texts are different, there is no disagreement among scholars that the absolute terms of a text cannot be qualified by the *muqayyad*. For example, Allah's saying,

"[As for] the thief, the male and the female, amputate their hands," (Q. 5: 38), where the word, 'hands' is absolute and can be qualified by Allah's saying, "and your forearms to the elbows." Q. 5: 6.[214]

But if the cause of the two texts is different but both have the sam ruling, the absolute has to be restricted by the *muqayyad* if they have something in common. Some scholars maintained that it may be restricted by the *muqayyad* even if they do not have something in common. Our view is that there must be some common feature. For example, our [Mālikī] companions relied on Allah's saying, "then the freeing of a believing slave," (Q. 4: 92) to prove that one of the conditions of a slave which can be emancipated in expiation of *ẓihār* is to be a Muslim because it has been qualified in the verse on the expiation of erroneous homicide (Q. 4: 92). The companions of abū Ḥanīfa maintain that they should not refer the verse of *ẓihār* to the verse of murder due to their different causes.

Our [Mālikī] companions counter argue by saying that both are intended to be expiations while emancipation is an act of charity. A condition of the one who receives charities is to be a Muslim. Such is the case of *zakat*, which is only payable to Muslims. This is the reason of making Islam a condition for the emancipated slave for the expiation of erroneous murder, which is also identified with respect to the expiation of *ẓihār*. Therefore, one of the conditions of a slave to be emancipated is being a Mulsim.

When the causes [of both the *muṭlaq* and *muqayyad*] are one but their rulings are different, scholars differed on whether to override the absolute by the *muqayyad* or not. An example is whether to consider the average standard of clothing of needy persons [as an expiation for broken oaths]? Those who stipulate that referred to Allah's saying, "So its expiation is the feeding of ten needy people from the average of that which you feed your [own] families." (Q. 5: 89) which is followed by his saying, "or clothing them." Q. 5: 89. Clothing is expressed in absolute terms but it is qualified to be of the average [clothing of an expiator's family]. It is as if he says, "So its expiation is the feeding of ten needy people from the average of that which you feed your [own] families or clothing them of the average that which you cloth your own families with", because the cause of both [alternatives] is the same.

But it may be stated that an absolute text can be restricted by a *muqayyad* except if their issues are similar or even identical. Otherwise, they cannot. It is evident that fasting has to be consecutive as an expiation for *ẓihār* in Allah's saying, "And he who does not find [a slave]—then a fast for two months consecutively before they touch one another." (Q. 58 :4), but it is not required, unanimously, to consecutively feed sixty needy persons. One has not to feed them immediately one after another. The reason is that both [fasting and feeding] are of different categories.

Proponents of the first view argue by stating that different things may share the same ruling. In this case, there is no consideration for being identical or different. This issue has elaborate discussion which may be held irrelevant.

Some people regarded the verse of ablution is of this type. Allah says, "[wash your faces and your forearms to the elbows." It is deemed that it restricts the absolute terms of the clause, "[then seek clean earth and wipe over your faces and hands with it]" Q. 5: 6. The cause of both cases is one, that is, rising to perform prayers. But shaykh abū Bakr al-Anbarī, of the Mālikī school of Iraq differentiates between both clauses by stating that the verse with regard to ablution the verse included the addition of a limb that is, the forearm. It did not include a qualification of the absolute. In the previous verse it included the addition of a qualifier but this discussion is [similarly] irrelevant.

A part of our discussion of [*muṭlaq* and *muqayyad*] is when an absolute clause includes one specific ruling for one specific cause, then it is followed by two rulings based on two causes.

Such is the case of our [Mālikī] companions' proving that apostasy invalidates ablution. So, if an apostate reverts to Islam, he has to reoffer ablution even if he does not make a ritual invalidator, due to Allah's saying, "If you should associate [anything] with Allah, your work would surely become worthless." (Q. 39: 65) and Allah's saying, "And whoever denies the faith—his work has become worthless."

Q. 5: 5. But an opponent of this view amongst our [Mālikī] companions argue that even if this verse is of absolute terms, it must be restricted to be applicable to those who die on their state of apostasy. They based their view on Allah's saying, "And whoever of you reverts from his religion [to disbelief] and dies while he is a disbeliever—for those, their deeds have become worthless in this world and the Hereafter, and those are the companions of the Fire, they will abide therein eternally." Q. 2: 217. This is because a *muṭlaq* must be referred to *the muqayyad*.

Conclusion

In order to transfer from a *ẓāhir* meaning of a text to its susceptible interpretation, the text has to fulfill the following three conditions: First, a locution can be possibly used in language for this *interpretation*. Second, the interpretation must be intended [by the lawgiver] by evidence. Third, the evidence provided to support a specific interpretation must be stronger than the evidence which supports the primary manifest meaning.

If it fails to fulfill any of these conditions, such a [proposed] interpretation would be void. A manifest text may vary in its strength. It may, sometimes, be compelling to the extent it approximately reaches the implication of univocal text. In such a case, it is hardly interpretable except if one introduces an evidence presuming that interpretation is stronger than the *ẓāhir*. An example of a strong [*ẓāhir*] is the Prophet's saying, "Whichever woman married without the permission of her guardian her marriage is invalid, her marriage is invalid, her marriage is invalid." The generality of this clause as expressed by the word 'whichever,' as used to express inclusiveness and to the repetition of the phrase 'is invalid' weakens the interpretation proposed by Ḥanafīs to exclude pubescent sane girl of its general terms. They confined it to only include insane and minor girls. But restricting the terms of a general clause to be meant for limited members turns the report into a mystery. Similarly, the Ḥanafīs' interpretation of the sentence 'her marriage is invalid' to mean that the status *quo* of this contract is validity but it may become void in case the girl marries an unqualified suitor and her guardian causes discord. However, the repetition of this sentence in the text for three times invalidates this interpretation.

An example of a text that implies a weak *ʿamm* and may be, therefor, specified by a weak evidence is the Prophet's saying, "On land that is watered by rain there is a tenth. On irrigated land there is a twentieth [to pay]".[215] Abū Ḥanīfa maintained that *zakat* is due on vegetables and based his view on the text of this report. However, the report's general indication is weak because it is basically issued to explain the ratio paid for *zakat*; not to explain the amount liable to zakat. When the amount liable to *zakat* is not mainly intended in this text, its general indication became weak to the extent that some scholars held that it does not provide a general indication, though it rightly does. Based on that you can give more examples. This is the conclusion of *muʾawwal.*

1.2.1.2. *Mafhūm* (Implied Meaning)

M*afhūm* is of two types, namely, *mafhūm al-mwāfaqh* (convergent meaning) and *mafhūm al-mukhālafa* (divergent meaning). *Mafhūm al-mwāfaqa* is defined as the implicit meaning on which the text may be silent but it is more worthy of the [stated] ruling than the meaning explicitly conveyed. It is similarly known as *faḥwā al-khiṭāb* (superior meaning). For example, Allah says, "say not to them '*uff*'" (Q. 17: 23). If the law prohibits the saying of a word of contempt [for parents], beating them would be more heinous. Such is the case of Allah's saying, "So whoever does an atom's weight of good will see it." (Q. 99: 7). So, we recognized that whoever does an elephant's weight of good will see it. Similarly, Allah says, "And among the People of the Scripture is he who, if you entrust him with a great amount [of wealth], he will return it to you." (Q. 3: 75). So, whoever returns a great amount of wealth is easier to return a single silver coin. Likewise, Allah says, "And among them is he who, if you entrust him with a [single] silver coin, he will not return it to you unless you are constantly standing over him [demanding it]." (Q. 3: 75). Therefore, whoever does not return a single silver coin would not rather return a large amount of wealth.

1.2.1.2.1 [Convergent Meaning]

Mafhūm al-mwāfaqh is of two types. It may be explicit or implicit. The former's examples are those which we have proceeded. An example of the latter is ramified in our [Mālikī] companions' position that one who deliberately misses a prayer has to make it up, due to the Prophet's saying, "Whoever sleeps past or forgets a prayer, let him pray it when he remembers it.[216]" They stated that one who misses prayer because he was in a state of sleep or forgetfulness has to make it up although he is not in a state of legal responsibility. Therefore, the one who deliberately leaves prayer is more worthy to make it up.

Similarly, Shāfiʿī scholars state that a dipping oath, in which one deliberately swears on a lie,[217] necessitates penance due to Allah's saying, "Allah will not impose blame upon you for what is meaningless in your oaths, but He will impose blame upon you for [breaking] what you intended of oaths." (Q. 5: 89). If penance is due on one who breaks an oath while not being sinful[218], it is more worthy for one who is sinful.

Such is the statement of Shāfiʿīs who obligated a penance on a deliberate murderer. They maintain that since a penance is incumbent on erroneous murder, it is more worthy to be due on intentional homicide.

However, the indication [of the foregoing examples] is implicit because someone may argue that making up prayers by a sleeping or a forgetting person does not necessarily require offering it by one who deliberately neglects it, because a belated performance is a means of restoration which can be hardly made in the case of deliberate abandonment. Similarly, the heinousness of a deliberate murder is hard to be obliterated by a penance. This is the reason scholars differed on [the ruling of] this case. These are mostly discussed in matters of disagreement among scholars.

1.2.1.2.2. [Divergent Meaning]

As for *mafhūm al-mukhālafa* (divergent meaning), it is a meaning derived from the words of the text in such a way that its ruling diverges from meaning pronounced.[219] It is also called *dalīl al-khiṭāib.* Scholars disagreed [on its authority]. The majority of Mālikīs and the companions of Shāfiʿī held it [authoritative] while the majority of Ḥanafīs reject it. Our [Mālikī] companions relied on reports from prominent figures of philology to prove it [authoritative]. Proponents of *mafhūm* held it acceptable only when it fulfills five conditions as follows:

1. The cases implied by *mafhūm al-mukhālafa* should not be infrequent or rare. For example, Allah says, "And do not compel your slave girls to prostitution, if they desire chastity." (Q. 24: 33). By way of *mafhūm al-mukhālafa*, this verse might be taken to mean that slave girls are to be forced to practice prostitution in case they do not wish for chastity. But this would be based on a rare situation, because unchaste girls are not in need to be compelled to practice prostitution.
2. [If it is based on an answer for a question], the divergent meaning should not go beyond the limits of an answer to this specific question. For example, the Prophet's saying, "The night prayer consists of pairs," is reported as a response on a question raised to the Prophet on how to perform night prayers. The Prophet replied by saying, "The night prayer consists of pairs and when one fears of dawn, he makes this number odd by one *rakʿa*.[220]" When this report was specifically issued on the context of a response to a question on night prayer, it's convergent meaning cannot be extended to include day prayers.
3. The text must not be intended to show emphasis or intimidation. For example, Allah says, "There is no blame upon you if you divorce women you have not touched nor specified for them an obligation. But give them [a gift of] compensation—the wealthy according to his capability and the poor according to his capability—a provision according to what is acceptable, a duty upon the doers of good." (Q. 2: 236), and He says, "Prescribed

for you when death approaches [any] one of you if he leaves wealth [is that he should make] a bequest for the parents and near relatives according to what is acceptable—a duty upon the righteous." (Q. 2: 180). It does not necessarily imply that those who are impious or unrighteous are not addressed by this ruling.

The Ḥanafīs state that this is the same reason the Prophet's specific mentioning of believing women in the context of his saying, "It is not permissible for a woman who believes in Allah and the Last Day to mourn for anyone who dies for more than three days except for a husband; she should mourn for him for four months and ten (days)[221]" does not imply a divergent meaning. Therefore, they made it obligatory for a *dhimmī* widow to mourn over her deceased husband. Similarly, the Prophet's saying, "It is not permissible for a woman who believes in Allah and the Last Day to make a journey of one day and night unless she is accompanied by a *Maḥram* (husband or any other relative to whom she is prohibited to marry),[222]" and his saying, "It is not permissible for a Muslim who believes in Allah and the Last Day to shun his brother for more than three nights.[223]"

4. A pronounced meaning must not be mentioned as a result of clearing a problem in understanding a given text. For example, the companions of abū Ḥanīfa[224] maintain that the penance is mentioned in the context of an erroneous murder in order to remove any confusion that may arise by presuming that an erroneous murderer is not liable for any type of punishment. The Lawgiver removed this confusion by decisively stating that he is liable to penance. It is not intended to differentiate between deliberate and unintentional murder with respect to penance.
5. The pronounced meaning must not be applicable for extension to other similar cases through analogy. For example, the Prophet says, "There are five trespassers that can be killed in the sanctuary of Mecca: rats and mice, scorpions, crows, kites and wild dogs.[225]" If we apply the divergent meaning of this report, it would mean that no further animals are permitted to kill. But the Lawgiver intends to extend the ruling to other similar harmful animals and insects. Such is the case of the Prophet's saying, "Avoid the seven destructive things: Associating anyone or anything with Allah in worship; practicing sorcery, killing of someone without a just cause, whom Allah has forbidden, devouring the property of an orphan, eating of usury, fleeing from the battlefield and slandering chaste women who never think of anything impairing chastity and are good believers.[226]" The Prophet (may God exalt his mention) did not intend to exclusively give a definite number of all major sins. He just defined them to include further similar cases.

The last two conditions are only referred to implicit divergent meaning. Some scholars concluded [those two conditions by saying that] the meaning on which the text is silent must not be equal or more worthy of a ruling than the pronounced meaning. Otherwise, it may be meant to be *mafhūm al-mwāfaq* (a convergent meaning).

A divergent meaning is an acceptable method of deduction when it only occurs in any of the following seven forms, some extended them to be ten. They include *mafhūm al-Ṣifa* (implication of an attribute), *mafhūm al-sharṭ* (implication of a condition), *mafhūm al-ghāya* (implication of the extent), *mafhūm al-ʿadad* (implication of the stated number), *mafhūm al-zamān* (implication of time), *mafhūm al-makān* (implication of place) and *mafhūm al-laqab* (implication of the stated noun). We are going to discuss each form separately.

i. Implication of an Attribute[227]

For example, our [Mālikī] companions hold that when an owner sells palm trees which he has already pollinated, its fruits should be possessed by him [not by the purchaser] due to the Prophet's (may God exalt his mention) saying, "If somebody sells pollinated date palms, the fruits will be for the seller unless the buyer stipulates that they will be for himself [and the seller agrees][228]." By the implication of a divergent meaning, if a palm tree is not pollinated, the fruit should be given to the purchaser.

Similarly, our [Mālikī] companions maintained that a virgin is compelled [by father or a grandfather] on marriage after reaching puberty. They based their view on the Prophet's saying, "A woman who has been previously married (*Thayyib*) has more right to her person than her guardian; and a virgin's father must ask for her consent.[229]" By convergent meaning, a woman who has not been previously married has no more right to her person. Therefore, a father may compel her to marry.

ii. Implication of a Condition[230]

Our [Mālikī] companions maintained that one who possesses financial means is not allowed to marry a slave girl. They based their view on Allah's saying, "And whoever among you cannot [find] the means to marry free, believing women, then [he may marry] from those whom your right hands possess of believing slave girls." (Q. 4: 25). By way of *mafhūm al-mukhālafa*, it is concluded that one who have enough means cannot get married to slave girls.

iii. Implication of the Extent[231].

For example, our [Mālikī] companions concluded that the performance of a ritual bath can efficiently replace ablution due to Allah's saying, "O you who have believed, do not approach prayer while you are intoxicated until you know what you are saying or in a state of *janabah*, except those passing through [a place of prayer], until you have washed [your whole body]." (Q. 4: 43). By way of *mafhūm*, if you have washed the whole body you can approach prayer.[232] Had *ghusl* not been efficient to replace ablution, a performer of a bath had not been allowed to approach prayers [after immediately having a full bath].

iv. Implication of the Stated Number[233]

For example, al-Shāfiʿī maintained that when an impurity falls in water below the amount of two *qullas,*[234] it should be rendered impure. He based his view on the Prophet's saying, "If there is enough water to fill two pots (*qullas*), it carries no impurity," Another version reads: "It does not become unclean.[235]"

v. Implication of the Time[236]

Ẓāhirites, for instance, hold that supererogatory prayers offered at daytime does not have a minimum number each time one engages in prayer. They based their view on the Prophet's saying, "The night prayer is offered in pairs." By *mafhūm*, it implies that daytime prayers are not offered in pairs. We could not apply *mafhūm* [in this context] because it is a response for a specific question.

vi. Implication of the Stated Place[237]

The Ẓahirites, for example, permitted one who has already engaged in ritual retreat to have sexual intercourse outside a mosque due to Allah's saying, "And do not have relations with them as long as you are staying for worship in the mosques." (Q. 2: 187). By *mafhūm*, it implies that if you are outside mosques, you can have relations with wives. We have not applied this implication in this context because *iʿtikāf* (spiritual retreat) is exclusively practiced in mosques. One who is engaged in *iʿtikāf* is not permitted to go outside a mosque except in cases of necessity. We have explained before that a *mafhūm* should not go against that which is dominant and customary in favor of something which is infrequent and rare.

vii. Implication of the Stated Noun

The Shāfiʿīs, for instance, hold that *taymmum* cannot be offered without dust due to the Prophet's saying, "The whole earth has been made a mosque for us, and its dust has been made a purifier for us.[238]" By way of *mafhūm*, any material other than dust cannot be regarded as purifying.

Those forms of *mafhūm* are of varying degrees of strength as elaborated in other compendiums. But the implication of noun was not supported by anyone except al-Daqāq and some Ḥanbalī scholars.

1.2.2. The Prophet's Actions

1.2.2.1. Introduction

It has been confirmed in Islamic theology that all Prophets (peace be upon them) are infallible to commit any sin.[239] So, when a Prophet acts upon something, it means that such a deed could not be a sin. Scholars differed on legal] significance of the Prophet's (may God exalt his mention) actions. The most popular view is that they entail obligation.[240] This is the view reported by ibn Khuwayz Mindād on the authority of Mālik. He further said, "I saw Mālik in his *Muwaṭṭa*ʾ referring to the Prophet's actions as well as to his sayings [as legal proofs]." Those scholars maintain that the Prophet's actions imply obligation.[241] They based their view on Allah's saying, "Say, [O Muhammad], 'If you should love Allah, then follow me.'" (Q. 3: 31), and His saying, "And whatever the Messenger has given you—take; and what he has forbidden you—refrain from." (Q. 59:7).

However, the most accepted view is that when the Prophet (may God exalt his mention) intended to do an act for devotion, it should be *mandūb* (recommended)[242] because offering it in devotion better suggests that it is a recommended act. Claiming it is obligatory is contrary to the default rule.

When something is not proved to be an act of devotion, the prophet's action implies that it is permissible. When it is proved to be offered by him, it implies that it is permissible. There is no indication in its primary significance to suggest recommendation. This is the meaning of *ibāḥa* (permissibility).

1.2.2.2. Authority of the Prophet's Actions

Having mentioned [these premises], the Prophet's actions have to fulfill the following conditions in order to be of legal authority:

1. Such an act must not be a part of the Prophet's instinctive behavior such as eating, drinking, sleeping, standing and sitting. We do not have to imitate him in those act of natural disposition. We are not assumed to eat when he eats or sleep when he sleeps.
2. An act must not be peculiar to the person of the Prophet (may God exalt his mention) such as supererogatory prayer during night which was obligatory for him or polygyny above the limit of four which was permissible for him. Similarly, the Prophet (may God exalt his mention) emancipated Ṣafiyya and regarded her emancipation a dowry. Such a practice is not permissible for others according to our [Mālikī] school. An opponent of this

view may argue that such an act is not peculiar to the Prophet (may God exalt his mention).

3. His act must not be a clarification of an ambivalent concept approved by *sharia*. A clarification of [an ambivalent] takes its very ruling. An explanation may be in the form of a statement such as the Prophet's saying, "Pray in the same way you saw me praying,[243]" which is a clarification of Allah's saying, "And establish prayer," (Q. 2: 43), and the Prophet's saying, "Receive from me how to offer your rituals [of hajj].[244]"

   Sometimes a clarification may be provided through a clue such as the Prophet's practice of cutting off hands [of thieves] from wrists. It provided a clarification for Allah's saying, "As for the thief, the male and the female, amputate their hands." (Q. 5:38).
4. The ruling of the Prophet's practice must not have been previously enacted by a *sharia* proof. If it has been already identified as obligatory or recommended, his followers are like him [in responding to the text].

1.2.2.3. Classification of the Prophet's Actions

In case those four conditions are fulfilled we may proceed [to classify the Prophet's acts as follows]:

The first category includes the Prophet's actions which are intended for devotion. They may be expressed in ambivalent (*mujmal*) way or as clarification for an ambivalent text. An example of the former is the Shāfiʿīs' position that wiping head three times is recommended. They based their view on the report of the Prophet (may God exalt his mention) that he offered ablution [by purifying each limb] three times.[245] However, our [Mālikī] companions argue that [the report] does not explicitly state that the Prophet wiped his head three times. The text did not mention that in explicit terms because *wuḍū* is [literally] derived from *waḍāʾa* which means cleanliness, which is confined to washing [not wiping]. The report, therefore, signifies that that the Prophet washed [limbs of ablution] three times. But Shāfiʿī scholars counter back that the legal definition of *wuḍūʾ* includes the act of wiping head. This is further confirmed by the report that the Prophet (may God exalt his mention) offered ablution one time for each [limb]. He, then, said, "This is the only [correct way of] ablution upon which Allah accepts prayers." It is well-known that *salat* is only valid upon the observance of ablution that includes the wiping of head. Therefore, the ablution mentioned in this report must have included wiping head [thrice].

An example for [a prophetic action,] which clarifies the meaning of an ambivalent text is the position of our [Mālikī] companions who maintained that purification is a prerequisite for *ṭawāf*[246] (circumambulation around the *ka'ba*) due to the report, "The Messenger of Allah (may God exalt his mention) made *ṭawāf* around the House while being in a state of ritual purity." But Ḥanafīs would argue that it does not entail obligation, since the Prophet's actions do not imply obligation.[247]

Our [Mālikī] companions counter back by stating that the Prophet's actions entail obligation. They based their view on [verses which generally confirm obedience of the Prophet] discussed in *fiqh* methodology. Furthermore, the report is a clarification of a text which purports obligatory *ṭawāf* as mentioned in Allah's saying, "and perform *ṭawāf* around the ancient House." (Q. 23: 29). *Ṭawāf* is one of the rituals included in the Prophet's saying, "Receive from me how to offer your rituals [of *hajj*]." The clarification of an ambivalent text that mentions an obligatory rite has to be obligatory as well.

[Similarly], our [Mālikī] fellows argued that it is obligatory for an *imam* to stand while reciting Friday sermon due to the report that the Prophet (may God exalt his mention) used to make the Friday sermon while standing. Ḥanafī scholars do not interpret the Prophet's standing as obligatory but our [Mālikī] companions confirm it to be obligatory due to what has been illustrated in in the realm of *uṣūl al-fiq*. They further affirm that it is a clarification of Friday prayer which is [primarily] obligatory. A clarification of an ambivalent text which mentions an obligatory rite has to be obligatory as well.[248]

Similarly, Shāfi'īs and some of our [Mālikī] companions hold that offering ablution in a sequential order is obligatory. They based their view on the report that the Prophet (may God exalt his mention) offered ablution by washing his face [first]. Then, he washed his hands [up to elbows]. Then, he wiped his head and he [finally] washed his feet. If he had [regularly] offered it in reverse, it would have been obligatory to imitate him because his action is a proof for obligation.[249]

The second category includes all actions of the prophet which are not intended for devotion. [In general,] they are permissible. For example, Ḥanafī scholars maintain that it is permissible to marry while being involved in a state of *iḥrām*. They based their view on the report that the Prophet married Maymūna while being *muḥrim*.[250] Since it is permissible for the Prophet, it should also be permissible for us. When Allah permitted the Prophet to get married of his adopted son's former wife in His saying, "So when Zayd had no longer any need for her, We married her to you," (Q. 33: 37), He provided the reason in His saying, "in order that there not be upon the believers any discomfort concerning the wives of their adopted sons." (Q. 33: 37). The reason given indicated that we follow the Prophet in [both] permissibility and in removing any discomfort [resulting from getting married to the wife of one's adopted son].

1.2.2.4. Conclusion

The Prophet's abandonments are also attached to our discussion of the Prophet's actions. Once the Prophet acted upon something, it is an indication that this certain act is not prohibited. Similarly, when the Prophet does not do a certain act, it is an indication that such an act cannot be held obligatory. For example, our [Mālikī] companions maintained that the observance of ablution is obligatory upon eating something cooked by fire. They based their view on the report of the Prophet (may God exalt his mention) that he cooked mutton from the shoulder region of a sheep and prayed without offering ablution again. Similarly, they argued that cupping does not invalidate ablution. They based their view on the fact that the Prophet (may God exalt his mention) had blood extracted from his body and then he offered prayer without performing (new) ablution.

It is also included in the discussion of the Prophet's silence on a specific ruling. For example, the Shāfiʿīs concluded that whoever forgetfully breaks his fasting should not make up the fasting of that day due to the report that a man said to the Messenger of Allah (may God exalt his mention) "I ate and drank in forgetfulness when I was fasting." He said "Allah had fed you and given you drink.[251]" Had it been obligatory for the man to fast this day later, the Prophet would have explained that for him.

They also proved that a woman who voluntarily has a sexual intercourse with her husband in a day time of Ramadan while fasting is not requested to give an expiation. They based their view on the report of a man who said to the Prophet, "I have done a sexual relation with my wife [while fasting] in Ramadan.[252]" The Prophet (may God exalt his mention) commanded him to emancipate a slave. Had expiation been obligatory for his wife, the Prophet (may God exalt his mention) would have explained it for him, because the Prophet [in another occasion] commanded Unays to go to a woman who committed adultery and said to him, "Go to the wife of this [man] and if she confesses, stone her to death.[253]"

But there is a condition for the validity of this evidence, that is, to prove that instruction was urgently needed when the Prophet did not give further clarification. Therefore, any delay of instruction may be held a sin. According to Mālikīs, one who forgetfully breaks his fast is not exempted from making up fasting of that day. Nor did we drop expiation of a woman who had intercourse [during the daytime of Ramaḍān]. We counter back the Shāfiʿīs' argument stating that *qaḍāʾ* and expiation are not due promptly. The Prophet's delay of issuing a verdict cannot be deemed as leaving the case unresolved. He commanded Unays to promptly go to the woman because it is an offence that came to a ruler's awareness. Clarifying the legal stand necessitates immediate execution.

This is the end of our discussion on [the Prophet's] actions.

1.2.3. The Prophet's Tacit Approvals

1.2.3.1. Introduction

Know that the Prophet (may God exalt his mention) does not approve something wrong or sinful since the approval of an evil deed is a sin. The One who preserved him from making a sin has also protected him to err in his approvals. To be an authoritative proof, the Prophet's approval must fulfill the following conditions:

- The act must be known to the Prophet and he must be in full capacity to forbid it.
- He must not have explained its ruling before. Otherwise, prohibition is dropped.

1.2.3.2. [Classification of the Prophet's Tacit Approvals]

Having confirmed [those two conditions], a tacit approval may be issued past a ruling or after an act. Both are going to be discussed in the following two sections:

The first section is when a ruling is issued before the Prophet (may God exalt his mention) and he approves it, it is an indication that [this ruling] is in compliance with the law. For example, our [Mālikī] companions argued that a penalty is prescribed for a husband who falsely accuses his wife [with adultery] but *li'ān* (public imprecation) drops it. This is in conflict with the view of the Ḥanafīs who maintained that *li'ān* drops the punishment [of accusation], but if it is unfeasible, the husband has to be imprisoned [until he swears *li'ān*] due to the statement of al-'Ajlānī who said to the Prophet, "If a man finds a man along with wife and declares (about her adultery) you will flog him. Or if he kills, you will kill him or if keeps silent he will keep silence in anger." The Prophet did not comment, which means that the man gave the right ruling.

Apart of the Prophet's tacit approval is when he approves an evidence used to prove something in his presence such as the case of Mujaziz al-Mudlijī who referred to resemblance [based on physiognomy as an evidence of proving paternity] and said when he saw the feet of Usāma and Zayd covered with a rug, "These feet are related to one another." The Prophet (may God exalt his mention) was, then, pleased [with what he said].[254]

Know that when the Prophet showed no opposition for something, the Companions recognized that it is the right thing to do.

You should have reviewed the report of Jābir who said, "I swear by Allah that ibn Ṣayyād is the antichrist because I heard 'Umar taking an oath before the Prophet (may God exalt his mention) that he is the antichrist and the Prophet has not disapproved him.[255]"

The second section is when a specific action can be made in the presence of the Prophet (may God exalt his mention) or during his time. It may also be popular or unknown. These are three cases:

1. An event may occur at the Prophet's presence. For example, Shāfiʿī scholars maintain that supererogatory prayers may be offered as *qaḍāʾ* even at times of proscription, due to what Qays ibn Qahd (may God be pleased with him) relates. The Prophet (may God exalt his mention) asked him about two *rakʿas* he offered upon finishing the dawn prayer. Qays said, "I did not pray the two *rakʿas* before the dawn prayer. Hence I offered them now." The Messenger of Allah (may God exalt his mention) kept silent.
2. An event may occur at the Prophet's life without being popular. For example, the Shāfiʿī scholars proved that it is permissible for a worshiper offering obligatory prayer to join a congregation led by an *imam* offering his supererogatory prayers due to the report of Muʿādh who used to offer *ʿishāʾ* with the Prophet (may God exalt his mention) and then go to his people to lead them, holding it *nafl* for himself while his followers intended to observe their obligatory prayer. This is not as strong as the previous case because it is probable that the Prophet have not heard about what happened. But most probably he heard about it, especially, he specifically knew *imams* leading the tribes of Medina. Furthermore, it is reported that a Bedouin complained about Muʿādh to the Prophet due to his prolongation of prayers. The Prophet, then, said, "Do you want to cause hardship to people?[256]"
3. An event may occur during the Prophet's time without being popular. For example, some scholars proved that sexual intercourse without ejaculation does not necessitate the observance of a ritual bath due to some Companions' saying, "We used to have intercourse without ejaculation at the time of the Prophet, with no need to have baths." It is strongly assumed that the Prophet had no knowledge about it. The correct view is that it is, however, not a valid proof, contrary to the two previous cases.

This is the conclusion of our discussion of tacit approvals [of the Prophet] and the conclusion of [our elaboration of the second condition of holding a proof authoritative, that is, a proof] must be evidently indicative for the intended ruling.

1.3. On the Continuity of Transmitted Proof

It means that [a revealed evidence] should not have been abrogated. So, we are going to discuss abrogation and will focus on a preface which will explain its definition and then we will discuss significant and relevant issues which jurists usually undertake in their discourse.

1.3.1. Introduction

Abrogation is defined as the [suspension or] replacement of one *sharia* ruling by another ruling of a subsequent origin. It is also [defined as] the expiry of a *sharia* ruling. Abū Bakr ibn al-Ṭayyib stated that according to the correct definition of abrogation it signifies suspension [of a legal ruling by virtue of another]. He further differentiated between suspension and expiry. For example, when someone rents a house for a year. Upon the completion of this year the lease contract expires. It cannot be called that the contract suspends. In case the house collapses within the year, it is said that the contract has been suspended. It cannot be stated that the contract has terminated.

Suspension is effected because of a new ruling, which is deemed stronger than its predecessor. A weak [evidence] can hardly suspend a relatively stronger [evidence]. Expiry of a ruling does not necessarily mean that an evidence is stronger than the other but a ruling comes to an end by itself.

Based on their disagreement on this precept, our [Mālikī] fellows differed with the companions of abū Ḥanīfa on [how to count the number of divorces for] a woman who has reunited with her ex-husband after being married to another. Does the number of divorces that her ex-husband issued count on her?[257] Our [Mālikī] companions maintain that the number of divorces count as long as they do not reach three because [upon divorcing her three times, she becomes prohibited to him until she] marries another man which is a prerequisite for the removal of such a prohibition.[258] This is due to Allah's saying, "And if he has divorced her [for the third time], then she is not lawful to him afterward until [after] she marries a husband other than him." (Q. 2: 230). So, [marrying another man] is an effect of three divorces and it is not effected by less than three.

Ḥanfīs state that prohibition [to reunite to her first husband] has been uplifted [and all three divorces are dropped] when she married another man. [Therefore, if the first husband divorces her twice only and then she marries another man, such two divorces will not count in case she returns back to her first husband]. Two divorces will not count because three were abolished upon her marriage to the second husband. A less number is more worthy to be abolished.

We stipulated that the abrogated rule must have been proved through a legal evidence. If it is proved through *istiṣḥāb*,[259] a change of its status cannot be held abrogation. Otherwise, all legal determinations would be regarded as abrogating of all rulings of *sharia*.

Similarly, we stipulated that the abrogating rule must have been enacted through a legal proof. It cannot be enacted through a legal impediment. For example, when a human agent falls into a state of sleep or insanity [he cannot be held liable for his actions]. A ruling in this case is suspended not due to a legal evidence.

We further put the condition that an abrogating rule must be of a subsequent origin to exclude the termination of a ruling by coming to its end. Fasting, for example, ends by the commencement of the night and one, therefore, breaks his fasting. We cannot say that prescribed fasting has been abrogated because Allah says, "Then complete the fast until the sunset." (Q. 2: 187).

This is the conclusion of the preface. Let us discuss the main questions.

1.3.2. The Supplement of a *Muṭlaq*

A supplement of an absolute text is not an abrogation according to Mālikīs and Shāfiʿīs. Ḥanfīs are on the contrary. Our companions [of Mālikī scholars] maintain that such a supplement does not replace the original ruling [but it restricts its meaning]. This is explained by the following two examples:

First, the recitation of *al-fātiḥa* during prayer is an obligatory act of prayer according to the view of Mālikīs. They based their view on the Prophet's saying, "Whoever does not recite *al-fātiḥa* in his prayer, his prayer is invalid,[260]" and his saying, "Each prayer in which the Opening of the Book is not recited, it is deficient, it is deficient.[261]" Moreover, reposing in bowing and prostration is obligatory according to our view due to the Prophet's saying to the Bedouin, "and then bow, and remain in this state till you feel at rest in bowing,[262]" and ritual purity is a condition for the validity of *ṭawāf* because of the Prophet's saying, "*Ṭawāf* of the House is a form of *salat*.[263]" The Prophet, furthermore, offered *ṭawāf* when he was in a state of purification. His action is an evidence that it is obligatory.

According to Ḥanfī scholars, a mere recitation [of any part of the Quran] is obligatory due to Allah's saying, "So recite what is easy from it," (Q. 73: 20), while recitation of *al-fātiḥa* is just a supplement. A mere bowing is obligatory due to Allah's saying, "O you who have believed, bow and prostrate," (Q. 22: 77), while reposing therein is an addition. Similarly, *ṭawāf* is obligatory due to Allah's saying, "Then let them end their untidiness and fulfill their vows and perform *ṭawāf* around the ancient House," (Q. 22: 29) while purification is additional. If we hold those supplements as obligatory, they must be abrogating of the original absolute texts of the Quran. Texts, which enact those supplements are solitary reports which cannot qualify as to abrogate the Quran because a probable source cannot abrogate a definitively authentic text.

Secondly, according to [Mālikī] scholar's view, exile is obligatory after lashing [for fornicators]. We based our view on the Prophet's saying, "When an unmarried male commits adultery with an unmarried female (they should receive) one hundred lashes and banishment for one year,[264]" but the Ḥanafīs maintain that banishment is an addition to lashing which is not mentioned in the Quran. It should be regarded as abrogating the text of the Quran. For them, abrogating the Quran by a solitary report is not possible.

The distinction between the first and the second example is that the former's supplement is an attribute of the original ruling while the addition at the latter example is independent from the original ruling. We cannot claim that purification is distinguished from *ṭawāf* because we do not mean by purification the observance of ablution but we mean the state of purification, which accompanies the observance of *ṭawāf*. So, if one offers ablution and then nullifies it he cannot, then, engage in *ṭawāf* because the state of purity is not extant at the time of observing *ṭawāf*. Our companions do not regard [those supplements] as abrogation because the original act of worship does not contradict any of those conditions. [At the revelation of an absolute text,] if the act is offered without a specific condition, it should be legally efficient. When a further condition has been supplemented, it is regarded an addition to the original ruling such as an act of worship added to another act of worship. The latter cannot be regarded as abrogating the former.

1.3.3. [The Abrogation of *manṭūq*]

When a pronounced meaning is abrogated, does it necessarily require the abrogation of its *mafhūm*[265]? It is, however, a controversial issue. As for *mafhūm al-mwāfaqh* (convergent meaning), the Ḥanafīs proved that a free man has to be retaliated for slaying a slave due to the Prophet's saying, "Whoever kills his slave, we will kill him and whoever injures his slave we will injure him.[266]" So, if retaliation is due on recompense of killing one's slave, it is more worthy when one kills another person's slave. But our [Mālikī] companions state that this report is abrogated because the Ḥanafīs do not maintain that a free man is to be retaliated for killing a slave. Ḥanfīs counter that they based their view on *faḥwā al-khiṭāb* (superior meaning of the text)[267] even the original text has been abrogated.[268] They further maintained that the abrogation of a text does not necessarily require the abrogation of the meaning subsequent of its inference.

As far as *mafhūm al-mukhālafa* (divergent meaning) is concerned, our [Mālikī] companions maintain that a legal will assigned for non-relatives is not obligatory. They based their view on Allah's saying, "Prescribed for you when death approaches [any] one of you if he leaves wealth [is that he should make] a bequest for the parents and near relatives according to what is acceptable—a duty upon the righteous." (Q. 2: 180). By inference of *mafhūm*, it implies that a will for anyone other than parents or relatives is not obligatory.

However, Ẓahirī scholars maintain that this verse has been abrogated. They based their view on the Prophet's saying, "No bequest is to be made to an heir.[269]" Our companions [among Mālikīs] counter that the verse has two implication; namely, *mafhūm* and *manṭūq*. The abrogation of one implication does not necessarily require the abrogation of the other.

1.3.4. Proof of Abrogation

A revealed proof is claimed to be abrogated for reasons some of which are agreed upon and others are not. Of those reasons [which are agreed upon] is when the Prophet (may God exalt his mention) is reported as stating that [the text] is abrogated such as his saying, "I forbade you before to store the sacrifice, but now store up. I forbade you before to make *nabīdh* (by soaking raisins or dates in water), but now make *nabīdh*. I forbade you to visit graves, but now visit them.[270]" The abrogated ruling is known through this report.

Our [Mālikī] companions based their view on the purity of tanned skin of dead animals on the Prophet's saying, "Any skin tanned has been purified.[271]" However, Ḥanbalī scholars maintain that this report has been abrogated by the Prophet's saying, "I have previously permitted you to use the skin of dead animals, but when my letter reaches you, do not make use of the untanned skin and sinew of dead animals.[272]"

Our [Mālikī] companions counter that the report refers to the Prophet's permission he gave when he passed by a dead sheep. He said, "Why do not you make use of its skin?" They said, "O Messenger of Allah! It is dead." He said, "It is the eating [of a dead animal] which is prohibited.[273]" The Prophet permitted unrestricted use of skin without exempting tanned skins [in his saying, "Any skin tanned has been purified"]. He referred in this report to the permission of using skin after tanning. It is alluded by reference to the word '*ihāb*,' which is used for kin before tanning. So, the Prophet's saying, "Do not make use of the untanned skin and sinew of dead animals" refers to the prohibition of using skins before tanning, not using it after tanning.

Similarly, a consensus of Muslim scholars may issue a ruling in conflict with that included [in a text] without recognizing the real abrogating text. A consensus cannot abrogate a text by itself but it includes the evidence, which proves abrogation. For example, the Prophet (may God exalt his mention) commanded that a drunkard is to be killed if he drinks for the fourth time.[274] Consensus has been held that he has to be penalized [according to the prescribed penalty after] the fourth time. We realized [through consensus] that the report has been abrogated.

This is similar to the practice of the Medinese [which may prove the abrogation of a report] according to the view of Mālik.

Likewise, a narrator may explicitly declare that a specific ruling has been abrogated. For example, our [Mālikī] companions hold that a pregnant and breast feeding mother can break their fast and feed [a needy person as an expiation]. They based their view on Allah's saying, "And upon those who are able [to fast, but with hardship]—a ransom [as substitute] of feeding a poor person [each day]" (Q. 2: 184).

A proponent of this view may argue that the text has been abrogated by the report of Salma ibn al-Akwaʿ who said, "People has been given the choice at the advent of Islam either to fast or not. Then it has been abrogated by Allah's saying, 'So whoever sights [the new moon of] the month, let him fast it.[275]'" (Q. 2: 184.). If the narrator did not state that they have been given the choice at the advent of Islam, [his statement would not be an explicit evidence for the occurrence of abrogation]. But if he says that such a text has been abrogated by another text, [his statement is not an explicit evidence for abrogation]. A lot of *uṣūlīs* do not regard the saying of a narrator as evidence for the occurrence of abrogation because it may be based on his own personal reasoning, not on a reference to a text.

Similarly, [scholars presume the occurrence of abrogation] when a narrator issues an ambivalent statement to confirm that a specific text has been revealed prior to another. For example, our [Mālikī] companions maintained that a ruler has option to either free [the captives of war] or to ransom them based on Allah's saying, "and either [confer] favor afterwards or ransom [them]." (Q. 47: 4). The companions of abū Ḥanīfa, however, maintain that the verse has been abrogated by Allah's saying, "Then kill the polytheists wherever you find them." (Q.9: 5). [They based their view on the assumption that] the former verse is a part of Surat *al-Qitāl* (Q. 47) while the latter is a part of Surat Barāʾa (Q. 9). The latter is of a subsequent revelation to the former.

Likewise, [abrogation may be proved by] confirming the date of an abrogated text and defining the date of an abrogating text by relating it to the date of a narrator's embracement of Islam. For example, the companions of abū Ḥanīfa hold that touching penis does not invalidate ablution. They based their view on the report of Ṭalq ibn ʿAdiyy who said, "I came to the Prophet (may God exalt his mention) while founding the mosque of Medina and a man asked him on touching the penis, does it invalidate one's ablution?" He said, "No, it is only a part of your body.[276]" But our [Mālikī] companions argue that this [report] has been abrogated by the report of abū Hurayra (may Allah be pleased with him) who related that the Prophet (may God exalt his mention) said, "If any of you touches his penis he has to do *wuḍū.*[277]" It is well-known that abū Hurayra accepted Islam years after building the mosque. Abū Hurayra said, "I came to Medina while the Prophet was in Khaybar and Simāʿ ibn ʿUrfuṭa was [assigned to be] the ruler on Medina on his behalf."

If the exact date of an abrogated report is not identified, we cannot ascertain its abrogation by relating its revelation or issuance to the narrator's time of conversion to Islam or by [just claiming that] one of the two reports has been issued immediately before the Prophet's death.

For example, the Prophet prohibited turning face towards *qibla* while urinating or defecating. A proponent of this [ruling] may say that the report has been abrogated by the report of Jābir who said, "I saw the Prophet (may God exalt his mention) a year before his death urinating while facing the *qibla*." The former report cannot be, certainly, abrogated because it may be of a subsequent origin of Jābir's report.

When the reason for enacting a specific ruling is removed, it does not indicate that such a ruling has been abrogated. For example, our [Mālikī] companions maintain that a vessel licked by a beast has to be washed [seven times]. They based their view on the report of abū Hurayra (may Allah be pleased with him).[278] But the Ḥanafīs state that the [Companions] were extremely accustomed with dogs. It has been very difficult to break up with them. Therefore, [the Lawgiver] aggravated [the ruling] in order to [to incite them to] dissociate themselves from dogs. When their attachment to dogs no longer exists, the ruling [on washing seven times] has been removed.

Similarly, our [Mālikī] companions maintained that changing wine to vinegar is prohibited. They based their view on the report of Anas (may Allah be pleased with him) who said that the Messenger of Allah (may God exalt his mention) has been asked about [the ruling of] a wine that turns to vinegar. He said, "No.[279]" But the Ḥanafīs state that it is their status when they have been extremely attached to wine, so that the Prophet prohibited possessing it [even] for making it vinegar in order to block the avenue of evil. When those evil avenues have been blocked the ruling of possessing it for the purpose of turning it to vinegar does not exit any more. The Prophet (may God exalt his mention) commanded them [at the beginning] to destroy vessels and break utensils [for the earlier reason] though it is not obligatory now [to destroy vessels that contained wine] according to the unanimous agreement of all scholars.

Our companions counter that when a ruling is enacted for a reason, it cannot necessarily be canceled when this reason is suspended. The Prophet (may God exalt his mention), for example, commanded them to rot on *ṭawāf* in order to show their strength when the people of Quraysh said that the Muslims have been fatigued by the fever of Yathriibn Though the cause no longer exists, rotting has not been suspended. The Prophet (may God exalt his mention) rotted at the farewell *hajj*. His Companions rotted later while none of the polytheists was in Mecca then.

The question of changing wine to vinegar is relevant to whether it is possible to abrogate a hadith by means of analogy or not. It is, however, a controversial issue. For example, our [Mālikī] companions hold that wild beasts' leftover is pure. They based their view on report of Jābir ibn ʿAbdullah who stated that the Prophet (may God exalt his mention) was asked whether to offer ablution from the leftover of donkeys. He said, "Yes and of the leftover of beasts too.[280]" But the companions of abū Ḥanīfa argue that it was permissible when beasts were lawful to eat. When the edibility of beasts has been abrogated, the purity of their leftovers has been suspended. They extended the legal ruling [of beasts' edibility] to [the purity of their leftovers] due to the existence of common effective cause between both rulings. When a ruling is abrogated, its effective cause is subsequently suspended. Afterwards, the new ruling [extended through analogy] is abrogated.

But we maintain that an abrogation of a ruling does not necessarily require the abrogation of another, because an attribute may be identified as a common cause for two rulings. When it is no longer considered in a case it does not necessarily require its suspension in the other.

Therefore, when an evidence or a report is valid to entail two legal rulings, does the abrogation of one of them result in suspending the other? The view of the majority of scholars is that when the two rulings are irrelevant but they have just been proved or mentioned in one report of the Quran or Hadith, the abrogation of one ruling does not affect the other. For example, our [Mālikī] companions maintained that selling a dog is prohibited due to the Prophet's saying, "The earnings of a cupper are impure and the price of a dog is impure[281]." But a proponent may say that the impurity of a cupper's earnings has been abrogated by the report of abū Tayba who cupped the Prophet (may God exalt his mention) and he gave him a compensation.[282] If the impurity of a cuppers' earnings has been abrogated, the impermissibility of a dogs' price should be abrogated as well. But such a case and its likes are of weak indication. But if the two rulings are relevant and contingent, an abrogation of one ruling requires the abrogation of the other.

For example, we may claim that the penalty of wine drinking may be extended to *nabīdh* by means of analogy. But the Ḥanfīs would say that the penalty of *nabīdh* has been suspended by the Prophet's (may God exalt his mention) saying, "I forbade you before to make *nabīdh* [by soaking raisins or dates in water], but now make *nabīdh*.[283]" When the prohibition of making *nabīdh* has been abrogated, the penalty on its drinking has been suspended.

There are several other examples such as the case of a witness who is impugned because of perpetrating a prohibited act, but later such an act, for which he has been impugned, becomes permissible. In this case criticism of this witness must be suspended.

Sometimes, the correlation between two rulings is implicit and speculative and in such a case, disagreement among scholars occurs. For example, Shāfiʿī (God bless him) maintained that a dog's price is prohibited. He based his view on the Prophet's command to kill dogs. He further stated that whatever to be killed cannot be compensated for a causality. Whatever does not have a legal value [in case of damage or causality] must not be given a price.

But the Ḥanafīs state that the command to kill dogs has been abrogated. Therefore, its value has to be paid in case of damage. If its value has to be paid, its price becomes permissible. But such conclusion is implicit so that it may presume prohibition [of a dogs' price], though imposing a killer to pay the value of what he kills does not justify the permissibility of selling such [an animal or a slave] that has been killed.

1.3.5. Conclusion

An abrogating text may be again abrogated by either restoring the first ruling or by another text such as the fasting of ʿAshūrāʾ (10th of Muḥarram) which has been abrogated by giving choice either to fast the month of Ramaḍān or feeding [a needy person on each day]. Then, the choice has been abrogated by the prescription of fasting Ramaḍān. Similarly, temporary marriage has been permitted by Allah and then it has been prohibited. Then, it has been permitted again before being finally prohibited. So, it has been finally established that it is prohibited. This is reported from ibn Ḥazm who is an authority in citing reports [in support of his argument].

1.4. On the Predominance of a Transmitted Proof

[In case of a seeming contradiction between two legal evidences,] the preference of one to another may be based on the chain of transmission or on the text [of a report]. We are going to discuss this in two sections as follows:

1.4.1. Preference Based on the Chain of Transmission

There are ten reasons for preferring a text to another based on their chains of transmission. They are as follows:

1.4.1.1. Seniority of a Narrator

For example, our [Mālikī] companions maintain that offering *hajj* alone before *ʿumra* is preferred [to other forms such as joining them together]. They base their view on the report of ibn ʿUmar in which he said, "The Prophet (may God exalt his mention) offered *hajj* alone when he commenced on the state of *iḥrām*.[284]" But the Ḥanafīs argue that this report conflicts with the report of Anas who heard the Prophet announcing *hajj* and *ʿUmra* together. Our [Mālikī] companions counter that ibn ʿUmar was older than Anas, so that they preferred the report of ibn ʿUmar. Moreover, reliable narrators reported Zayd ibn Aslam and others who related that a man came to ibn ʿUmar asking him, "How did the Prophet commence on the state of *iḥrām?*" He said, "Have not you attended *hajj* last year?" He said, "I did but Anas ibn Mālik claims that the Prophet has intended both *hajj* and ʿUmra together." Then, ibn ʿUmar said, "Anas ibn Mālik used to [be so young that he could] enter into women of uncovered heads while I was below the Prophet's camel where its saliva falling on my shoulders and I heard him reciting *talbiya* where he commenced on hajj [alone].[285]" The report of a senior is preferred because he is [supposed to be] more exact and firm in what he relates.

1.4.1.2. Knowledge and Exactitude

For example, our [Mālikī] companions maintained that offering *hajj* alone before *ʿumra* is better due to the report of ʿĀisha.[286] If it is contradicted by the report of Anas, we may say that ʿAisha has better knowledge and is more accurate than Anas.

1.4.1.3. Witnessing the Incident

In this case the report [of a direct witness] should be preferred to the one who has not attended the incident. For example, our [Mālikī] companions preferred the report of abū Rāfiʿ to the report of ibn ʿAbbās. Abū Rāfiʿ said, "The Messenger of Allah married Maymūna while he was *ḥalal*,[287] and he stayed with her while he was *ḥalāl*, and I was the messenger between the two of them,[288]" but ibn ʿAbbās related that the Prophet (may God exalt his mention) married Maymūna while he was in the state of *iḥrām*, but he consummated that marriage after finishing that state.[289] Abū Rāfiʿ was an eye witness of the story, so that his report is preferred.

1.4.1.4. Being a Part of the Incident

For example, our [Mālikī] companions preferred the report of Maymūna who said, "The Prophet (may God exalt his mention) married me while we were both *ḥalāl*.[290]" to the report of ibn ʿAbbās, which has been mentioned before.

1.4.1.5. Constant Companionship

For example, our [Mālikī] companions preferred the reports of ʿAisha and Umm Salama that "the Prophet would wake during Ramadan (fasting) in a state of major impurity without a wet dream, but on account of sexual intercourse and he would take a bath before dawn,[291]" to the report of abū Hurayrah, "Whoever begins the morning in a state of ritual impurity has to break the fast of that day." The reason is that the one who has a longer period of companionship is more aware of perspicuous and abrogated practices of the Prophet. Therefore, when Marwān sent to abū Huraya to verify his report by referring him to the reports of ʿĀʾisha and Maymūnah, abū Hurayra asked, "Have they related the report?" He said, "Yes." Thereupon, abū Hurayra said, "They are of more knowledge.[292]"

1.4.1.6. Greater Number of Narrators

For example, our [Mālikī] companions preferred the report which confirms the necessity of offering ablution due to the touching of one's penis to the report of Ṭalq ibn ʿAdiyy who reported the Prophet's saying, "It is only a part of your body.[293]" The former report is related by abū Huryara, ibn ʿUmar, Zayd ibn Khālid, Saʿd ibn abī Waqqāṣ, Jābir ibn ʿAbdullah, ʿĀʾisha, Umm Salama, Umm Ḥabība and Arwā [bint Unays]. A report related through a greater number of narrators overweighs other reports which are related through a less number. It is said that a greater number of narrators is not as effective as the number of witnesses and does not give an extra weight to a report.

1.4.1.7. Close Contact with the Prophet

For example, our [Mālikī] companions preferred the report of ibn ʿUmar to that of Anas on confirming that the Prophet observed *hajj* alone [without joining it with *ʿumara*].

1.4.1.8. Direct Reception

For example, our [Mālikī] companions preferred the report of al-Qāsim and ʿUrwa from ʿAisha that Barīra was emancipated while her husband was still a slave[294] to the report of al-Aswād from ʿĀʾisha that she was freed while her husband was free.[295]

1.4.1.9. [VariantTexts from the Same Teacher]

When two reports are transmitted through the same teacher; one conforms to the the majority of students while the other is not, preference is given to former. An example is preferring the report of ibn ʿUmar, "If the camels are over a hundred and twenty camels, on every forty camels, one '*bint labūn*[296]' is due and on every fifty camels, one *ḥiqqah*[297] is due[298]", to the report of ʿAmr ibn Ḥazm, "If the camels are over one hundred and twenty camels, restart the proportion due.[299]" The reason is that ʿAmr ibn Ḥazm has reported another version which is consistent with the report of ibn ʿUmar.

1.4.1.10. Late Embracement of Islam

In this case, the report of the one who accepted Islam lately is less susceptible to abrogation. For example, our [Mālikī] companions preferred the report of abū Huryara, "The Prophet [forgot and] recited the final *taslīm* (salutation marking the end of prayer) after offering two *rakʿas*, and then he talked [with his companions] and then he [resumed and] completed his prayer[300]" to the report of ibn Masʿūd, "We used to greet the Prophet (may God exalt his mention) while he used to be in prayers, and he used to reply to our greetings. But when we came back from our visit to Negus (the King of Abyssinia) we greeted him (while he was praying) and he did not reply to us. We said, "O Allah's Messenger (may God exalt his mention)! We used to greet you in the past and you used to reply to us." He said, "Verily the mind is occupied and busy with more important matter during the prayer.[301]" [So one cannot return one's greetings during prayers]. According to another version, he is reported as saying, "Allah, the Almighty, creates new command as He wishes, and Allah, the Exalted, has sent a fresh command that you must not talk during prayer. He then returned my salutation.[302]" The Ḥanafīs used this report to maintain that talking in prayer nullifies it absolutely exactly like one who has a state of minor ritual impurity during prayer.

1.4.2. Textual Preferences

1.4.2.1. Saying vs. Action

In this case, a narration of the Prpohet's statement is preferred to a report of his action. For example, our [Mālikī] companions preferred the report of ʿUthmān in which the Prophet (may God exalt his mention) said, "A *Muḥrim* must not contract marriage, nor help others contract marriage, nor get engaged to marry,[303]" to the report of ibn ʿAbbās that the Prophet married Maymūna while being in the state of *iḥrām*.[304] The reason [for preferring a statement to a narration of an action] is that an action may be performed by the Prophet as one of his peculiar acts [which are not permissible for the Muslims to do]. Moreover, it does not indicate that the ruling has not been abrogated.

1.4.2.2. *Manṭūq* vs. *Mafhūm*

In this case, the former takes precedence over the latter. For example, the Ḥanfīs prefer [to act upon] the Prophet's saying, "A neighbor has the best claim to the house or land of the neighbor.[305]" to the Prophet's saying, "The right of preemption is due in property which had not been divided up.[306]"[307] But if the implied meaning of a text is substantiated by the pronounced meaning of another text, the latter should predominate, because indication is, then, confirmed by two proofs. For example, our [Mālikī] companions preferred the Prophet's saying, "Preemption takes effect in all cases where land has not been divided. But if the boundaries have been set and the roads laid out, then there is no preemption." to his saying, "A neighbor has the best claim to the house or land of the neighbor,[308]" because the former confirms through both *mafhūm* and *manṭuq* that a neighbor does not have the right of preemption.

1.4.2.3. [Legal Precedent vs. Non-legal Practice]

A report may be intended for legislation while the other is not. For example, our [Mālikī] companions preferred the report of Gerbil that he lead the Prophet (may God exalt his mention) for *ʿaṣr* prayer when the shadow of an object became similar to it in length,[309] to the report which is upheld by the Ḥanafīs to prove that the beginning of *ʿaṣr* is when a shadow on an object becomes double its size. It is the report of ibn ʿUmar, "Your example and the example of the people of the two Scriptures (that is, Jews and Christians) is like the example of a man who employed some laborers and asked them, 'Who will work for me from morning till midday for one *qirāṭ* (proportionate reward)?' The Jews accepted and carried out the work. He then asked, 'who will work for me from midday up to the *ʿaṣr* prayer for one *qirāṭ*?' The Christians accepted and fulfilled the work. He then said, 'Who will work for me from the *ʿaṣr* till sunset for two *qirāṭ*s?' You, Muslims have accepted the offer. The Jews and the Christians got angry and said, 'Why should we work more and get lesser wages?' (Allah) said, 'Have I withheld part of your right?' They replied in the negative. He said, 'It is My blessing, I bestow upon whomever I wish.[310]" Ḥanafīs state that the report implies that the time between *ʿaṣr* and *maghrib* should be shorter than the time between *ẓuhr* and *ʿaṣr*. It can only make sense if the time for *ʿaṣr* starts when the shadow of an object is double its size. Our [Mālikī] companions maintain that this report is primarily intended to strike a parable, not to impart a law, but the report of Gabriel is primarily issued for enacting a rule.

1.4.2.4. [A Text's Being General or Issued in Particular for a Special Incident]

A text may be issued with respect to a specific occasion or has a general meaning. The former is preferred to be a suitable evidence for similar cases while the latter may be better suited for others. An example of the former is the preference of Maymūna's report, "When the skin is tanned it becomes purified,[311]" to the Prophet's saying, "Do not make use of the skins and sinew of dead animals.[312]" The former report is preferred to prove the permissibility of using the skin of edible animals. It is like a decisive rule which has been mentioned in its occasion in particular. But the latter report is preferred to support the argument that the skin of inedible animals cannot be used even when it is tanned. The reason is that scholars differed on the applicability of a general statement, which has been issued in connection to a specific occasion if it is intended to be applied in cases other than the original situation in which it has been issued. This is an example of the fifth reason [on preferring a report due to its textual implication]. Therefore, we mentioned two reasons in this paragraph.

1.4.2.5. *Ẓāhir* vs. *Mu'awwal*

A text with manifest meaning is preferred to a text susceptible to various interpretations. Examples of this reason are included in the chapter where we discussed *ẓāhir.*

1.4.2.6. *Mu'awwal* vs. *Ẓāhir*

A text susceptible to various interpretations is preferred to a text with a manifest meaning (*ẓāhir*) if there is a strong clue in the text. We have discussed examples of this category when we elaborated the *muʾawwal.*

1.4.2.7. Affirmative vs. Negative

If a text provides a an affirmative evidence, it takes precedence to a text with negative evidence. For example, our [Mālikī] companions preferred the report of Bilāl that the Prophet (may God exalt his mention) entered into *kaʿba* and offered prayers therein[313] to the report of Usāma who said, "The Prophet (may God exalt his mention) entered the House without offering prayers therein.[314]"

1.4.2.8. [A Default Rule Takes Precedence]

A text may affirm the state of original freedom from liability while the other postulates liability. The latter takes precedence. For example, our [Mālikī] companions preferred the report of abū Huryara, which necessitates ablution due to one's touching of his penis to the report of Ṭalq ibn ʿAli which does not necessitate it, because the former poses a shift from the original state of freedom from liability. Moreover, if we gave precedence to the report of Ṭalq, it would be abrogating the report of abū Hurayra, but we by doing the opposite there would be no abrogation.

1.4.2.9. [Precautionary Content is to Prevail]

A text that indicates precaution takes precedence. For example, our [Mālikī] companions preferred the saying of the Prophet (may God exalt his mention),"Do not start the fast or break it until you see the new moon. If the new moon is obscured from you, then complete a full thirty days,[315]" to the other version which states, "Start fasting after you have seen it (that is, the new crescent) and end the fast (at the end of the month) when you see it. If it is overcast and cannot be seen, then estimate its sighting (that is, presume that Sha'bān lasted for twenty nine).[316]"

Notes

1. *Tawātur* is the transmission of a *mutawātir* narration according to its conditions.
2. A *mutawātir* narration must fulfill four conditions: (1) its transmitters must have been so numerous during each generation or period that it is inconceivable for all of them to have conspired to propagate a lie; (2) the locality of narrators should be diverse so as to preclude the possibility of collusion to fabricate the report; (3) the report would fail to qualify as *mutawātir* if its reporters are found to be biased or associated with one another through a political or sectarian movement; (4) the report must convey certain knowledge based on what is perceived by the senses, rather than thoughts and feelings. Likewise, rational axioms or commonly accepted facts are not regarded as *mutawātir*.
3. Ibn Mujāhid (d. 324AH/936AD) stipulated three basic conditions that must be met for the acceptance as part of the Quran: (1) the reading should be in accordance with one of the 'Uthmanic codices of the seven cities to which it was sent; (2) its chain of transmission should be *mutawātir*; and (3) it should conform to the rules of Arabic grammar (Ibn Mujāhid, 1979, 47; Zarkashī, 1994, 1, 474). A recitation that lacks any of these conditions is classified as *shādh* (abberant) (Zarkashī, 1994, 1, 474). Some Muslim scholars reported *ijmā'* regarding the impermissibility of using abberant readings in prayer (Ibn 'Abd al-Bārr, 1967, 8, 293) but such consensus is controversial (Al-Ḍuwayḥī, 2010, 238). Although an anomalous reading does not meet the prerequisites of *tawātur*, its authority is equal to that of an authentic solitary report, with regard to application, according to Abū Ḥanīfa (Sarakhasī, n.d., 1, 281; Kāsānī, 1986, 4, 11). Mālikī scholars held three varying views regarding citation of an abbarent reading: (1) it cannot be relied upon as a sound proof in legal rulings (Ibn al-'Arabī, 1999, 3, 79); (2) it is equal in authority to a solitary report with respect to application, but it is not definitive (Ibn al-Ḥājib, 2006, 2, 138); (3) it is recommended to use it as evidence in legal rulings. Shāfi'ī scholars also differed regarding use of abbarent readings as evidence in legal rulings (Juwaynī, 1, 427), but Shāfi'ī, himself, did accept them as legislative evidence (Subkī, 2004, 1, 231). As for Imam Aḥmad, he cited abbarent readings as evidence, considering them to be an authentic, solitary report attributed to the Prophet through a Companion (Ibn Qudāma, 1968, 1, 63).
4. Muslim jurists differed regarding the minimum number of times a child must be breastfed to render marriage unlawful between the child and the wet-nurse and between the child and all of the wet-nurse's family members with whom marriage would be prohibited. According to Mālik, his followers, 'Alī, and Ibn Mas'ūd, and in one of the two views of Ibn 'Umar and Ibn 'Abbas, any amount of breastmilk is sufficient to prohibit marriage. On the other hand, according to Shāfi'ī, Imam Aḥmad, Ibn Ḥazm, 'Ā'isha, Ibn Mas'ūd, Ibn al-Zubayr, Ṭāwūs and others, marriage is only prohibited by five known breastfeeding sessions. According Abū 'Ubayd and Abū Thawr, however, breast feeding must take place three times to effect the prohibition of marriage

(Shīrāzī, 1983, 3, 142). The reason for their disagreement stems from the conflict between that which is specified in a number of hadiths and between the general meaning of the phrase "your foster mothers who nursed you" in Q. 4: 24). It reads as follows, "Prohibited to you [for marriage] are your mothers, your daughters, your sisters, your father's sisters, your mother's sisters, your brother's daughters, your sister's daughters, your [foster] mothers who nursed you."

There are basically two conflicting hadiths: (1) The abovementioned hadith related by ʿĀʾisha specifying the five breast-feedings which includes an aberrant Quranic variant; (2) The hadith that was narrated on the authority of ʿĀʾisha, in which the Prophet said, "One or Two sucks or feedings do not effect prohibition [of marriage]" (Muslim, n.d., 2, 1073). Those who referred to the general meaning of the Quran without reference to any of these *hadiths* did not specify the minimum amount of milk that effects prohibition of marriage, while those who specified the meaning of the verse differed. The first group assigned preponderance to the literal meaning of ʿĀʾisha's hadith specifying five breast-feedings over the indirect meaning of her other *hadith* that indirectly implies that anything over more than two breast-feedings is sufficient to effect prohibition of marriage. (Ibn Rushd, 2004, 3, 60). In conclusion, specification of general Quranic meanings should be based on reliable hadiths, and literal meaning of texts should be preferred over indirect meanings.

5. This means that the second abrogation took place so late that a great number of the Companions did not come to known of the abrogation until after the Prophet's death. ʿĀʾisha, moreover, accepted that the verses had been abrogated because she accepted the authenticity of the codices collected during the time of ʿUthmān that gained the unanimous consensus of all Companions, even those who had variant copies including verses which had been abrogated, unbeknownst to them.
6. The word "consecutive" only occurs in Ibn Masʿūd and Ubay's reading (Mālik, 1992, 3, 436; Saʿīd ibn Mansūr, 1997. 4, 1562; ʿAbdur-Razzāq, 1983, 4, 241).
7. Mālik and Shāfiʿī were of the opinion that it is recommended to perform the fasts consecutively. Abū Ḥanīfa and Aḥmad, however, considered consecutive observance of the fasts to be obligatory. Their disagreement stems from two issues. The first is whether it is permissible to take an aberrant narration as a source of legislation to be followed. This is applied to Ibn Masʿūd's reading which states, "then three days of *consecutive* fasts." The second reason stems from their disagreement over whether a restricted command to fast can be interpreted to mean consecutive fasting, based on the fact that the obligatory fasting prescribed by *sharia* must be observed consecutively (Ibn Rushd, 2004, 2, 180).
8. *Īlāʾ* (foreswearing) is when a husband, who has the capacity to divorce his wife, instead swears that he will abstain from sexual relations with his wife for an unrestricted period, or for more than four months (Nawawī, 2011, 432). The husband must either resume relations with his wife before the expiry of the four months and expiate for his remitted oath or, upon the expiry of the four months, he will be forced by a judge to divorce his wife if he does not resume relations with her. Scholars differed with regard to whether a woman is immediately considered divorced upon the completion of the period of the four months specified in the narration, or whether the husband is given time either to return or to divorce. The latter is the view of Mālik, Shāfiʿī, Aḥmad, Abū Thawr, Dāwūd and al-Layth, who referred to the general meaning of the Quranic verse, "*For those who swear not to have sexual relations with their wives is a waiting time of four months, but if they return [to normal relations]—then indeed, Allah is Forgiving and Merciful.*" (Q. 2: 226).
Abū Ḥanīfa, however, relied on the aberrant narration of Ubayy ibn Kaʿb, which qualifies the meaning of the general injunction. According to Ubayy's variant, the verse reads: "For those who

swear not to have sexual relations with their wives is a waiting time of four months, but if they return [to normal relations] *within* the period [of four months] indeed, Allah is Forgiving and Merciful."

9. There are three major views regarding the validity of wiping over leather socks when performing ablution (instead of washing the feet). The dominant majority of Sunni Muslim scholars view that it is permitted both in cases of residence as well as during travel, while some hold the position that it is only permissible during travel (Ibn Rushd, 2004, 1, 25). The Shiites, however, believe that this practice is invalid. The reason for their disagreement is the supposed contradiction between the verse of ablution (Q. 5: 6), commanding the washing of feet, and the hadiths that permitted wiping. Moreover, because the verse was revealed after the *hadith*, they rule that it abrogates wiping. But this view is overruled by the report related by Muslim, on the authority of Jarīr ibn ʿAbdullah, who confirmed to them that he had seen the Prophet (peace be on him) wiping his boots (Ibn Qudāma, 1968, 1, 206.) Jarīr also attested, "I converted to Islam after the revelation of *al-Māʾida* [i.e. after the revelation of the *aya* pertaining to washing the feet]" (Bukhārī, 2001, 1, 87; Muslim, n.d., 1, 227). In response to those who prohibit wiping over leather socks, Sunni scholars present three arguments: (1) There is no contradiction between the verse and the *hadiths*, as the command to wash the feet is directed toward those who are not wearing leather socks, whereas the permission to wipe over them has been granted to those who are. Thus, there is no contradiction considering that the two cases are different with respect to subject, predicate, time and place. (2) Though all the reports concerning wiping over leather socks were reported as solitary narrations, they all have one common *mutawātir* theme, that is the legality of wiping over boots. (3) More than eighty of the Prophet's Companions, including the ten who were promised Paradise, reported that the Prophet wiped over boots (Ibn ʿĀbidīn, 1992, 1, 77).
10. *Mutawātir* hadiths are classified into three categories:

    1. *mutawātir lafẓī* (consecutive verbatim *hadith*), a report quoted verbatim with the exact wording uttered by the Prophet (may God exalt his mention) himself) consecutively transmitted from one large group of people to the next such as his saying, "Whoever deliberately lies about me, let him occupy his seat in the hellfire." (Bukhārī, 2001, 2, 80; Muslim, n.d., 1, 10). This hadith was reported by a large number of Companions including, ʿAlī, Al-Zubayr, Anas, Salama and Abū Hurayrah. Moreover, many other Companions narrated it from these Companions. While the exact number of verbatim *mutawātir* hadiths is a subject of disagreement, it is suggested that there are no more than ten.
    2. *Mutawātir maʿnawī* (continuously recurrent in meaning): When a large number of the transmitters of *hadith* narrate reports which agree in meaning but differ in wording or in form, their common meaning is considered *mutawātir*. This type is called *mutawātir maʿnawī*, or conceptual *mutawātir*. An example is raising hands in supplication, which was reported by many solitary hadiths, all of which share one common theme, which is that the Prophet (may God exalt his mention) raised his hands or mentioned raising hands when making invocations.
    3. *Mutawātir ʿamalī* (consecutively recurrent practice): This refers to practices that are recurrently transmitted by one large group of people to the next throughout ages. Examples of *mutawātir* practices are the five daily prayers, fasting, zakat, Ḥajj, and recitation of the Quran. "According to the majority of scholars, the authority of a *mutawātir ḥadīth* is equivalent to that of the Quran." (Kamali, 1991, 94).

11. Scholars agreed on the permissibility of acting according to a solitary report in testimonies, religious verdicts and secular affairs. Therefore, one may have one witness or a scholar issuing a religious opinion or a single reporter for narrating an event or incident respectively. They differed on acting according to solitary reports in religious matters. The massive majority of scholars accepted it in both creedal and juristic matters while Qadariyya (those who negate God's predestination) and Ẓāhirites did not.
12. Aḥmad, 2001 4,1121; Tirmidhī, 1998, 2,398; abū Dāwūd, n.d., 2, 229.
13. Mālik, 1992, 2, 59; Aḥmad, 2001, 11, 648; abū Dāwūd, n.d., 1, 46; Tirmidhī, 1998, 1, 139.
14. Aḥmad, 2001, 4, 382; Tirmidhī, 1998, 3, 335; Ibn Mājah, n.d., 2, 1124.
15. It is a kind of beverage made of dates, raisins; that is must; and of honey; that is mead; and of wheat, and of barely; that is wort or made of dates, or of raisins which one throws whence its appellation, into a vessel or skin of water until it ferments and becomes intoxicating, or not so long as to become intoxicating. Before it becomes so it is lawful (Lane, 1984, 2757). Jurists have unanimously agreed on the prohibition of large and small amounts of *khamr* 'wine derived of grape juice.' They have further agreed that an amount of other beverages including *nabīdh* that actually intoxicates is similarly prohibited. They differed on small amounts of *nabīdh* that do not intoxicate.
16. Bukhārī, 2001, 1, 43; Muslim, n.d., 1, 233.
17. A vessel hallowed out of stone. By this, Ibn ʿAbbās means that due to the weight of the vessel it would be impossible for one to pour water out of it before immersing his hands therein.
18. Bukhārī, 2001, 9, 75; Mulsim, n.d., 3, 1291.
19. The source of ʿAmr's statement could not be found.
20. Aḥmad, 2001, 40, 435; Abū Dāwūd, 1999, 2, 220; Tirmidhī, 1998, 3, 339.
21. It is called *'man ḥaddatha wa nasī'* (whoever relates reports and then later forgets).
22. A *wasaq* is unanimously estimated to 60 *sāʿs* (2175 g.). A *wasaq* is then estimated to be 2175 × 60 = 130.500 kilograms. So, five *wasaqs* are estimated as 652.5 kilograms (Manīʿ, 1999, 184). The minimal quantity on which *zakat* is payable for crops is five *wasaqs* [652.5 kilograms] of net dried weight, free of husks or chaff, though for rice and wheat, which are stored in the kernal, the *zakat* minimum, including husks, is ten *wasaqs* [1305 kilograms] of dried weight (Miṣrī, 1997, 874).
23. Integrity is an acquisition which impels a person to act with decisiveness and maturity. By 'decisiveness' scholars mean the turning away from evil deeds of idolatry, impiety and heresy while 'maturity' means exemption from certain major sins and vices which shock the sensibility and judgment (Salisbury, 1862, 64.).
24. Scholars labeled a reporter as liar either when he frequently or occasionally lies. If a decisive proof is established, or a confession is declared against a specific reporter, his uprightness is completely impaired (ibn abī Ḥātim, 1952, 1, 37).
25. A narrator is classified as *munkar al-ḥādīth* when he quotes disclaimed or rejected reports. He is a transmitter who does not possess reliability and exactitude sufficient to allow him to transmit a report by himself. He usually commits excessive errors or apparent inattentiveness (Ar-Rahawān, 2014, *199*)
26. Tirmidhī, 1998, 2, 73.
27. Those versions refer to the practice of ibn Masʿūd as in ʿAbdur-Razzāq's *Muṣannaf* (1983, 2, 178) and al-Bayhaqī (2003, 2, 180) or to that of ibn ʿUmar as related in Mālik's *Muwaṭṭaʾ* (1992, 2, 122) or to ibn ʿAbbās as in Aḥmad (2001, 5, 15). A Companions' practice is not as authoritative as the Prophet's. Moreover, if we regard the report of Khālid as authentic, it cannot be used

as a proof for the illegality of a brief sitting after the second prostration and before rising because of two reasons:

1. The text of this hadith does not explicitly show any contradiction between sitting and rising on the tips of one's feet. The Prophet might have sit for rest first and when he started rising he rested on the tips of his feet. This is, the view of the Ḥanābila who recommended sitting for rest before rising and getting up on the tips of his feet (ibn Qudāma, 1968, 1, 279).
2. The Prophet's sitting on the tips of his feet is classified according to some scholars as non-legal *Sunna* (*Sunna ghayr tashri'iyya*) mainly consists of the natural and instinctive activities of the Prophet (*al-af'āl al-jibilliyya*) such as the manner which he ate, slept, dressed, and such other activities as do not seek to constitute a part of the *sharia* (Kamali, 1991, 53). Activities of this nature are not of primary importance to the Prophetic mission and therefore do not constitute legal norms. According to the majority of *ulema*, the Prophet's preferences in these areas only indicate the permissibility of the acts in question (Shaltūt, 2001, 5; Khallāf, n.d., 43).

28. The exact wording of the quoted hadith is as follows:
On the authority of abū Hurayra (may Allah be pleasded with him) who reported that the Messenger of Allah (may God exalt his mention) made obligatory the rinsing of the mouth and snuffing three times (Dāraquṭnī, 2004, 1, 207; ibn 'Adiy, 1997, 2, 324).
29. His full name is Baraka ibn Muḥammad al-Ḥalabī al-Anṣārī. He is accused of being a liar. Ibn Ḥibbān said, "[Scholars] informed us that he used to plagiarize traditions, and sometimes he inverted phrases at hadith texts. His reports are not a reliable source of law when he solely reports them" (ibn abī Ḥātim, 1952, 2, 433). According to ibn 'Adiyy, his reports are null and void (ibn 'Adiy, 1997, 2, 324).
30. Aḥmad, 2001, 23, 12; ibn Māja, n.d., 2, 33; Ṭāḥāwī, 1994, 1, 217; Dāraquṭnī, 2004, 2, 107; Bayhaqī, 2003, 2, 228.
31. His full name is Jābir ibn Yazīd ibn al-Ḥārith al-Ju'fī, one of the well-known Shī'ī scholars of Kūfa. He is accused of reporting lies (Bukhārī, 2005, 29; ibn ābī Ḥātim, 1952, 2, 497; Ibn Ḥibbān, 1976, 1, 208).
32. *Al-Raj'a* is cyclic rebirths based on transmigration of the human soul from one physical body to another. This process of reincarnation allegedly continues until the soul reaches its full maturity and perfection when it joins its source—God or the "Universal Soul". This theory is one of the tenets of Shī'a (Baghdādī, 1977, 39). They believe that 'Ali transmigrate by coming back in the flesh after his death (Dhahabī, 1963, 2, 147). Shī'a claim that upon the reappearance of Mahdī, Prophet Muhammad, 'Alī, al-Hasan, al-Ḥusayn, abū Bakr and 'Umar will reincarnate to have retaliation before their second death before the day of resurrection (al-Shaykh, 1989: 101).
33. *Majhūl al-ḥāl* is a narrator whose integrity is not verified. *Majhūl al-'ayn* is a narrator whose report was received by only one student and is not known in the literary circles.
34. It is the greater treatise of Imām Mālik ibn Anas (d. 179AH/795AD). It is transmitted through Saḥnūn 'Abdus-Salām ibn Sa'īd al-Tannūkhī (d. 256AH/869AD) from Abdu-Raḥmān ibn al-Qāsim (d. 191AH/806AD), one of the disciples of Mālik. It is a list of questions that were raised by Asad ibn al-Furāt (d. 213AH/828AD) and were directed to ibn Qāsim. Saḥnūn conveyed those questions to ibn al-Qāsim upon abridging and correcting the content. He, then, spread it in Andalusia, where the Mālikī school of law became widespread. It is the most trustworthy source of Mālik's views (Ibn Farḥūn, n.d., 162).
35. There are means of proving the integrity of a narrator such as being well known among scholars of Hadith, being recommended by renown scholars or being examined in Hadith circles.

Scholars differed on narrators who are *majhūl al-ḥāl* 'of unverified integrity'. The majority of jurists rejected the report of a *majhūl al-ḥāl,* but the rest including Ḥanafī scholars accepted it without restrictions relying on the legal maxim that the original state of people is their freedom of liability. The majority of Hadith scholars accepted the report of *majhūl al-ḥāl* basing their verdict on the statement that "a narrator who is quoted by two trustworthy students will have his *jahāla* 'want of information' will be uplifted and his integrity proven" (Shawkāwī, 1999, 2, 54). A third view maintains that if the students who quoted him are known for electing their teachers, his integrity is proven (Tilmisānī, 2013, 376).

Scholars of Hadith maintained that a narrator's uprightness is also proved if his reports have been circulated among students, especially those who elect their teachers and only report on the authority of well-known and trustworthy narrators (*Ibid*). Khālid ibn Abī al-Ṣalt is declared as trustworthy due to the fact that Mubārak ibn Faḍāla and Wāṣil ibn abī ʿUyana in addition to Khālid al-Ḥadhā' and Sufyān ibn Husain narrated from him. Those names are known for quoting hadiths only from trustworthy narrators.

36. If a narrator is chronically forgetful, his reports will be rejected. If poor memory results from his old age, or of being sightless, or because of having his notebooks burnt, his reports are called jumbled (*mukhṭalat}*). His transmissions reported before the occurrence of his occasional forgetfulness or such problems will be accepted. Otherwise he will be either rejected or suspended. Scholars defined reports received from chronic forgetful narrators (*sayyi' al-ḥifẓ)* as jumbled (*mukhṭalaṭ*) traditions. To have his reports rejected, the amount of errors he commits must be excessive. Minor and accidental mistakes do not make his reports rejected (Shāfiʿī, 1940, 382; Shīrāzī 2003, 76; Baghdādī, n.d., 281).
37. There are four branches for the Mālikī school of law:
    1. The Medinese branch which represented the origin of the Mālikī school of law. The most influential scholars of this branch are ibn al-Mājishūn and Muṭṭarif ibn ʿAbdullah. The main methodology of this branch is that it preferred *hadith* to the Medinian practice "ʿ*amal ahl al-madīnah*'. They, therefore, differed with the majority of Mālikīs.
    2. The Iraqi branch which is an extension of the Medinian branch was founded by al-Qaʿnabī and ʿAbdur-Raḥmān ibn Mahdī.
    3. The Egyptian branch which was founded by ʿUthmān ibn al-Ḥakam al-Juẓāmī and ʿAbdur-Raḥīm ibn Khālid al-Jumaḥī, ʿAbdullah ibn ʿAbdul-Ḥakam, Ibn Wahb and ʿAbdur-Raḥmān ibn al-Qāsim. The latter is the most reliable source of Mālik's views, which was included in the *Mudawanna.* Though its origin is the Western branch of the school, it was refined, edited and elaborated by ibn al-Qāsim. This is the reason that the Western branch of the school gives much credit to the views of ibn l-Qāsim. It is very much related to the Western branch.
    4. The Western branch which spread in Western provinces including Andalusia, Morocco and western parts of the Muslim state. To this school is credited the final standardization of the *mudawannah*, which is the main source of the Mālikī school of law.
38. This is the dominant view of Mālikīs because it is the most popular view of Mālik as recorded by ibn al-Qāsim in *al-mudawwana*. Mālikīs of the Western provinces give much credit to ibn al-Qāsim because of his long stay with Mālik. The recommendation of raising hands on the commencement of prayer is also the view of abū Ḥanīfa.
39. Ḥumaydī, 1996, 741; abū Dāwūd, *Musnad*: 753; Ṭaḥāwī, 1994, 1, 224; Dāraquṭnī, 2004, 2, 438; al-Bayhaqī: 2528. They all related it from Yazīd ibn abī Ziyād from ʿAbdur-Raḥmān ibn abī

Lyala from al-Barā' ibn 'Azib (*d. 72/691*). Reliable transmitters agreed that the phrase, **but he did not repeat it [again]**' is an interpolation of Yazīd who was well known of inserting extraneous words and phrases to the texts of *hadiths*. Aḥmad, Bukhārī, Ḥumaydī, ad-Dārimī and others graded it as weak *hadith* (Zayla'ī, 1997, 1:402; Shawkānī, 1993, 2:210).

40. His full name is abū 'Abdulalh Yazīd ibn abī Ziyād al-Qurashī al-Kūfī. He is of the renown Shī'ī scholars of Kūfa. He was reliable but when he became old of age he had a poor memory, became jumbled and his students started to interpolate extraneous materials in his books. He died in 137AH/705AD (Ibn Sa'd, 1968, 6, 340).
41. Ibn abī Ḥātim, *al-Jarḥ wa al-Ta'dīl*, 9:265; Dhahbī, 1963, 4, 423.
42. It is related by 'Aṣim ibn Kulayb from his father that 'Alī (may Allah be pleased with him) used to raise his hands on the commencement of prayer but he did not repeat it again (Ṭaḥāwī, 1994, 1, 225). There is another variant version of the report which is related by Sufyān from 'Aṣim ibn Kulayb from 'Abdur-Raḥmān ibn al-Aswad from 'Alqama who reported 'Abdullah ibn Mas'ūd saying, "Should I lead you in prayer in the same way I saw the Messenger of Allah praying?" 'Alqama said, "He lead them in prayer raising his hands only at the beginning of prayer." It is related by Aḥmad (2001, 6, 203) and abū Dāwūd (1999, 1, 199). This version was graded as fairly authentic by some scholars such as al-Tirmidhī and ibn Ḥazm (Al-Muḥalla, n.d., 2, 265). There are, however, other more reliable traditions which prove that the Prophet raised his hands on bowing down and on standing from *rukū'* as we will show in discussing scholars' disagreement on this issue.
43. This type of defect is called *idrāj* 'interpolation'. *Mudraj* 'interpolated' is a hadith whose *isnād* has been changed, or that which has something interpolated into its text, which is not part of it (Ibn al-Ṣalāḥ, 1986, 45). Interpolation may occur in the chain of transmitters by incorporating various texts of different narrators. There are other forms of this interpolation. It may also occur by inserting words or phrases in the text. This is the intended meaning of *idrāj* in this book. *Idrāj* may be justifiable if the narrator demarcates the inserted phrase or words. It may in this case serve the text by explaining a word.
44. Ṭaḥāwī, 1994, 1, 335; ibn Māja, n.d., 2, 250; Ibn Khuzayma, n.d., 2, 221; abū Dāwūd 1999, 2, 25.
45. His full name is abū 'Abdul-Karīm ibn 'Ubayda ibn Mu'attib al-Ḍabbī al-Kūfī. He became senile at the end of his age. This is the reason critics of Hadith narrators regarded him unreliable (Bukhārī, n.d., 6, 127).
46. He is one of the erudite Ḥanfī jurists. Ibn Ma'īn labeled him a liar. Scholars of Hadith have unanimously agreed that his reports cannot be used as legal proofs due to his weakness and telling lies. He died in 189AH/804AD (Bukhārī, n.d., 8, 338).
47. Aḥmad, 2001, 18, 512; 'Abd ibn Ḥumayd, 1988, 1, 104; Ṭaḥāwī, 1994, 1, 335.
48. This is the general meaning of *inqiṭā'*, which includes disseverance of the line of transmission at any point of the *isnād*. This definition includes a report of a missing link at the beginning of the chain at the point of the compiler, or at the end of the chain immediately before the Prophet, or at the middle. This is the definition used by most jurists and traditionists. According to early traditionists, it is called a report with an incoherent *isnād* at the level below the Followers (al-Baghdādī, n.d., 37; ibn 'Abdul-Barr, 1967, 1,22; Ibn al-Ṣalāḥ, 1986, 26). The problem in a *munqaṭi'* is that the missing link is unknown. He may be an unreliable transmitter.
49. According to this definition, the only problem of a *mursal* report is that the missing link is the Prophet's Companions, though it is not a problem according to the scholars of Hadith. Not

knowing the Companion does not impair the authenticity of a report because all Companions occupy the highest grades of integrity. The proper definition of *mursal* is a report with a broken link in its *isnād* at the level of a Companion. A *Tābi'ī* (Follower) reported it directly from the Prophet (may God exalt his mention) (Ar-Rahawān, 2014, 69).

50. *Mawqūf* is a report which is transmitted by the Companions concerning their words, deeds and the like, which is not attributed to the Messenger (Ar-Rahawān, 2014, 63).
51. It is a disseverance at any point of a transmission chain.
52. If it is pronounced *salasil;* it is the name of a well where the battle occurred in the third year after *hijra.*
53. Aḥmad, 2001, 29, 346; abū Dāwūd, n.d. 1, 249; ad-Daraquṭnī, 2004, 1, 327. It is an authentic hadith (Albānī, 1985, 1, 181).
54. Daraquṭnī, 2004, 1, 327; Haythamī, n.d., 1, 76; Bayhaqī, 2003, 1, 345.
55. It is when one, who has not accompanied the Prophet, ascribes a report to the Prophet (may God exalt his mention).
56. Aḥmad, 2001, 32, 280; ibn Māja, n.d., 3, 79; abū Dāwūd, 1999, 1, 429; Sa'īd ibn Mansūr, 1982, 1, 177.
57. His full name is abū Burda 'Amir ibn abū Mūsa al-Ash'arī. He is one of the Followers and a son of abū Mūsa al-Ash'arī; the well-known Companion of the Prophet.
58. Ḥanafī scholars accept the *mursal* report. They only differed on the type of *mursal* which is accepted as a legal proof. Karkhī, for instance, generally accepts *mursal* reports, while Sarakhsī unrestrictedly accepts *mursal* of the first three generations. A third group of Ḥanfīs rely on *mursal* after fulfilling specific conditions (Sarakhsī, n.d., 435). Therefore, I think this argument may be raised by some Ḥanafīs, or the writer presumes so for the sake of argument.
59. Followers of the Prophet who witnessed the Prophet's Companions.
60. His name is Moḥammad ibn Yaḥya ibn 'Abdullah ibn Khālid ibn Fāris ibn Dhu'ayb al-Naysābūrī (d. 258AH/871AD).
61. It is when report is attributed to a *ṣaḥābī.*
62. Spiritual retreat in a mosque.
63. Dāraquṭnī, 2004, 3, 184; Bayhaqī, 2003, 4, 521. It is related from Suwayd ibn 'Abdul-Azīz through Sufyān ibn Ḥusayn from al-Zuhrī from 'Urwa from 'Aisha who attributed it to the Prophet. Daraquṭnī stated that Suwayd is the only student of Sufyān who related it on his authority. Suwayd is a weak narrator whose report cannot be accepted if it is solitarily transmitted by him (Bukhārī, n.d., 4, 148; ibn abī Ḥātim, 1952, 4, 238).
64. Scholars disagreed on the Validity of *i'tikāf* without fasting as follows:

    1. Abū Ḥanīfa, Mālik and a group of jurists made fasting a condition for *i'tikāf.*
    2. Shāfi'ī and Aḥmad hold that fasting is not a condition for a person engaging in *i'tikāf.*

    The reason of their disagreement is whether there is a coincidence between fasting and *i'tikāf* or not. The former view identified a coincidence by maintaining that the Prophet made *i'tikāf* only during the month of Ramaḍān. Furthermore, the verse of fasting includes instructions on *i'tikāf.* This coincidence is further confirmed by the tradition of 'Ā'isha. Shāfi'ī and Aḥmad disregard any coincidence between fasting and *i'tikāf* because when the Prophet swore not to fulfill his *i'tikāf* during Ramaḍān and made up the ten days at the beginning of *Shawwāl* (Bukhārī, 2001, 3, 51), it is not conceivable that he was fasting because the first day of Shawwāl is the day of feast which is prohibited to fast. Furthermore, when 'Umar asked the Prophet on the vow he took on himself before embracing Islam to stay a night in the sacred mosque of Mecca (Bukhārī, 2001,

3, 48; Muslim, n.d., 3, 1277), the Prophet commanded him to fulfill his vow while night is not a time for fasting. Furthermore, the hadith of ʿĀʾisha is unauthentic (Albānī, n.d., 6, 58).

65. When a scholar issues a religious verdict he does not necessarily provide full *isnād* or references for his quotations. This is the reason that ʿĀʾisha might have provided the statement of the Prophet without giving full details of *isnād*.
66. The reason of scholars' disagreement on the authority of this statement is the ambiguity of the word '*sunna*'. It may refer to a practice of the Companions, the normative practice of the Rightly Guided Caliphs as mentioned in the Prophet's *hadith* (Aḥmad, 2001, 28, 367; ibn Māja, n.d., 1, 28; ibn Ḥibbān, 1988, 1, 178) or the normative precedent of the Prophet. The majority of jurists maintain that a Companion's saying, "*sunn*a has preceded that ..." is as authoritative an elevated statement of the Prophet, because when a word vacillates between two meanings, the legal connotation prevails. Furthermore, the Companions usually mention this phrase when they prove a certain act's legal ruling. They use it as an authority. Abū Bakr al-Ṣayrafī and abū al-Ḥasan al-Karkhī of the Ḥanafī scholars, Juwaynī of the Shāfiʿīs in addition to ibn Ḥazm did not regard this phrase as authoritative. Shāfiʿī has two conflicting views regarding this issue (abū al-Ḥusayn, *al-Muʿtamad*, 1983, 2:667; ibn Ḥazm, n.d., 2, 72; Abū Yaʿlā, 1990, 3, 991; Juwaynī, 1997, 1, 649).
67. *Liʿān* is public imprecation. It consists of the Islamic magistrate (or his equivalent) telling the husband to repeat four times, "I testify by Allah that I am truthful in charging her with adultery."
68. The majority of scholars including the Mālikīs, Shāfiʿīs and Ḥanbalīs maintain that separation immediately occurs by *liʿān* and there is no need for a judge to effect it. Ḥanafī scholars made the decree of a judge necessary for effecting separation (ibn Rushd, 2004, 3, 140).
69. The literal meaning of the word *qunūṭ* is being obedient or humble. It also means standing. In the context of prayer, it implies special supplication made either in *witr* or in other prayers as the Muslims are overtaken by a calamity.
    According to Shāfiʿī scholars, *qunūt* includes the following words according to the reliable *hadith* of al-Ḥasan ibn ʿAlī in which the Prophet taught him the words of *qunūt*: "O Allah, guide me among those You guide, grant me health and pardon among those You grant health and pardon, look after me among those You look after, grant me grace in what You have given me, and protect me from the evil [A: here, one turns the palms down for a moment] of what You have ordained; for You decree and none decrees against You; and none is abased whom You befriend. 0 our Lord, who are above all things sacred and exalted, all praise is Yours for what You decree. I ask Your forgiveness and turn to You in repentance."
    Malik preferred that it be with the words: "O Allah, we seek Your help, we seek Your forgiveness, we seek Your guidance, we believe in You, we bow and humble ourselves before You, we devote ourselves to You, and we shun him who denies You. O Allah, You it is we worship, and for You we pray and prostrate ourselves, toward You we strive and hasten, seeking Your mercy, and fearing Your torment, for Your torment is about to chase the disbelievers" (Ibn Rushd, 2004, 1, 141).
70. I could not find the statement of ibn Masʿūd. It is a statement of ibn abī Lyala as being related by ibn abī Shayba in his *muṣannaf* (1989, 2, 104). Ibn Masʿūd did not use to recite *qunūt* in *fajr* prayer (ʿAbdur-Razzāq, 1983, 2, 110, *al-Ṭaḥāwī,* 1994, 3, 62; Bayhaqī, 2003, 4, 48).
71. Scholars disagreed on the recitation of *qunūt* supplication in *fajr* prayer as follows:

    1. Mālik: it is recommended
    2. Ash-Shāfiʿī: It is emphatically recommended (*sunna*)
    3. Abū Ḥanīfa and Aḥmad: It is not permitted in *fajr* prayer, but it is recommended in *witr*.
       The reason for their disagreement is the apparent conflict among the following traditions:

(a). Anas related that the Prophet made supplications for a month against a group of people and then stopped. But he continued reciting *qunūt* in fajr prayer till he passed away (Ibn Mājah, 2009, 2, 297; Dāraquṭnī: 2004, 2, 372; Bayhaqī: 2003, 2, 278). The report has many variant versions. Al-Nawawī (n.d., 4, 147) and Bayhaqī authenticated this report. Ibn al-Jawzī criticized al-Rabī' who received the report from Anas (ibn Ḥajar, 1908, 2, 239).

Ibn Abū Hurayra related that the Prophet did not recite *qunūt* except when he prayed for or against people (ibn Khuzayma, n.d., 1, 313) A'ẓamī, the editor of ibn Khuzayma's *Ṣaḥīḥ* graded it authentic. There are other repots which confirm the same meaning. The problem lies in Anas' tradition which was graded as *mu'ḍal* (perplexing) due to deficiencies in its narrators (Shawkānī, 1993, 2, 400). There is a version of Anas' tradition which supports the meaning of abū Hurayra's report (ibn Khuzayma, n.d., 1, 314). Moreover, the tradition of Anas may be interpreted to refer to special *qunūt* supplications at times of calamities. Confirming that the Prophet continued reciting *qunūt* until he passed away is weakened by the perplexity of reports which mentioned it and its opposition to other more authentic reports.

72. Bukhārī, 2001, 1, 124; Muslim, n.d., 1, 278.
73. Muslim, n.d., 3, 1153; abū Dāwūd, n.d., 3, 254; Tirmidhī,1998, 2, 523; Nasā'ī: 1986, 7, 262; ibn Māja, n.d., 3, 313.
74. The word is derived from *shafa'a* 'to join' [because the property is joined to the *shāfi'* [pre-emptor]. In the terminology of the jurists, it is the right to take possession of a house and land to prevent the harm of a neighbor, for example if a man sells his house or land and tells his neighbor or partner about this sale, the partner/neighbor has a right to object to the sale. He can take what was sold at the price at which it was sold. The one who has this right is called a *shafī'* [pre- emptor] (Qudūrī, 1997, 106).
    Scholars agreed on establishing the right of preemption for a partner, but they differed on proving it for a neighbor. The majority of scholars including Mālik, Shāfi'ī and Aḥmad did not include the neighbor. Abū Ḥanīfa extended the right of preemption to an adjacent neighbor, but priority is given to a partner in a sold item and a partner in land or a house (Ṭaḥāwī, n.d., 4, 239).
75. The wording of this *ḥadīth* is not extant in any Hadith compilation. The correct text of the hadith reads as follows:
    On the authority of Jābir who said, "The Messenger of Allah (my God exalt his mention) decreed [the right of] preemption and [the right of] neighborhood" Nasā'ī, 1986, 7, 321. Al-Albānī graded it as *ṣaḥīḥ li ghayrih* (sound by virtue of extraneous evidence). There are other authentic traditions which confirm the neighbor's right in preemption.
76. Ibn Māja, n.d., 2, 561; ibn Khuzayma: n.d., 3, 204; ibn Ḥibbān: 1988, 8, 351; Tirmidhī, 1998, 2, 63; abū Dāwūd: n.d., 2, 300.
77. Muslim, n.d., 1, 234.
78. Both *manṭūq* and *mafhūm* are derived from the words and sentences of the text. The former form the obvious text and the latter come through logical and juridical construction thereof (Kamali, 1991, 125).
79. The full text of the hadith is related by Bukhārī (2001, 7, 68) and Muslim (n.d. 3, 1599). The wording of Bukhārī is as follows: It is related that 'Umar ibn abī Salama said, "I was a boy in the care of the Messenger of Allah, may Allah bless him and grant him peace, and my hand used to go all around in the plate. The Messenger of Allah, may Allah bless him and grant him peace, said to me, 'Boy, say the name of Allah and eat with your right hand and eat from what is in front of you.' That has been the way I have eaten ever since."

80. It is an ironic expression which apparently shows respect but intended to contempt.
81. It is adding raisins and dates to water to better change its taste.
82. Aḥmad, 2001, 7, 341; Muslim, n.d., 3, 1584; Tirmidhī, 1998, 2, 361; ibn Māja: n.d., 2, 511; Nasāʾī: 1986, 7, 234.
83. There is a third view not mentioned by the author, but it is regarded the most preponderant view among scholars. It maintains that a command following proscription removes prohibition and restores the prior status. So, if it indicates obligation prior to prohibition it is restored be obligatory. If it is recommended, it will return to be recommended. This is the view of Zarkashī, ibn al-Humām, ibn Taymiya, ibn Kahthīr and Shaykh al-Amīn (Shinqīṭī, 2001, 192).
84. It is an order devoid of any contextual clue to provide a decisive connotation.
85. Scholars disagreed on witnessing upon recourse of marriage. Abū Ḥanīfa, Mālik, Shāfiʿī according to his most updated view and Aḥmad in one of his variant views held that it is only recommended. According to old view of Shāfiʿī and one of the variant views of Aḥmad, it is obligatory (Shāfiʿī, 1990, 5, 245; Shīrāzī, n.d., 2, 14, Ibn Rushd, 2004, 3, 104). The reason of their disagreement is referred to their disagreement on the meaning of a command in the verse which states, "And when they have [nearly] fulfilled their term, either retain them according to acceptable terms or part with them according to acceptable terms. And bring to witness two just men from among you and establish the testimony for [the acceptance of] Allah." (Q. 65: 2).
    Command primarily vacillates between obligation and recommendation. The first view stated that analogy requires that recourse of marriage is like other transactions which do not necessitate witnessing. The other view referred to the primary meaning of a command, that is obligation to prove that it is compulsory to witness even on the revocation of marriage.
86. Bukhārī, 2001, 1, 45; Muslim, n.d.,1, 234.
87. He based his view on the hadith related by Bukhārī (2001, 9, 94) and Muslim (n.d., 2, 975) from Abu Hurayra that the Prophet, may Allah bless him and grant him peace, said, "Leave me alone regarding what I have not mentioned to you. People before you were destroyed on account of their questioning and disagreeing with their Prophets. If I forbid you something, then avoid it. If I command you something, then do it as much as you can." When the Prophet stated that the implementation of his commands is dependent of one's ability it gave the impression they imply mere recommendation. In fact abū Bakr al-Abharī had two variant views on this issue and the most popular view is that both commands of Allah and His messenger mean obligation (Subkī, 2004, 2, 26; 2003, 1, 376).
88. Muwaṭṭaʾ, 2004, 2, 53; Bukhārī, 2001, 2, 4.
89. Scholars disagreed on the immediate performance of *hajj* as follows:
    1. Moḥammad ibn al-Ḥasan, Moḥammad ibn Shujāʿ and the majority of Ḥanfī scholars upheld its delayed performance (Samarqandī, 1994, 1, 578; Kāsānī, 1986, 1, 119). This is one of the variant views of Mālik as related by ibn al-Qaṣṣār (ibn Rushd, 2004, 2, 86) and the view of the majority of Shāfiʿī scholars (Shirāzī, n.d., 1, 206).
    2. Abū Ḥanīfa, abū Yusūf and al-Karkhī upheld its immediate observance. Abū Ḥanīfa was once asked which should be offered first: *hajj* or marriage, he stated that *hajj* is to be offered first (Samarqandī, 1994, 1, 578; Kāsānī, 1986, 1, 119). This is the variant view of Mālik as reported by Ashhab and the view of Ḥanābila (ibn Qudāma, 1968, 3, 241). The reason of their disagreement is whether an unqualified command entails immediate or deferred observance.
        1. According to a view of Mālik and Ḥanbalī scholars, absolute command entails immediate performance. They based their rule on this principle.

2. Ḥanafis and Mālik according to one of his views stated that it does not necessitate immediate performance.
3. Shāfiʿī scholars stated that it does not necessitate either, but they relied on further evidences to prove its delayed performance such as the Prophet's delay of hajj to the ninth year though it was obligated two years earlier (Ibn Rushd, 2004, 2, 86).

90. The majority of scholars including Ḥanfis, abū al-Ḥusayn al-Baṣrī, al-Rāzī, al-Āmidī and ibn al-Ḥājib is that an absolute command which is devoid of any contextual clue does not indicate single or multiple executions. This is the view of al-Tilimsānī. The majority of Shāfiʿīs, Mālikīs, abū Isḥāq al-Isfrāinī, Shīrāzī, al-Ghazālī and ibn Qudāma stated that an absolute command requires single execution of an act. Doing it for multiple times needs further evidence outside the context. The view of Ḥanbalīs and Khuayzmandād is that a command requires multiple execution of an act provided that it is within the limits of one's ability and it is possible to do so (Ghāzalī, 1993, 2, 2; Shīrāzī, 2003, 1, 219).
91. This is a mistake since the hadith is related by Burayda al-Aslāmī as it is shown in the previous footnote. The hadith of Yaʿlā is on the shortening of prayers, when he exclaimed to Umar, "Allah said: That you shorten the *salat* if you fear and the people are safe (Q. 4: 101)." So ʿUmar said: "I wondered about that just as you have wondered. So I mentioned that to the Messenger of Allah (may God exalt his mention), and he said: "It is charity which Allah has given to you, so accept His charity" (Muslim, n.d., 1478; abū Dāwūd, n.d., 2, 3; Trimidhī, 1998, 5, 93).
92. This question has been raised in different occasions by both al-Aqraʿ ibn Ḥābis (Muslim, n.d., 2, 975; Nasā'ī,1986, 5, 110) and Surāqa ibn Mālik (Muslim, n.d. 2, 975; Nasāʾī, 1986, 5, 110).
93. Subkī said in his *al-Ibhāj* (2004, 1, 95):
"This opinion has been attributed to some of our [Shāfiʿī] companions but fellows of Shāfiʿī *madhhab* asked about those who advocated it. It is not found in any of the books of Shāfiʿīs after a long time of searching. I think someone misunderstood one of our companions' statement that prayer is held obligatory at the beginning of its prescribed time but at an extended time [to the time of the next prayer].
94. This is the view of the majority of Irāqī Ḥanfis.
95. Shirbīnī, 1994, 1, 315.
96. The popular view of Mālikī scholars is that prayer must be made up (Ḥaṭṭāb, 1992, 1, 410).
97. The majority of scholars including Mālikīs, Shāfiʿīs, Aḥmad, al-Thawrī and al-Awzāʿī maintained that a non-traveler who is free of any diseases and lacks water cannot perform *tayammum* to offer a supererogatory prayer.
98. Muslim, n. d., 1, 471; abū Dāwūd, n. d., 1, 118; Tirmidhī, 1998, 5, 170.
99. *Mafhūm al-mukhalafa* may be defined as a meaning which is derived from the words of the text in such a way that it diverges from the explicit meaning thereof (Kamali, 1991, 124).
100. Abū Isḥāq al-Isfrāyīnī was a medieval Sunni Islamic theologian, Shāfiʿī jurist, legal theoretician and commentator on the Quran. Al-Isfrāyīnī's scholarship was focused on the sciences of *ʿAqida*, Hadith and *Fiqh*. He was along with Ibn Furak the chief propagator of Sunni Ash'ari theology in Nishapur at the turn of the 5th Islamic century. (Jonathan A.C. Brown, 2007, 156).
101. ibn Rushd, 2004, 1:125.
102. It means that once an act like a contract of sale is prohibited by a text, it does not entail any legal consequences since it is regarded null and void. For example, A sells B an item which involves usurious interest. Such a contract becomes null and void. B cannot own this item based on this invalid contract. There is an exception to this rule. For example, when a contract is prohibited but such a prohibition does not entail invalidity. The Prophet prohibited *najsh* (artificial bidding to

raise the price of a certain community), but if a contract of sale is concluded after *najsh* it is still effective and valid.

103. It is to marry by trading daughters or sisters. It means a man gives his daughter in marriage on the condition that the other gives his daughter to him in marriage without any dower being paid by either.
104. It is a sale contract in which an unusual condition is added to give an extra or undue benefit to the seller or to the buyer (Khan, 1990, 31). The report is related by al-Ḥākim (1990, 1, 103), al-Khāṭṭābī, (1932, 3, 744) and ibn Ḥazm (n.d., 8, 415) from Muḥammad ibn Sulaymān al-Dhuhī from ʿAbdul-Wārith ibn Saʿīd from abū Ḥanīfa. The report does not have a genuine origin. Ibn Taymiya maintained that is not found in any of the compilations of Hadith (Ibn Taymiya, 1987, 29, 132).
105. A sale transaction in which a seller says: 'I shall sell you this product for such and such price if you lend me so much money' (Khan, 1990, 31).
106. (Bukhārī, 2001, 3, 70; Muslim, n.d., 3, 1153).
107. Pertinent particulars of a legal decision include the action suggested by a legal ruling, its description, its time of performance and place. They further include the subject matter of a ruling. For example, the Prophet's saying, "Five types of animals are all vicious and can be killed in the sacred sanctuary," the text provides a ruling that is permissibility of killing such named animals, and other relevant particulars of this ruling that is the place where it is permissible to kill them, the description such animals as vicious and their number.
108. *Mafhūm* means 'expression of the one thing in a text is exclusion of the other' (Ahmad, 2006, 41) By *mafhūm* in this context, the author refers to *mafhūm al-mukhālafa* which is "inference based on the assumption that a case whose judgment was not mentioned in a text must be decided in a manner opposite to the one mentioned in the text" (Ahmad, 2004, 129). A legal ruling may be connected with a definite number such as the recommendation of killing those five stated animals mentioned in the report. By *mafhūm*, prohibition is extended to all other animals which do not fall within the scope of this number. It is however controversial among scholars.
109. The number provided in this report is not a part and parcel of the legal ruling, nor is it intended by permissibility. It is a description of the vicious animals permitted to kill. The number 'seven' in the former example is a *naṣṣ* (univocal) in the sense that the command to wash vessels licked by dogs stipulated that the number of washings must be seven. But the number 'five' mentioned in the other report is not *naṣṣ*. It suggests that animals which are harmful and may be killed are five. The number is pertinent to the reason for a ruling. It is not intended to exclusive.
110. It refers to the name of the two stars β and γ of Usra Minor.
111. Bukhārī (2001, 1, 151).
112. *Mujmal* literally means a word or a phrase implying many things and unexplained (Rāghib, 1992, 203). Technically it denotes a word or text which is inherently unclear and gives no indication as to its precise meaning. The cause of ambiguity in *Mujmal* is inherent in the locution itself (Kamali, 1991, 99). It may also be defined as a word or a phrase that inherently conveys two equal meanings; none of which is given preference to the other (Shinqīṭī, 2001, 215).
113. Semantic ambiguity may be a result of using a homonym; a word inherently used to share two or more meanings; none of them is figurative.
114. This is the view of Mālik, Shāfiʿī, Aḥmad according to one of his two variant views, abū Thawr and the majority of Medinian scholars. A waiting period according to this view expires by the immediate start of the third menstruation. According to abū Ḥanīfa, his disciples and Aḥmad in one of his views, a waiting period expires by the end of the purification period following the third menstruation.

115. The verse is attributed to abū Baṣīr Maymūn ibn Qays al-Bakrī, known as al-Aʿshā al-Akbar (d. 7AH/629AD). It means that he engages in battle each year but it always results in affluence of properties he takes up and the praise he receives from people because of missing his pleasure during days when his women were pure of menses.
116. In all reported traditions, the word *qurʾ* was only used to mean menstruation.
117. The Prophet's Companions differed on interpreting the meaning of *qurʾ*. Abū Bakr, ʿUmar, ʿUthmān, ʿAlī, ibn Masʿūd, abū Mūsā al-Ashʿarī, ibn ʿAbbās, ʿUbada ibn al-Ṣāmit and abū al-Dardāʾ maintained that it is used to mean menstruation period. ʿĀʾisha, Zayd ibn Thābit and ibn ʿUmar are reported as interpreting it to mean purification period (ibn Rushd, 2004, 3, 108).
118. It is related by Daraquṭnī, 2004, 1, 394 and Bayhaqī, 2003, 2, 184. Ibn Ḥajar graded it as weak (ibn Ḥajar, 1998, 1, 170), but Albānī authenticated it (Albānī, 1985, 1, 225).
119. The verse is mentioned by al-Bājī, n.d., 4, 94; Qurṭubī, 1964, 4, 94.
120. It refers to two Arabic words pronounced in the same way but their meaning is different. Discrepancy of their meanings is not a result of being homonyms but because of difference in their morphological origin. Due to morphological reasons, one form may refer to two distinct nouns. For example, the word *mukhtār* is used as passive part noun to mean 'selected, elected, chosen or preferred' and as an active part noun signifying 'the one who has free choice'.
121. Aḥmad, 2001, 19, 383; Muslim, n.d., 3, 1213; Tirmidhī, 1998, 2, 547; abū Dāwūd, n.d., 3, 249; Nasāʾī, 1986, 7, 279.
122. When gold is traded for gold three conditions are binding: (a) exact equivalence in amount, which must be made certain of, this condition precluding exchanges of foodstuff, gold or silver in which the amounts are not known, for such sales are not valid even if the two quantities transacted subsequently turn out to be equal, because of ignorance of their equivalence at the time of the transaction, since ignorance of it is the same as actual non-equivalence. (b) the properties transacted must be in the respective possession of buyer and seller before they part company. (c) and immediate such that the agreement does not mention any delay in the exchange even if brief (Miṣrī, 1982, 152).
123. This report is not extant in Hadith compilations. Ṭaḥāwī's version reads, "separate them from each other" Ṭaḥāwī, 1994, 15, 378. Some editors introduced it as "Trade them with greater weight in some." But it is an apparent typo, which is mostly absent in other editions of *Sharḥ Mushkil al-Athār*.
124. *Maḥfūẓ* is an authentic and accepted *hadith* related by reliable narrators versus the anomalous, which is related by less accurate or less retentive transmitters.
125. It means that it should be read *ṣād* by default and should be presumed to be without a dot until the addition is certain.
126. It refers to a situation where a sentence may be interpreted in more than one way due to ambiguous sentence structure. Syntactic ambiguity arises, not from the range of meanings of single words, but from the relationship between the words and clauses of a sentence, and resulting implied sentence structure. When a reader can reasonably interpret the same sentence as having more than one possible structure, the text meets the definition of syntactic ambiguity.
127. *Nabīdh* is a beverage made of dates, and of raisins; that is, must; and of honey, that is mead; and of wheat and of barely; that is wort: or made of dates or of raisins which one throws whence its appellation into a vessel or skin of water and leaves until it ferments and becomes intoxicating. Before it has become so, it is a lawful beverage (Lane, 1984, 2757).
128. Instead of reading the text as '*nabīdh* is wholesome dates and a pure water [to drink],' they read the text literally by interpreting as '*nabīdh* as wholesome dates [to drink] and [it] is a pure water [to wash with].'

129. An ambivalent locution imparts two distinct meanings such as the word *qur'* which may be used to mean menses or the period between two menstruation periods. An ambivalent word or phrase cannot be an effective evidence before lifting ambivalent which is possible by preferring one of those two meanings. Such a preference must be based on a clue either from ambivalent word itself or the text in which it has been mentioned or through an external evidence, through which are known by scholars as locutionary, contextual and paratextual respectively.
130. In Arabic grammar, a preceding adjective which indicates number must be masculine if the noun is feminine and vice versa. For example, we say '*khamsu banāt*' (five girls) but we say '*khamsatu awalād*' (five boys). The feminine suffix *tu* is added to the number adjective of boys.
131. It does not necessarily mean that the intended referee of the word *juththa* or *jasad* to be the body of female or a male. The word had a suffix peculiar for feminine but it does not mean that it is female.
132. The subject of a legal decision is an action. The action may be described as obligatory, recommended, permissible, disliked or prohibited. A subject cannot be a human agent. For example, you cannot say A is prohibited and B is permissible. In the Quran, Allah says, "Prohibited to you are your mothers." (Q. 4:23). Mothers cannot be described as prohibited or permissible but there must be a meaning on which the text itself is silent and yet which must be read into it if it is to fulfill its proper objective. So the text must read "Prohibited to you [for marriage] are your mothers." This is called *iqtiḍā' al-naṣṣ*; the required meaning, which is a logical and necessary meaning without which the text would remain incomplete and would fail to achieve its desired purpose (Kamali, 1991, 118). This is the reason scholars differed on such a text either to regard it ambivalent that need elucidation or it is evident by itself.
133. For example, the word "lion" in the sentence, "I saw a lion" is clear enough, while it is possible, although less likely, that the speaker might mean a brave man.
134. The relationship between the real and metaphorical meaning is that a brave man is similar to a lion in this feature.
135. It is the right to nullify the agreement at any time before purchasing parties physically part company, or both waive the right to cancel, or until one of them cancels the sale (Miṣrī, 1982, 151).
136. Aḥmad: 2001, 1, 455; Abū Dāwūd: 3456.
137. Aḥmad, 2001, 8, 346; Bukhārī, 2001, 3, 69; Muslim, n.d., 2, 1032; ibn Māja, n.d., 3, 298; Abū Dāwūd, n.d.,2, 228; Nasā'ī,1986, 7, 258.
138. Aḥmad: 2001, 8, 346; Bukhārī, 2001,3, 69; Muslim, n.d., 2, 1032; Abū Dāwūd, n.d., 3, 112; Nasā'ī,1986, 7, 258.
139. State of consecration to perform major or minor pilgrimage.
140. Aḥmad, 2001, 1, 508; Muslim, n.d., 2, 1030; Nasā'ī, 1986, 5, 19.
141. Aḥmad: 2001, 10, 284; ibn Mājah, n.d., 3, 77; Bayhaqī, 2003, 7, 183.
142. Scholars disagreed on the validity of marrying a virgin without seeking her consultation. The reason for their disagreement is an apparent conflict of reports which resulted in a disagreement on identifying the reason for legal determination:

    1. Mālikīs, Shāfi'īs and Imām Aḥmad according to his most famous view maintain that a virgin can be forced by her guardian, but taking her permission is recommended. According to them virginity is the cause of this ruling. They based their view on an indication derived by means of *mafhūm al-Mukhālafa,* where the report purports that a *yatīma* should not be given in marriage except after her permission. By means of a divergent implication, a girl who has a father, may be given in marriage without being consulted. They, however, based their view on other evidences such as the report of ibn 'Abbās where the Prophet classified

women into a previously married and a virgin, "A previously married woman has more right (to decide) about herself (with regard to marriage), and a virgin should be consulted by her father, and her permission is her silence." (Aḥmad, 2001, 3, 384; Muslim, n.d., 2, 1037; Abū Dāwūd, n.d., 2, 232). Furthermore, Abū Bakr gave ʿĀʾisha to the Prophet in marriage without seeking her consultation (Bukhārī, 2001, 7, 17; Shāfiʿī, 1990, 5, 17). Similarly, many companions of the Prophet and followers of the second Islamic century gave their daughters in marriage without asking them for permission. Mālik reported that al-Qāsim ibn Muhammad and Sālim ibn ʿAbdullah were marrying off their daughters and they did not consult them. Malik said, "That is what is done among us about the marriage of virgins." (Mālik, *Muwaṭṭāʾ*, 2004, 3, 750.

2. Ibn Ḥazm, Ḥanafīs, Imām Aḥmad according to one of two reported views maintain that a virgin cannot be compelled by a guardian to get married. They based their view on the Prophet's saying, "A previously married woman should not be married until she has been consulted. A virgin is not married until she has been asked for her permission." When being asked on how to seek her permission, the Prophet said "It is when she remains silent." (Bukhārī, 2001, 7, 17). The text of this report does explicitly require the permission of a virgin before getting married. This is further confirmed in ʿĀʾisha's report (Aḥmad, 2001, 42, 199; Muslim, n.d., 2, 1037). The report of ibn ʿAbbās express it in the form of a command, " A woman who has been previously married is more entitled to her person than her guardian, and a virgin must be asked for her consent for herself, and her consent is her silence." (Mālik: 888; Aḥmad, 2001, 3, 377; Muslim, n.d., 2, 1037). This is further asserted by the report of ibn ʿAbbās where a virgin came to the Prophet (may God exalt his mention) and mentioned that her father had married her against her will, so the Prophet (may God exalt his mention) allowed her to exercise her choice. By comparing the denotation of *mafhūm* to that of the pronounced meaning of those texts, the latter should take precedence.

143. *Mutʿa* is an amount paid by the husband and determined by the Islamic judge through his own personal reasoning. (Miṣri, 1982, 205).
144. *Ẓihār* is an injurious dissimulation. It is an oath by the husband that his wife is like his mother's back, meaning she is unlawful for him. It was a form of divorce in pre-Islam, not permitted in Islam (Belewy, 1998, 130).
145. *Hysteron proteron* is a figure of speech in which the normal order of two sentences, clauses, etc, is reversed, as in *bred and born* (*for born and bred*) www.Collinsdictioanry.com.
146. Scholars criticized this definition as not being denotative in the sense that it gives mention to *genus* but it neglects *differrentia*. *ʿĀmm* is better defined as 'a word which applies to many things, not limited in number, and includes everything to which it is applicable (Ghazali, *1993*, 2, 12).
147. *Mawāt*, which is translated as 'waste land', signifies any piece of land incapable of yielding advantage, either from a want of water, an inundation, or any other cause, such as it prevents tillage; and it is termed *mawāt*, or dead, because, like the dead, it is of no use (Mirghinānī, n.d., 4, 833).
148. Mālik, 2004, 5, 1134; Tirmidhī, 1998, 3, 57 on the authority of Jābir. Tirmidhī graded it as authentic. It is further related by abū Dāwūd, (n.d., 3, 187); Tirmidhī, (1998, 3, 55) on the authority of Saʿīd ibn Zayd. The report is further reported by ʿĀʾisha, Samura and ʿUbāda.
149. Scholars differed on the execution of a female apostate as follows: (a) Abū Ḥanīfa maintains that if a Muslim woman become an apostate, she is not put to death, but she is imprisoned, until she returns to the faith. (b) Mālikīs, Shāfi'īs and Ḥanbalīs maintain that both man and woman must be executed upon apostasy. The reason of their disagreement is how to deal with the text under

discussion. Abū Ḥanīfa holds that it is specified by the Prophet's prohibition of slaying women, without making any distinction between those who are apostates, and those who are original infidels. A female apostate, therefore, is the same as an original female infidel; and as the killing of the one is forbidden, so is the killing of the, other also. She is however to be imprisoned, until the return to the faith; because, as she refuses the right of Allah after having acknowledged it, she must be compelled, by means of imprisonment, to render Allah his right, in the same manner as she would be imprisoned on account of the right of the Individual (*Mirghinānī*, n.d., 2, 406).

The majority of scholars keep hold of the general terms of the report relying on further proofs such as the Quran using same words for men and women in terms of punishment and reward, such as Allah's saying, "And whoever does righteous deeds, whether male or female, while being a believer—those will enter Paradise and will not be wronged, [even as much as] the speck on a date seed." (Q. 4: 124). They further confirm that early companions of the Prophet understood texts as being applicable to both men and women. For example, the Prophet is reported as saying, "Whoever arrogantly drags his garment, Allah will not look at him on the Day of Judgment." So Umm Salama said: "What should the women do with their hems?" He said: "Slacken them a hand span." So she said: "Then their feet will be uncovered." He said: "Then slacken them a forearm's length and do not add to that." (Bukhārī: 2001, 5, 6; Aḥmad, 2001, 4, 280; Tirmidhī, 1998, 3, 275 and others).

It is well-known that the Mālikīs, Shāfi'īs and Ḥanbalīs accept the possibility of a report specifying the general terms of other texts. Why have not they exempt women of the general terms of the report though prohibition of killing women which is authenticated? Moreover, the Prophet is reported as prohibiting the execution of an apostate woman. They state that the report on the prohibition of killing women in war is not qualified to specify the terms of the general since it is issued for a special reason in a specific occasion, where women do not engage in warfare. So, prohibition is restricted to women participating in battlefield. Moreover, a woman has forsaken her religion in the battle of Uḥud, but the Prophet commanded that she is invited to repent and if she refuses, she has to be executed (Daraqūṭnī: 2004, 4, 128). The report on prohibition of killing apostate women is not, however, reliable.

150. Bukhārī, 2001, 1, 69; abū Dāwūd, n.d., 1, 96; Tirmidhī, 1998, 3, 111; Nasā'ī, 1986, 7, 104; ibn Māja, n.d., 3, 574.
151. Aḥmad, 2001, 33, 338; Tirmidhī, 1998, 3, 39; abū Dāwūd, n.d., 4, 26; ibn Māja, n.d., 3, 565.
152. Bukhārī, 2001, 8, 150; Muslim, n.d.,3, 1233.
153. This issue is common among scholars as whether the performance by the follower of the part of the prayer he has missed, from the imam's prayer, amounts to *adā'* or *qaḍā'*? According to the former, a follower just makes up missed parts without exact imitation of how his *imam* offered them while *qaḍā'* indicates that he has to imitate his imam regarding actions and recitations. Scholars differed on this issue as follows:

(a) According to a variant view of Aḥmad, the part a follower observes after the imam's conclusion of his prayer is regarded *qaḍā'* while the parts he observed with the imam cannot be reckoned as the first part of his prayer. According to this view, person who is able to catch one *rak'a* of the sunset prayer has to stand up when the imam ends his prayer and offer two rak'ahs reciting the opening chapter in addition to another chapter in each *rak'ah*. He has not to adopt the sitting posture in between the two. He just copy what he missed of the congregation (ibn Qudāma, 1968, 2, 303). Ḥanafis, Shāfi'īs, Ḥanbalīs and a variant view of Mālik maintain that whatever a follower observes after the imam's conclusion of his prayer is regarded as *adā'* in the sense that whatever he observed with the imam is reckoned as the first part of a follower's own prayer. According to this view a person missing two *raka'ats* of the sunset prayer has to stand up for one *rak'a* reciting the opening chapter in addition to another *sūra* and then adopt the sitting posture, after which he will rise for another *rak'a* and recite in it only the opening chapter. He regards the amount he catches up of congregation as the first part of his own prayers, so he does not have to recite a short *sūra* in the third *rak'a* (Mirghinānī, n.d., 3, 79; Nawawī, n.d., 4, 220; ibn Qudāma, 1968, 2, 303). According to the dominant view of Mālik, a distinction is made between words and acts. Therefore, a follower should perform the recitations as *qaḍā'* while the actions of prayer as *adā'*. In accordance with the this view, a follower will stand up for a *rak'a* reciting in it the opening chapter and another short *sūra* and then takes the sitting posture, after which he will rise for the second *rak'a* also reciting in it the opening chapter in addition to a short *sūra* (ibn Rushd, 2004, 1, 198).

According to the author, there is a disagreement among Mālikīs. The majority of them hold the third view while a few of them adopt the second. The reason of their disagreement is whether to regard the report quoted as general or specific. The majority of them including Mālik restricted its application to recitations only that must be made up exactly as performed by the imam, while the minority view supported the general application of the report to include both acts and sayings.

154. Aḥmad, 2001, 31, 346; Abū Dāwūd, n.d., 1, 55.
155. Dāraquṭnī, 2004, 2, 52, 196. It is graded as a weak hadith by Dāraquṭnī.
156. Aḥmad, 2001, 40, 435; abū Dāwūd, n.d., 2, 229; Tirmidhī, 1998, 3, 479.
157. Aḥmad: 1895; abū Dāwūd: 4125; Tirmidhī: 1728; Nasā'ī: 4214. Shu'ayb al-Anā'ūṭ and Albānī graded it as authentic that meets conditions of Muslim's *Ṣaḥīḥ*.
158. It refers to a disagreement among Mālikī scholars. According to the view of Mālik, as related by ibn Ḥabīb, the best slave to free is the most expensive. Asbagh differed by stating that freeing a Muslim is more rewarded even it is less priced (al-Bājī, n.d., 6, 287. The reason of their disagreement is whether to regard the report of the Prophet as general or it is specified by the terms of other reports. According to Mālik, it is general. Aṣbagh relied on (Q. 2: 221) to confirm that price is considered in case that both slaves are equal with regard to religion.
159. Aḥmad, 2001, 15, 40; Bukhārī, 2001, 3, 144; Muslim, n.d., 1, 89.
160. Muslim, n.d., 3, 1235.
161. When a person owns a capital of any wealth which is liable to *zakat* but it increases by a lapse of time, scholars classified this excess into three categories:

    1. Excess which is a profit of this wealth such as an increase in the number of sheep a person owns by multiplication. Scholars are unanimous that at the end of the year, a Muslim is supposed to pay *zakat* on both capital and the excess (ibn Qudāma, 1968, 2, 468).
    2. Excess is different from capital such as a person who owns 100 grams of gold at the beginning of the year, but he is gifted another 1000 grams of silver the mid of the year. In this case he has to calculate a full year for each type of wealth.
    3. Excess is of the same kind of a *zaktable* wealth he owns but the increase is not a result of multiplication. An example is a person who owns 40 sheep at the beginning of the year but someone gifted him another 40 at the middle of year. This is a case of disagreement. Jurists disagreed on whether a full lunar year has to elapse for this increase on capital or not:

        1. Shāfi'ī and Aḥmad held that a year is to be calculated from the day it accrues either capital has reached the minimum ratio of *zakat* or not. This the view of 'Umar ibn

ʿAbdul-ʿAzīz, who gave the instructions that the profits accrued from trade should not be liable for *zakat* until a full year has passed.

2. Mālikīs differentiated between gold and silver on one side and cattle on the other side. For the former they agreed with Shāfiʿī and Aḥmad while they accepted the view of abū Ḥanīfa with regard to cattle. Therefore, silver added to gold through the year cannot be subject to *zakat* until it remains for one full year but if cattle is added during the year both capital and the excess must be subject to *zakat* without consideration of a new year for the excess.
3. Al-Awzāʿī, abū Thawr and abū Ḥanīfa made a distinction between whether a capital amounts to the minimum ratio or not. In case it reaches the minimum ratio zakatable, both capital and profit are subject to *zakat*. If capital does not amount the minimum ration, both are not *zaktable*.

The reason of their disagreement is whether to regard the statement of the Prophet, " *zakat* does not have to be paid on property until a year has elapsed over it " is general to include both capital and accrued wealth or it is specified by virtue of other proofs. According to Ḥanfīs, the general terms of the report are specified by analogy through a comparison between accrued wealth with *zakat* on cattle and trade where multiplication and profit are added to capital. Mālik exempted cattle from the general terms of the Hadith.

162. Aḥmad, 2001, 44, 53; abū Dāwūd, n.d., 2, 329; Tirmidhī, 1998, 2, 100; ibn Māja, n.d., 2, 598; Nasāʾī,1986, 4, 196.
163. Scholars discussed this issue by raising this question: Is it a prerequisite to intend fasting before dawn even in supererogatory fasting? (1) Mālik maintained that fasting is not valid except by an intention formed before the break of the dawn. According to him, it applies to both obligatory and supererogatory fasting. (2) Abū Ḥanīfa Shāfi'ī and Aḥmad stated that intention formed after dawn is valid in supererogatory fasting (ibn Rushd, 2004, *2, 56*; Bahūtī, 1993, 1, 480). The reason for their disagreement arises from a seeming conflict of traditions on the issue. The report of Ḥafṣa: "One who does not form the intention to fast during the night has no fast" is general to include both obligatory and supererogatory fasting. This is the reason Mālik stipulated intention before dawn for both types of fasting. The Majority of scholars relied on the practice of the Prophet where he intended fasting after dawn when 'Aisha informed him that they do not have anything to afford for him to prove that supererogatory fasting is exempted. This is further confirmed by the report of Muʿāwiya who said, "O people of Medina, where are your learned men? I heard the Messenger of Allah saying, 'Today is the day of ʿAshūra and its fast has not been prescribed for us. I am fasting, so those of you who wish to fast may do so and those who like may continue to eat".
164. It is a part of a hadith related by ibn ʿAbbās; Aḥmad, 2001, 6, 379; Ṭabarānī, 1994, 2, 52.
165. Dāraquṭnī, 2004, 1, 101; Bayhaqī, 2003, 1, 377.
166. It is a drink made of dates.
167. Bukhārī, 2001, 5, 161; Muslim, n.d. 3, 1365.
168. The wording of this report as mentioned by the author are not correct. It has been related by Dāraquṭnī (2004, 4, 321) as follows: It is related from ʿĀ'isha that the Prophet said, "A [valid] marriage must have four; a guardian, a husband and two witnesses." This version is weak.
169. Bukhārī, 2001, 1, 103; Muslim, n.d., 1, 450.
170. It is literally translated as 'a dipping oath' because, according to a report from the Prophet, it dips one who pronounces it in the fire of hell.

171. This report is not recorded in this wording. It has been related from the Prophet as follow: "Allah has rid this *umma* of three things: inadvertence, forgetfulness and an act done in coercion." (ibn ʿAdiy, 1997, 3, 95; 2, 573; Ḥākim, 1990, 2, 198; ibn Māja, n.d., 3, 199). In his commentary on ibn Mājah, Albānī regarded it as *ṣaḥīḥ*.
172. Analogy should include an original case which is regulated by a given text and a new case whose legal ruling cannot be found in the text in addition to an effective cause which should be a common attribute and should be extant in both the original and the new cases. When the effective cause is general, its application extends to a general ruling. For example, Q. 17: 23 obviously forbids the utterance of the slightest word of contempt to the parents. The effective cause of this prohibition is avoiding offence or harm to them. There are, of course, other forms of offensive behavior to which the effective cause of this prohibition would apply. Therefore, the general application of the effective cause extends to apply to all forms of abusive words and acts which offend parents.
173. When he did not include an object in his oath, all possible objects became generally included in his phrase, so he is regarded as breaking his oath if he eats fish, meat, fruit, etc. This is a form of *ʿamm* which is expressed by two linguistic patterns: (a) deletion of an object. When he gave no mention of any object, it means that he intended all possible objects. (b) A negative form which precedes an indefinite phrase which means that the act of eating has not occurred by all means. When an object does not appear, scholars differed on whether to regard it as general that may be specified by the intention of a speaker or not to regard it as general due to reference to common sense.
174. There is a disagreement between the majority of scholars including Mālikīs, Shāfiʿīs, Ḥanbalīs on one side and the Ḥanafis on the other side. Qurṭubī, a Mālikī scholar and al-Rāzī; a Shāfiʿī jurist opted for the Ḥanafī view. The main reason of their disagreement is that whether to regard the expression, 'by Allah I have not eaten' as linguistically general or as general by common sense. The difference is that if we regard it as general by reference to language, it means that a person has taken an oath not to eat all possible foodstuffs. Therefore, there is a possibility of intending some items and not thinking of others because it is an expression that indicates generality and is applicable to many possible things. If we regard it as general by common sense it means that that the swearer negates the act of eating *a priori*. He does not refer to the negation of items of food. The act of eating cannot be regarded as general as it does not apply to many things. It is just the act of eating. Therefore, it is not open for specification according to Ḥanfis.
175. This is the view of the majority of scholars including Mālik, Shāfiʿī and Aḥmad. It is the view of ibn ʿUmar, ibn ʿAbbās, ibn al-Zubayr and others. According to abū Ḥanīfa, imam Moḥmmad and abū Yūsuf, a divorce under coercion is effective.
176. The Arabic word *ghalaqa* means 'became disquieted by grief or angry'. *Yamīn al-ghalq* is the oath of anger. Ghalq, thus refers to straitness (Lane, 1984, 2284).
177. The correct wording of the hadith is as follows: "There is no divorce or emancipation of a salve [to be effective] at a state of *ighlāq*" (Aḥmad, 2001, 43, 378; ibn Māja, n.d., 3, 201; abū Dāwūd, n.d., 2, 258.
178. The author uses *ighlāq* for insanity but this is not found in Arabic lexicons. One common usage of *ighlāq* is severe madness.
179. This is commonly discussed by scholars as when a word is understood both literally and metaphorically. In such a case, should we regard both meanings as applicable in case of the absence of a clue to prefer one over the other, or should we limit our interpretation according to the either the real or the figurative?

180. Scholars have agreed that both the bearing and delivering of testimony is a communal obligation when more than one do afford it. They differed on the ruling of bearing testimony when the case is only witnessed by a specific group of people. Some Mālikīs and Ḥanblīs maintained that bearing testimony is obligatory. Other scholars stated that it is not. The reason of their disagreement is whether to regard the word 'witness' in the context of (Q. 2, 282) to be used in its real or metaphorical meaning or that it is used for both at once. The real meaning of the word witness refers to the person who has already witnessed the occurrence of something. The figurative meaning is to use it for one who is going to witness. According to the majority of scholars the verse refers to those who have already witnessed and are invited to deliver their testimony since a word that vacillates between a real and a figurative meaning must be meant for the real unless a clue diverts it to the metaphorical, but it cannot be used for both meanings simultaneously. According to some Mālikīs and Ḥanbalīs it may be used for both at once. Therefore, a witness is used to mean both the real and figurative meanings, that is both a bearer of witness and the one invited to see in order to later deliver it must respond to the obligatory command mentioned in the verse.
181. The word *shāhid* is used literally for 'the one who is going to witness an incidence' and figuratively to mean 'the one who has already witnessed the incident.' According to the majority of scholars, both meanings cannot be intended by the Lawgiver. The intended meaning according to them is that a *shāhid* who has already witnessed an incident has to appear before courts to deliver his testimony. He has not to respond initially to see an incidence and record it.
182. It refers to an example of using a word for its figurative meaning as in Allah's saying, "One of them said, "Indeed, I have seen myself [in a dream] pressing wine." (Q. 12: 36). He was actually pressing grapes which has not been made wine yet, but the Quran used the word wine in its figurative sense. It refers in this context for grapes but due to the fact that it is going to be wine in the future, the Quran used the term wine for it. This is a type of figurative speech.
183. This is the view of abū Ḥanīfa, ash-Shāfiʿī, Aḥmad and the majority of Ẓahirites and the heads of Muʿtazilah. This is the popular view of Mālik as related by Qāḍī ʿAbdul-Wahhāib (Abū al-Ḥusayn, 1983, 1, 231).
184. This is the view of Mālik as related by Muḥammad ibn Khuwayz Mindād, ibn al-Mājishūn, abū Isḥāq al-Isfrāyīnī, ibn Dāwūd aẓ-Ẓāhirī and al-Ghazālī. This is further the view of abū Bakr, ʿUmar and Zayd ibn Thābit (Abū Yaʿla, 1990, 2, 650).
185. Silver coin used in pre and early Islam. It weighs 3.15 g. according to Ḥanafī scholars and 2.975 according to the majority of Muslim scholars.
186. *Muṭlaq* denotes a word which is neither qualified nor limited in its application (Kamali, 1991, 110). For example, a Muslim breaking his oath must free a slave according to (Q. 5: 92). The word 'slave' is *muṭlaq* in the sense that it is not limited to any type of slave.
187. The difference between *muṭlaq* and *ʿamm* is that the latter comprises all to which it applies whereas the former can apply to any one of a multitude, but not to all (Kamlai, 1991, 110).
188. The majority of *uṣūlīs* classify implications derived through the pronounced meaning into three categories, namely *naṣṣ* (explicit meaning), *ẓāhir* (manifest meaning) and *mujmal* (ambivalent meaning). They do not usually add *Muʾawwal* since it is included in the three as we will show. Tilmisānī added it because it is of the types of a clear indication and sometimes is preferable to other layers of meaning. *Muʾawwal* is a word or a phrase which vacillates between two meanings one of them conveys a manifest while the other bears an indication derived through interpretation. The interpreted meaning predominates over other possible meanings due to an independent and external proof. Therefore, the reason that its indication is clear differs from that of manifest (*ẓāhir*).

189. In both *ẓāhir* and *mu'awwal* a word or a phrase vacillates between two or more meanings one of them predominates others. For *ẓāhir*, the reason of giving a preference to one meaning is due to the usage of the word or phrase itself while in *mu'awwal* we give preference to a specific interpretation due to an external proof. The word *nikāḥ*, for example, is legally used to connote both intercourse and marriage contract. Both usages are common in the text of the Quran and Hadith. Preference of one meaning to the other is related to propensity of the word or its context. If preference is due to an external text, it is, thus, called *mu'awwal*. One word may be of *ẓāhir* and *mu'awwal* meanings due to their respective sources of interpretation. For example, the word *nikāḥ* may refer to a marriage contract or intercourse. The former is *ẓāhir* which is based on its propensity, since the word is used in it's the primary legal meaning, that is marriage contract. When a word is used primarily to connote a meaning and sometimes used allegorically to imply another, it should be interpreted according to the primary usage. Using it to mean 'intercourse' is allegorical. This meaning is *mu'awwal* which is supported by virtue of other extraneous clues such as (Q. 4: 22) where Allah says, "And do not marry those [women] whom your fathers married, except what has already occurred." 'What has already occurred' refers to the pre Islamic practice of inheriting a deceased father's wife by cohabiting her without a contract. This external proofs give preference to the interpretation that *nikāḥ* in this context refers to intercourse.
190. Bankruptcy occurs when an Islamic magistrate makes a debtor bankrupt by declaring him so and forbidding him to dispose of his property. After being suspended, the magistrate sells the property in the most profitable manner and divides the proceeds according to the percentage of the total debt which is owed to each creditor (Miṣrī, 1982, 163).
191. Mālik, 1992, 2, 338; Bukhārī, 2001, 3, 118; Muslim, n.d., 3, 1193; abū Dāwūd, n.d., 3, 286, ibn Māja, n.d., 3, 447.
192. The author refers to a phenomenon common in Arabic linguistics where a word is called a meaning which existed in the past, such as calling a mature person an orphan in Allah's saying, "And give to the orphans their properties." (Q. 4: 2), though, after reaching the age of maturity and being capable to independently manage their wealth, orphanage no longer exists. If they are still orphans in the literal sense of the word, they cannot be entitled to take care of their properties. This linguistic feature of using a name which expresses a state in the past does not consistently apply to all cases. This is the reason the author stated that it is not possible to call a Muslim who has already accepted Islam a *kāfir* because he was a disbeliever immediately before his reversion. Therefore, the Ḥanafīs referred to the original and literal meaning of the words '*ṣāḥib al-matā'*' to interpret it to mean the recent owner who seizes a property, that is the bankrupt. The majority of scholars interpreted it to mean the original owner. Based on this various interpretation scholars differed on the explanation of the report. According to the majority of scholars, when A sells a property for B and B seizes it in his hand without paying off. When a magistrate declares suspending B of his properties due to bankruptcy, A can regain his property if he finds it intact. He does not have to share other creditors in a percentage of the bankrupt suspended wealth which may be less than the price of his property. According to the Ḥanafīs, A cannot regain his property but should share a percentage with the rest of creditors.
193. The reason is that he intended the primary literal meaning of the words, '*ṣāḥib al-matā'*' that is owner of a property. He does not intend to call it for the bankrupt.
194. The word *ẓihār* is derived from *ẓahr*, back. In the language of the law it signifies a man comparing his wife to any of his female relation, within such prohibited degree of kindred, whether by blood, by fosterage, or by marriage, as renders marriage with them invariable unlawful, as if he

were to say to her [by a peculiarity in the Arabic idiom], "you are to me like the back *[ẓihar]* of my mother" (*Mirghinānī*, n.d., 2, 265).

195. It means that her womb has not comprised or enclosed a fetus.
196. In Q. 2: 228, the verse used the verb *'yatrabaṣṣna'*, which means 'has to remain waiting'. Therefore, the Mālikīs confirmed that a woman has to start engagement in her waiting period immediately upon the issuance of divorce. Their opponents among Ḥanafīs counter argue that the word *'yatrabaṣṣna'* is used in Arabic language to indicate the existence of a gap between the time of issuing a command and the addressee's initiation of action. One may be addressed at noon to remain waiting for three nights. His initiation of stay commences with sunset which marks the beginning of a night.
197. It refers to animals illegally edible such as domesticated donkeys even if they are slaughtered and other animals not legally slaughtered.
198. Aḥmad, 2001, 31, 74; abū Dāwūd, n.d., 4, 67; Trimidhī, 1998, 3, 274.
199. The default rule is that each word must have a meaning which is unique for it, not being shared by other weods.
200. It means that words and articles are normally used for a meaning. To presume that they are used in specific contexts for emphasis without adding a new meaning is contrary to the norm and needs a strong proof to prove that.
201. It is a rhetorical device. It occurs when the first key word of the idea refers to something that happens temporally later than the second key word. The goal is to call attention to the more important idea by placing it first (Smyth, 1920, 679–680). An example of *hysteron proteron* encountered in everyday life is the common reference to putting on one's "shoes and socks," rather than "socks and shoes." By this deliberate reversal, hysteron proteron draws attention to the important point, so giving it primacy. Hysteron proteron is a form of Hyperbaton, which describes general rearrangements of the sentence.
202. Lit. it refers to extremity. It is a grammatical structure used to indicate the end of something or a period of time (*intihā ʾ al-ghāya*) such as the example, 'he purchased the land extending from the mosque *ilā* (to) the canal'.
203. In Arabic grammar, *istithnā ʾ* or exception is composed of *mustathnā* 'excepted' and *mustathnā minhu* 'general term'.
204. According to this implication, a confessor admits that he owes ten and then the makes an exemption from those ten. So, the ten are affirmed but the seven are negated. Therefore, he owes him 10–7 = 3.
205. The phrases of this report are not correct. Most probably, the author refers to the hadith of ʿUbāda b. al-Ṣāmit which reports the Prophet's forbiddence of seling gold by gold, silver by silver, wheat by wheat, barley by barley, dates by dates, and salt by salt, except like for like and equal for equal." (Muslim, n.d. 3, 1210).
206. Aḥmad, 2001, 12, 171; ibn Māja, n.d., 1, 250; abū Dāwūd, n.d., 1, 21.
207. Bukhārī, 2001, 1, 54; Muslim, n.d., 1, 234.
208. It refers to report narrated by abū Qatāda that the Messenger (may God exalt his mention) said about the cat that, "It is not unclean, but is one of those who intermingle with you." abū Dāwūd, n.d. 1, 19; Tirmidhī, 1998, 1, 151; Nasāʾī, 1986, 1, 55.
209. Aḥmad, 2001, 8, 265; Muslim, n.d. 2, 892; ibn Māja, n.d., 4, 259; abū Dāwūd, n.d., 1, 16; Tirmidhī, 1998, 2, 208. Though the report has been issued in the occasion where the Prophet (may God exalt his mention) instructed his companions on the way of running between Ṣafa and Marwa and which hill they should start with in reference to Q2:158, it is used by the Shāfiʿīs to prove the obligation of enjoining a sequential order when washing limbs of ablution.

210. Aḥmad 2001 4,1121; Tirmidhī, 1998, 2,398; abū Dāwūd, n.d., 2, 229.
211. Bayhaqī, 2003, 1, 433.
212. The version which does not include the phrase, 'two witnesses' is authentic (Tilmisānī, 2013, 542).
213. It is a part of a hadith related by Aḥmad, 2001, 2, 292; abū Dāwūd, n.d. 1, 16.
214. The two verses included two different rulings, namely, amputation of hands and washing of hands up to the elbows. The two rulings have two distinct causes. The former's cause is theft while the latter's cause is the state of ritual impurity which necessitates ablution.
215. Bukhārī (2001, 2, 126).
216. Muslim, n.d., 1, 471; abū Dāwūd, n.d., 1, 118; Tirmidhī, 1998, 5, 170.
217. A dipping oath is when one swears by Allah that something happened or he, for example, purchased such a merchandize for such a specific price but he lies. It is called a dipping oath (*yamīn ghamūs*) because it dips one who pronounces it in fire of hell.
218. A person does not incur a sin in case he swears on doing something in the future but it goes beyond his capacity or he found out that it is legally better not to do such a thing. He is supposed in this case to break his oath and give penance in expiation of his oath.
219. It is compatible with the "expression of the one thing in a text is exclusion of the other" or *expressio unius est exclusio alterius* (Ahmad, 2006, 41). It is inference based on the assumption that a case whose judgment was not mentioned in a text must be decided in a manner opposite to the one mentioned in the text (*ibid,* 129).
220. Bukhārī, 2001, 1, 102; Muslim, n.d., 1, 516.
221. Bukhārī, 2001, 1, 69; Muslim, n.d., 2, 1125.
222. Bukhārī, 2001, 3, 43; Muslim, n.d., 2, 977.
223. It has been related by Saʿd ibn abī Waqqāṣ as in Aḥmad, 2001, 3, 149. It is further related by Anas in a different wording. It is quoted by Aḥmad, 2001, 19, 128; Bukhārī, 2001, 8, 19; Muslim, n.d., 4, 1982. It is also related through a different wording by abū Ayyūb al-Anṣārī as in Aḥmad, 2001, 38, 550; Bukhārī, 2001, 8, 21; Muslim, n.d., 4, 1984. All the versions of Saʿd, Anas and abū Ayyūb do not include the phrase, 'who believes in Allah and the Last Day.'
224. This is a mistake at the original Arabic text. It should be the companions of Shāfiʿī.
225. Bukhārī, 2001, 4, 129; Muslim, n.d., 2, 856.
226. Bukhārī, 2001, 4, 10; Muslim, n.d., 1, 92.
227. It is when the ruling of a text is dependent on the fulfillment of a quality or an attribute then the ruling in question obtains only when that quality is present; otherwise, it lapses (Kamali, 1991, 128). For example, when a text specifying the amount of *zakat* to be collected from sheep owners mentions the adjective "grazing on natural grass" (*sāʾima*) after the noun "sheep," a jurist would infer, based on *mafhūm al-ṣifa*, that the case of sheep that are not grazing on natural grass must be decided in an opposite manner (Ahmad, 2006, 129).
228. Bukhārī, 2001, 3, 78; Muslim, n.d., 3, 1172.
229. Muslim, n.d., 2, 1037.
230. When the ruling of a text is contingent on a condition, then the ruling obtains only in the presence of that condition, and lapses otherwise (Kamali, 1991, 129).
231. When the text itself demarcates the extent or scope of the operation of its ruling, the latter will obtain only within the scope of the stated limits and will lapse when the limit is surpassed (Kamali, 1991, 129).
232. The text did not provide a condition to offer *wuḍūʾ* in addition to *ghusl* before engagement in prayers.

233. When the ruling of a text is conveyed in terms of a specified number, the number so stated must be carefully observed (Kamali, 1991, 129).
234. A *qulla* is a volume measurement which equals 108 liters. Two *qullas* equal 216 liters
235. Aḥmad, 2001, 8, 211; abū Dāwūd, n.d., 1, 17.
236. When the ruling of a text is observed in terms of a specified time, the time so stated must be carefully observed.
237. When the text specifies a place for the operation of its ruling, the latter will obtain only within the scope that place limits and will lapse when the limit is surpassed.
238. Muslim, n.d., 1, 371; ibn abī Shaybah, *Muṣannaf* 1989; 6, 304; Dāraquṭnī, 2004, 1, 323.
239. This is called *'Iṣma* which literally means 'protection'. In Islamic terminology it is defined as a spiritual grace of Allah to a person which enables him to abstain from sins by his own free will (Qāḍī ʿIyāḍ, 2001, 4, 93). Scholars are unanimous to the effect that all Prophets and Messengers are infallible with regard to what they deliver or convey from Allah. The majority of scholars maintain that they may commit minor sins but they do not insist on doing them. They are only infallible with regard to insistence on the perpetual of minor sins (Al-Fawzān, *Irshād*, 1999, 194). Infallibility is also possible for people whom Allah protects from committing sins.
240. This is the most popular view of Mālikī scholars.
241. It refers to his acts of devotion and excludes his *jibilllī* acts which are merely a result of his instinctive behavior.
242. This is the view of ibn al-Muntāb; a Mālikī scholar, the viw of Shāfiʿī and one of the variant views of Aḥmad in addition to Ibn Ḥazm, al-Fakhr al-Rāzī and al-Bayḍāwī (Shīrāzī, 2003, 1, 546; Ibn Ḥazm, n.d., 4, 39.
243. Bukhārī, 2001, 2, 128.
244. Aḥmad, 2001, 22, 312; Muslim, n.d., 2, 934, Abū Dāwūd, n.d., 2, 201.
245. Abū Dāwūd, n.d., 1, 27; Tirmidhī, 1998, 1, 98; Nasāʿī, 1986, 1, 62.
246. It is circumambulation around the *kaʿba.*
247. Scholars differed on the validity of *ṭawāf* without purification. Mālik, Shāfiʿī and Aḥmad maintained that it is not valid to offer *ṭawāf* without purification, either intentionally or unintentionally. Abū Ḥanīfa held that offering *ṭawāf* without purification is valid. Abū Thawr differentiated between offering it intentionally and unintentionally by making the former as valid and the latter invalid (Ibn Rushd, 2004, 2, 109). The reason for their disagreement is whether to regard the terms of (Q. 23: 29) as *'amm* to be of explicit and inclusive of all the rituals of *ṭawāf* or to regard it as *mumjmal* (ambivalent). The majority of scholars including Mālikīs, Shāfiʿīs and Ḥanbalīs maintain that the text is ambivalent. To clarify its terms, they referred to statements of the Prophet in addition to his performance of *ṭawāf.* Ḥanafī scholars do not specify or limit the terms of a *'amm* or a *muṭlaq* by virtue of a solitary report such as a prophetic tradition.
248. Scholars differed on the legal ruling of standing on the delivery of the two Friday sermons as follows: (1) Ḥanafīs, Ḥanbalīs and ibn al-ʿArabī; a Malikī scholar maintained that it is recommended for an imam to stand while reciting the Friday sermons. (2) Shāfiʿīs and the majority of Mālikī scholars held that it is one of the conditions of Friday sermons which is only obligatory when a person is able to do so. The reason of their disagreement is whether to regard a prophetic action which is related to prayer as obligatory in its absolute terms or to regard it as a mere indication of permissibility (Ibn Rushd, 2004, 1, 171).
249. Scholars disagreed on the observance of a sequence in the acts of ablution as follows: (1) Later disciples of Mālik, abū Ḥanīfa, al-Thawrī and Dāwūd maintained that it is recommended to offer ablution in a sequential order as illustrated in Q. 5: 6 and other reports which related the

exact ablution of the Prophet (may God exalt his mention). (2) Shāfiʿī, Aḥmad, and abū ʿUbayd stated that making obligatory constituents of ablution in order is obligatory while it is not with regard to supererogatory acts of ablution. There are two reasons for their disagreement: (1) The equivocality that arises from the conjunction *wāw* (and). It is sometimes used to indicate a sequential order, while at other times it is not. Kūfan grammarians assume the former while Baṣrans argue for the latter. Therefore, jurists differed on the implication of the verse of ablution, whether it necessitates a sequential order or not. (2) Scholars' disagreement on the legal authority of prophetic action which is devoid of a verbal statement whether it construes obligation of recommendation. Those who interpreted his actions as indicative for obligation maintained that offering *wuḍū'* in the sequential order indicated by the Prophet in a number of traditions strongly supports this view. Others held it is merely recommended (Ibn Rushd, 2004, 1, 23).

250. The report of ibn ʿAbbās has been contradicted by many other reports which confirm that the Prophet (may God exalt his mention) has not married Maymūna when he was in the sate of *iḥrām*. One of those reports is related by Maymūnh (Muslim, n.d., 2, 1032) in addition to the Prophet's statement which clearly prohibits marriage during the sate of *iḥrām* (Muslim, n.d., 1409).
251. Bukhārī, 2001, 3, 31; Muslim, n.d., 2, 809.
252. Bukhārī, 2001, 3, 32; Muslim, n.d., 2, 781.
253. Bukhārī, 2001, 3, 102; Muslim, n.d., 3, 1324.
254. Bukhārī, 2001, 5, 24; Muslim, n.d., 2, 1082.
255. Bukhārī, 2001, 4, 70; Muslim, n.d., 4, 2240.
256. Bukhārī, 2001, 1, 142; Muslim, n.d., 1, 339.
257. For example, A marries B and then divorces her two times. Then B marries C who divorced her. If she reunites with A do we count that he has already divorced her two times and only one divorce remains for her or should he resume the number of divorces?
258. By removal of prohibition, all previous three divorces do not count when her ex-husband likes to marry her again according to a new contract.
259. It is a rule of law and reason, whose existence or non-existence had been proven in the past, and which are presumed to remain so for lack of evidence to establish any change.
260. Bukhārī, 2001, 1, 151; Muslim, n.d., 1, 295.
261. Muslim, n.d., 1, 296.
262. Bukhārī, 2001, 1, 152; Muslim, n.d., 1, 297.
263. Nasāʾī, 1986, 5, 222; ibn Ḥibbān, 1988, 9, 143; Bayhaqī, 2003, 5, 138.
264. Bukhārī, 2001, 3, 171; Muslim, n.d., 3, 1394.
265. *Mafhūm* is of two categories; convergent and divergent meanings. The former is defined as an implicit meaning on which the text may be silent but is nevertheless in harmony with its pronounced meaning. For example, the Quran is silent about the ruling of physical abuse of parents but it has been implied by the *mafhūm* (convergent meaning) of Q. 17: 23 which prohibited saying the slightest word of contempt to parents. A divergent meaning is defined as an "inference based on the assumption that a case whose judgment was not mentioned in a text must be decided in a manner opposite to the one mentioned in the text." (Ahmad, 2004, 129). For example, when a hadith specifies the amount of *zakat* to be collected from sheep owners by providing the adjective "grazing on natural grass" after the noun "sheep," a jurist would infer that the case of sheep that are not grazing on natural grass must be decided in an opposite manner (*ibid*).

266. Aḥmad, 2001, 23, 296; abū Dāwūd, n.d., 4, 176; Nasā'ī, 1986, 8, 20; ibn Mājah, 2009, 3, 674; Tirmidhī, 1998, 3, 78.
267. It is when the implied meaning of a text is superior to the pronounced meaning. For example, the Q. 17: 23 forbids the utterance of '*uff*' to parents. It is, however, the slightest word of contempt. By means of *faḥwa al-khiṭāb* the meaning is extended to include all forms of physical abuse to parents. The implied meaning (the prohibition of physical abuse), is superior to pronounced meaning (the saying of 'uff').
268. Ḥanafī scholars maintain that retaliation of a free man in recompense of murdering a slave is proved by means of *faḥwa al-khiṭāb* (superior meaning) of the report. When a report is abrogated its pronounced meaning is only suspended. Abrogation does not preclude the continuity of a ruling deduced by means of superior meaning.
269. Abū Dāwūd, n.d., 3, 114; Ibn Mājah, n.d., 4, 18; Tirmidhī, 1998, 3, 504.
270. Aḥmad, 2001, 6, 56; Muslim, n.d., 3, 1562; Nasā'ī: 1986, 7, 234; ibn Ḥibbān, 1988, 13, 248.
271. Muslim, n.d., 1, 277; Tirmidhī: 1998, 3, 273; Nasā'ī, 1986, 7, 173.
272. Aḥmad, 2001, 31, 74; abū Dāwūd, n.d., 4, 67; Trimidhī, 1998, 3, 274; Nasā'ī, 1986, 7, 175; ibn Māja, n.d., 4, 604.
273. Bukhārī, 2001, 2, 128; Muslim, n.d., 1, 276.
274. Abū Dāwūd; n.d., 4, 164; Tirmidhī, 1998, 3, 101.
275. Bukhārī, 2001, 3, 34; Muslim, n.d., 3, 802.
276. Abū Dāwūd, n.d., 1, 46; Tirmidhī, 1998, 1, 142.
277. Aḥmad, 2001, 14, 130; ibn Ḥibbān, 1988, 3, 401.
278. Bukhārī, 2001, 1, 45; Muslim, n.d., 1, 234.
279. Aḥmad, 2001, 19, 226; Muslim, n.d., 2, 1573; abū Dāwūd, n.d., 5, 518.
280. Dāraquṭnī, 2004, 1, 101; Bayhaqī, 2003, 1, 378.
281. Aḥmad, 2001, 25, 123; Muslim, n.d., 3, 1199; abū Dāwūd, n.d., 5, 296; Trimidhī, 1998, 2, 565; Nasā'ī, 1986, 3, 39; Dārimī, 2000, 3, 1711.
282. Bukhārī, 2001, 3, 63; Muslim, n.d. 2, 862.
283. Aḥmad, 2001, 17, 429; Muslim, n.d., 3, 1562; Nasā'ī, 1986, 7, 234.
284. Tirmidhī, 1998, 2, 175.
285. Bayhaqī, 2003, 1, 387. Ibn Ḥazm and ibn al-Turkmānī argued that it is not possible for ibn 'Umar to say that because he is only one year older than Anas. They based their argument on the fact that Anas migrated to Medina at the age of ten and the Prophet died when he was twenty. Ibn 'Umar has been accepted to participate in the battle of the trench which occurred at the year four and ibn 'Umar was fifteen. So ibn 'Umar was twenty one years when the Prophet passed away and Anas was twenty (ibn al-Turkumānī, n.d., 5, 9-10).
286. Aḥmad, 2001, 40, 78; Muslim, n.d., 2, 870.
287. Not in state of consecration to perform major or minor pilgrimage.
288. Aḥmad, 2001, 45, 173; Ṭaḥāwī, 1994, 14, 514; Dāraquṭnī, 2004, 4, 390.
289. Bukhārī, 2001, 3, 15; Muslim, n.d., 2, 1031.
290. Aḥmad, 2001, 44, 397; Muslim, n.d., 3, 1032.
291. Bukhārī, 2001, 3, 31; Mulism, n.d., 2, 779.
292. Bukhārī, 2001, 3, 29.
293. Abū Dāwūd, n.d., 1, 131; Tirmidhī, 1998, 1, 142.
294. Aḥmad, 2001, 40, 58; Bukhārī, 2001, 3, 71; Tirmidhī, 1998, 2, 452.
295. Aḥmad, 2001, 40, 180; Bukhārī, 2001, 3, 117; Tirmidhī, 1998, 2, 452; Dārimī, 200, 2, 1471.
296. A young female camel, which is two years old and already starting the third year.

297. It is three years old and starting the fourth.
298. Aḥmad, 2001, 8, 256; ibn Mājah, 2009, 3, 16; abū Dāwūd, n.d., 3, 19; Tirmidhī, 1998, 2, 10.
299. The report has been falsely attributed to abū Bakr ʿAmr ibn Ḥazm. It has been related by ʿAli as in ibn Zanjawayh (1986, 2, 809) The report of ʿAmr ibn Ḥazm is identical to that of ibn ʿUmar. It is related in ibn Zanjawayh (1986, 2, 798; abū Dāwūd (1988, 1, 128); ibn Ḥibbān, (1988, 15, 42). According to the report of ibn ʿUmar when camels reach 120 a payer of *zakat* is to pay three *bint labūns* and then he does not have to pay any additional amount until they reach 160. According to the repot of ʿAlī, for every 125 five camels, an owner has to pay three *bin labūns* for the 120 and one sheep for the five. When they reach 130 three *bin labūns* are due on the 120 in addition to two sheep for the additional ten. When they reach 135 three *bint labūns* are to be paid in addition to 3 sheep for the additional 15, etc. Therefore he has to pay for amounts ranging from 120 to 160 according to normal calculation of *zakat* which starts with a sheep for each five camels.
300. Aḥmad, 2001, 11, 593; Bukhārī, 2001, 1, 88; Muslim, n.d., 303.
301. Aḥmad, 2001, 6, 248; Bukhārī, 2001, 2, 62; Muslim, n.d., 1, 382.
302. Bukhārī, 2001, 9, 152.
303. Aḥmad, 2001, 1, 463; Muslim, n.d., 2, 1030; Dārimī, 2000, 2, 1149; ibn Māja, n.d., 3, 140; abū Dāwūd, n.d., 2, 169.
304. Bukhārī, 2001, 3, 15; Muslim, n.d., 2, 1031.
305. Aḥmad, 2001, 22, 155; abū Dāwūd, n.d., 3, 286; Tirmidhī, 1998, 3, 44; Nasāʾī, 1986, 7, 320.
306. Bukhārī, 2001, 3, 79; ibn Māja, n.d., 3, 547; Tirmidhī, 1998, 3, 46.
307. *Shufʿa* signifies the becoming proprietor of lands sold for the price at which the purchaser has bought them, although he be not consenting thereunto (Mirghnānī, *n.d.*, 1, 356). For example, A and B each one owns a part of some dividable piece of real estate. B sells his part to C, a third party. In such a case, A can legally force C to sell the part for him by right of preemption. His purpose is to prevent the harm that would result if C were to subsequently go to the Islamic magistrate and demand that the property be divided to distinguish his property from A. According to the Ḥanfīs it is proved to be a right of a neighbor but according to Shāfiʿīs it is a right of a partner in indivisible properties. Ḥanfīs based their view on the pronounced meaning of the former report, which proves it as a right for a neighbor. They preferred it to the implied meaning of the latter report, which indicates by way of divergent meaning that once a property is divisible there is no reason for preemption. Mālikīs and Shāfiʿīs referred to the pronounced meaning of a third report to substantiate their argument, that is the Prophet's saying, "Preemption takes effect in all cases where land has not been divided."
308. Bukhārī, 2001, 3, 87; Muslim, n.d., 3, 1229.
309. Aḥmad, 2001, 5, 202; Trimidhī, 1998, 1, 217; abū Dāwūd, n.d., 1, 107.
310. Bukhārī, 2001, 3, 90; Muslim, n.d., 3, 1373.
311. Bukhārī, 2001, 2, 128; Muslim, n.d., 1, 276.
312. Aḥmad, 2001, 31, 74; abū Dāwūd, n.d. 4, 67; Trimidhī, 1998, 3, 274; Nasāʾī, 1986, 7, 175; ibn Māja, n.d., 4, 604.
313. Bukhārī, 2001, 1, 101; Muslim, n.d., 2, 966.
314. Bukhārī, 2001, 1, 88; Muslim n.d., 2, 968.
315. Bukhārī, 2001, 2, 45; Muslim, n.d., 2, 765.
316. Bukhārī, 2001, 3, 25; Muslim, n.d., 2, 759.

CHAPTER TWO

Inferred Proofs: *Istiṣḥāb*

By an inferred source we refer to *Iṣtiṣḥāb* (presumption of continuity). It is, however of two types:

1. Presumption of original presence or absence
2. Presumption of the continuity of the general rules and principles of the law

2.1. Presumption of Original Presence or Absence

The first type is considered a proof according to Mālikīs and Shāfiʿīs because whatever has been proved to exist, is presumed to remain as such. It can hardly be contradicted by another *istiṣḥāb* or be changed [by means of a new evidence].

An example of *istiṣḥāb* which is contradicted by another is the position our [Mālikī] companions who maintained that when an absent merchandize perishes before its reception by the purchaser and a conflict occurs between the two purchasing parties on whether it has perished before or after the conclusion of a contract. Liability lies on the purchaser because such a merchandize is proved as extant and sound of any defect before the conclusion of the contract. So, it is presumed to remain sound up to the time when we ascertain that it has perished, which is certainly affirmed to be after the conclusion of sale. Since it has perished in the possession of the purchaser, he is held liable for any damage.

But this view has been argued by opponents among our [Mālikī] companions who stated that the purchaser is originally free from liability, so that we have to presume its continuity. Reference [in settling this dispute] may be made to the preference of one *istiṣḥāb* to the other.

As for the latter, that is, a presumption of continuity unless a change is proved, our [Mālikī] companions maintain that a dog's leftover is pure as long as it is guarded of undertaking impurities before liking. Such an original state of purity must be presumed to continue until we prove that the dog has undertaken an impurity. But an opponent of this view may argue that such a presumption of continuity can be effective as long as no change occurs. In this case the act of liking strengthens the probability that the dog has undertaken an impurity because it is the dominant affair of dogs. In this case, we refer to the question on whether such an argument is valid to nullify the effectiveness of *istiṣḥāb*.

2.2. Presumption of the Continuity of the General Rules and Principles of the Law

For example, our [Mālikī] companions hold that nose bleeding does not invalidate ablution because all scholars are unanimous to the effect that one is held ritually pure before bleeding. We have to presume the continuity of this state unless a change occurs. But the companions of abū Ḥanīfa argue that such an *istiṣḥāb* is invalid because this ruling was based on consensus. We are not all in agreement that he is pure after his bleeding. So, how we presume the continuity of a rule even after undermining the evidence on which it has been based. Moreover, in this case, an invalidator of ablution is extant, that is, nose. The Prophet said, "Whoever vomits, bleeds through the nose, or released *madhiy* (urethral discharge) should go, perform ablution and then complete his *salat* (prayer) (by continuing from where he had stopped at) on condition that he does not speak in the process.[1]" This type of *istiṣḥāb* rarely occurs and it is less effective than the former type.

Note

1. Ibn Māja, n.d., 2, 281; Bayhaqī, 2003, 1, 222.

CHAPTER THREE

Evidence Corollary to a Legislative Source: *Qiyās*

An evidence corollary to a legislative source must refer to a legal determination. This legal determination may be congruous with the *aṣl* (original case)[1] or in contradiction to it. Sometimes it is neither congruous with nor opposing to it. If both rulings are compatible, there must be two distinct cases.[2] This is called *qiyās al-ṭard*[3] (coextensive analogy). If the new case is of a ruling different from that of the original case, both cases must be of two different attributes. This is *qiyās al-ʿaks* (coexclusive analogy). If both cases are neither compatible nor opposing, it is called *qiyās al-istidlāl* (analogy by indication). Therefore, our discussion is focused on *qiyās al-ṭard, qiyās al-ʿaks* and *qiyās al-istidlāl.*

3.1. *Qiyās al-Ṭard* (Coextensive Analogy)

Our discussion is focused on explaining its definition, constituent elements, classification and opponent arguments raised against it. This is going to be an introduction, two sections and a conclusion.

3.1.1. Introduction

Qiyās is defined as the appending of a case of unknown ruling to a case of known ruling due to a common effective cause. The case of a known ruling is called *aṣl* (original case), while the case of unknown ruling is called *far*ʿ (subsidiary case). An example is to compare *nabīdh* which is of unknown ruling to intoxicant grape juice which is of a known ruling. Intoxicant grape juice is the original case while *nabīdh* is the subsidiary case and the common cause is intoxication. The rule intended to prove for the subsidiary case is prohibition.

3.1.2. Constituent Elements of Analogy

They are four: *aṣl* (original case),[4] *ʿilla* (effective cause),[5] *far*ʿ (new case)[6] and *ḥukm* (ruling).

[3.1.2.1. The *Aṣl* (Original Case)]

The first element of *qiyās* is *aṣl* (original case). It has to fulfill the following five conditions:

(a) The ruling of an original case must be consistent. If it is not consistent, it cannot be extendable because the intent is to prove the same ruling for the new case. Proving a ruling for a new case is an offshoot of proving it in the original case. In polemical discussions, if one extends the ruling of an *aṣl*, which he himself does not accept, to other new cases, his argument will be untenable even if an opponent approves this *aṣl*. This is because a proponent admits the invalidity of this analogy.

An example is the Shāfiʿīs' argument against Ḥanafīs to prove that when one retains an intention to offer a supererogatory *hajj* while he has not observed the obligatory duty, his intention is valid [and it does not hold him liable to offer *hajj* again]. This is a contradiction to Ḥanafīs' position. The Shāfiʿīs relied on the Ḥanafī principle of holding a supererogatory intention of fasting efficient for the obligatory fasting of Ramadan. Shāfiʿīs extended the ruling of an original case which they themselves do not support.

(b) The [ruling of an] original case must be operative, that is, it has not been abrogated. If the ruling of an original case is abrogated and it is used to include a common attribute, such an attribute becomes no longer a [valid] rationale. The reason is that the ruling is no more effected by such a rationale. But if this common attribute is not [a priori a valid] rationale, a correlation [between *aṣl* and *far*'] cannot be established. The reason is that an invalid rationale cannot entail a rational ruling.

But if you argue that the original and the new cases may be correlated without an effective cause, we may state that the common similarity feature must include an *ʿilla*. If the common feature between them is not a valid rationale or does not include an *ʿilla*, a correlation cannot be established.

Sometimes, one of the rulings of an original case is abrogated so that one thinks that abrogation extends to the new case. An example is the argument of abū Ḥanīfa's companions that retaining intention during night for the one observing fast during Ramadan is not obligatory because fasting [of Ramaḍān] is discernible by itself [and does not need an intention]. They reached this conclusion by comparing the fast of Ramaḍān to the fast of *ʿashūrāʾ*,[7] where intention may not be retained at night according to the hadith on this regard.

But our [Mālikī] companions maintain that the ruling of the original case has been abrogated [that is, the fasting of *ʿashūrāʾ*]. A prerequisite of an *aṣl* is that it has not been abrogated. The Ḥanafīs counter them back by stating that they have not extended obligation [of fasting of *ʿashūrāʾ* which was abrogated], but they extended another ruling [that is, permissibility of retaining intention during day time]. The permissibility of retaining intention during day time is not necessarily abrogated along with the abrogation of the obligation of fasting *ʿashūrāʾ*.

Included in this discussion is also the *ẓihār* of a slave girl. It may be stated that *ẓihār* was a type of divorce [in pre Islam] particularly applicable to marriage. Had it not been abrogated, it would not have been applicable to a concubine, because divorce is not applied to a concubine. But when the ruling of divorce has been abrogated, *ẓihār* has been confined to mean a [vow] to prohibit [sexual] enjoyment of a woman. [Sexual] enjoyment is common in both a wife and a slave girl. Therefore, *ẓihār* is applicable to both a wife and a concubine

It may be argued that *ẓihār* had a particular ruling, that is, divorce and a particular subject, that is, a female marriage partner. Its ruling has been abrogated but it does not necessarily mean that its subject has also been abrogated. *Īlāʾ*[8] used to be a type of divorce [in pre Islam]. Its ruling has been abrogated but its subject that is, a female marriage partner has not been abrogated.

(c) The ruling must not be peculiar for the original case. In case it is peculiar for [the original case], it cannot be extendable to other cases. This condition is further ramified in three categories:
- A group of cases where the Lawgiver or consensus determined that their rulings are not extendable [to further cases].
- A group of cases where the Lawgiver has not specified such peculiarity but they are irrational in the sense that their ruling can hardly be extended to other cases, because the reason for their enactment is not rational.

- Rational rulings which lack similar instances to which a ruling may be extended.

The first category includes [issues like] the Prophet's decree that the testimony of Khuzayma alone is efficient. It was peculiar for him and it became known among the Companions (may Allah be pleased with them). If his case was extendable to other similar cases, analogy would be operative and the [current standard] number of witnesses would be revoked.

Similarly, the Prophet's statement to abū Burda on the young she-goat, "Sacrifice it in lieu of the first, but it will be not sufficient [as a sacrifice] for anybody else after you.[9]" Such is the case of Sālim who was particularly permitted to enter alone into ʿĀʾisha[10] after he was nursed by her upon reaching puberty.

In the same realm fell the peculiarities of the Prophet which were not shared by others. Scholars differed on the rule of some issues due to whether to regard them peculiar to him. Among those cases is the ruling of concluding the contract of marriage using the verbal form of a gift. Shāfiʿīs prohibit that because they held it is peculiar to the Prophet due to Allah's saying, "and a believing woman if she gives herself to the Prophet [and] if the Prophet wishes to marry her, [this is] only for you, excluding the [other] believers." (Q. 33: 50).

But the Ḥanafīs interpret it to mean that it refers to dropping dowry which is an indicative of elevating the Prophet's status and uplifting discomfort from him, not assigning him a verbal form to conclude marriage which can be substituted by other forms. The Shāfiʿīs maintain that Prophet's peculiarity to use a specific form of is subsequent to his getting married without dowry. Therefore, a disagreement occurred among the fellows of our [Mālikī] school.

An example of this is the validity of making the freedom of a concubine as [a form of] dowry. According to [Mālikī] school, it is one of the Prophet's peculiarities so that others cannot share him in this respect. However, there are numerous examples that belong to this section.

But if a conflict occurs on whether to regard a text as decisively referring to a peculiar case [which is exclusive of all other similar cases], then the manifest meaning should presume that it is not peculiar until peculiarity is proved by a text or *ijmāʿ*.

Such is the case of the scholars' disagreement on whether *iḥrām* terminates by death or not. Based on this is [the question on whether it is] permissible to apply perfume to one who dies in state of *iḥrām.* They further differed on a martyr, whether to wash his body and offer funeral prayer for him or not. It has been related that a Bedouin was killed by his camel, where the Prophet (may God exalt his mention) said, "Do not cover his head or perfume him because he is going to be resurrected as reciting *talbiya.*[11]" He, further said regarding the martyrs of Uḥud, "Wrap them up on their clothes that are stained with blood, for there is no wound that is sustained for the sake of Allah, but it will come bleeding on the Day of Resurrection: its color will be the color of blood, but its fragrance will be the fragrance of musk.[12]"

Ḥanafīs maintain that the is exclusive to the Bedouin and the martyrs of Uḥud so that it is not extended to others, while Shāfiʿī jurists state that it is not peculiar to them but it is inclusive of others. Our Mālikī companions differentiated between the case of the Bedouin by holding the ruling peculiar for him while regarding the case of martyrs of Uḥud as extendable to all martyrs.

The second category includes irrational rulings such as assigned proportions and prescribed numbers which are not extended [to other cases] by analogy.

It is argued that you have given an estimate of the minimum amount of a dowry by comparing it to the minimum amount of a stolen property [where a hand may be cut] and you have given a limit for the hand to be wiped in *taymmum* by comparing it to the part to be cut for theft according to the popular view of [Mālikī] school. Both cases have been proved by analogy.

We counter that this is not analogy, but it is a personal reasoning of the minimum amount considered [by the Lawgiver]. To explain, the Lawgiver obligated a monetary compensation for marriage by Allah's saying, "that you seek them [in marriage] with [gifts from] your property." (Q. 4: 24). This is due to the seriousness of a marriage contract. It cannot be shown by whatever is called a property, because a penny and a grain can be called a property. Therefore, we had to refer to a significant amount of wealth. Since it is controversial in law and custom, we had to refer to the law which obligated the payment of a monetary compensation in marriage. We had to consider the least significant amount of wealth [in *sharia*]. There is nothing less significant than the amount for which a hand may be cut off due to theft. When the law subjected it to amputation due to stealing a quarter of a dinar, it indicated that the amount of a quarter of a dinar has a significance. We have not found any less amount which is considered by *sharia*. This is the reason we assigned it as the minimum amount for a dowry.

As for assigning the wrist bone [as the limit of the part to be wiped in *tayamum*], we confirm that it is not by virtue of analogy but it has been reached through the same method. A 'hand' is an absolute [term,] which can be given different limits, but the minimum limit of a hand is the wrist. So, we regarded that wiping that limit is efficient according to the popular view [of our Mālikī school.] We further maintained that such one [who performs *taymmum*] has to redo his prayer if he finds water before the designated time for prayer elapses. There are, however, numerous examples of irrational rulings in *sharia*.

The third category includes rulings which are rational but do not have similar examples to which they may be extended. Their rulings may be based on a simple reason or a number of reasons. An example of the former is traveling. It includes difficulty which is the basis for shortening prayers, but this meaning cannot be held a basis for labor which includes hardship though it may be held a suitable reason for shortening prayers too. However, it is not attached to traveling. Illness is a basis for exemption from fasting and for combining two prayers. This is based on the text; not reached through analogy.

Difficulty resulting from illness does not fit as a basis for shortening prayers, but it may a basis for permitting a sick person to sit down and mime [instead of standing or sitting].

An example of this section is the right of preemption in real estate which has a rational cause, that is, the harm inflicted on a partner who does not like [a stranger] to share property with him. Similarly, the plaintiff initiates by swearing oaths in *Qasāma*[13] (compurgation by oath) to guard lives where a person is slain treasonably and it is difficult to find witnesses and the murderer would take false oaths lightly as he took murder lightly while persistently denying his crime. This is the reason plaintiffs initiate swearing oaths [instead of defendants]. This ruling may include a number of reasons. It is, therefore, belongs to the second category.

An example for a ruling which is based on a number of reasons not extendable to further cases is the obligation of a blood money for a murder's family in the case of erroneous homicide. It is a rational ruling. Therefore, Arabs in pre Islam used to practice it and Islam confirmed its enactment. The interest behind it is that there is a need for using weapons, training on battle works, archery and shooting. This is the reason why hunting is permissible even when there is no necessity or need. It necessitates the use of war instrument. But since [murdering] a soul is a grave sin which cannot be neglected and an [erroneous] murderer does not deliberately intend [to commit] the crime, people would dissociate themselves with weapons in case we execute them or burden them with the whole blood money. [Moreover,] there is no great injustice incurred on the family since the blood money is born by them proportionately. It is further substantiated by their mutual support and consolidation which is a natural disposition of the members of a tribe. For this same objective, *sharia* sanctioned the [bearing of] testimony by children [on a crime occurring] at [places] of play. There are numerous examples for this.

This is an explanation for the third prerequisite [of the original case]. Some *uṣūlīs* further express it as that [an original case] must not be inconsistent with the norms of analogy.

d. [The ruling of] an *aṣl* must not have been reached through a previous analogy. Such a proviso has been approved by *uṣūlīs* but Ḥanablīs and abū ʿAbdullah al-Baṣrī of the Mutazilites have been reported that it is not a prerequisite [of analogy]. For our [Mālikī] school, it is not a requirement.

It is justifiable to extend the ruling of an original case which was previously reached by another analogy.

For example the majority of scholars extended the ruling of one's saying to his spouse, 'You are divorced if you menstruate' to that of his saying, 'You are divorced by the commencement of the month'.[14] They based the ruling of the original case on analogy by comparing it to temporary marriage [which is prohibited]. The intended objective of marriage is affinity and tenderness which can only be attained through permanent relationship. Probable or certain expectation of dissolution upon the termination of an appointed term tends to undermine what is intended by marriage, that is, affection and attachment. But it is unlike slavery, where emancipation may be conditional to the expiry of a certain course of time. The reason is not to effect certain transactions by deferment such as giving a slave as a gift or hiring him [for someone else before emancipation].

Uṣūlīs maintain [in case of one *qiyās* constituting the *asl* of another] that when an effective cause [of the second] is identical to the original *ʿilla*, it becomes futile. An example is to compare quince to apple [as being usurious] due to the common cause of edibility. If the ruling [of usurability] is not operative in the case of apple, one has to compare [quince] directly to wheat [since both are edible]. It may be said that making apple an *aṣl* is futile. It is presumed to compare quince [directly] to wheat without any mention of apple. Those [scholars] maintain that a constituent element of any evidence cannot be pointless.

[If we have analogy A and Analogy B and each one of them has an original case and a new case, the new case of A becomes an original case for B, so] when the *ʿilla* between an intermediary [that is, the new case of A which turns to be the original case for B] and the original case of A is not identical to the *ʿilla* between the intermediary and its respective new case, therefore, the ruling of this *farʿ* cannot be extracted from the intermediary because the rationale between them is not identical to the rationale on which the intermediary was based.[15]

An example is when one extends the ruling of [a water change caused by the falling of] algae and the change effected by long standing to a change caused by the falling of dust. [In both cases] water is a ritual purifier, the common effective cause is the probability of a change and the emergent need [of people for using water in those cases]. If the ruling of the original case [that is, change by algae and long standing] is granted to [the *farʿ* that is, change of water by fall of dust], we can further extend the same ruling to the case of dropping pure [and ritually used[16]] water to pure water. The common cause would be then the purity of the additive in both cases.[17]

(e) The ruling must not be based on two different attributes advocated by two groups each claiming that his is the effective cause. The ruling of an original case cannot be maintained based on such [*an ʿilla*]. For example, our [Mālikī] scholars extended the ruling of one who murders a *mukātab* slave[18] to the case of one who kills a pure slave [in the sense that both murderers are not retaliated for the killing of any of them]. The Ḥanfīs agree with our fellows that a murderer of a *mukātab* is not to be executed. The *ʿilla* identified by our fellows is that the murdered is a slave [in both cases] but the *ʿilla* identified by Ḥanafīs is the indecisive state of the one who would claim right for retaliation and deserve blood money. The contract of emancipation rendered a *mukātab* in a position between slavery and freedom. In case of paying off, he is a freeman. Otherwise, he is still a slave. When he dies we cannot decisively regard him a slave to give the right of claiming retaliation to the master or to be treated as a freeman and thus grant that right to his heirs.

Ḥanafīs state that if the effective cause we identified was valid, extending the rule of the murderer of a pure slave to the murderer of a *mukātab* would be ineffective, because the claimant of a slave's blood is unknown. When *an ʿilla* is not operative, the ruling identified in the original case that is, the murderer of a *mukātab* should not be applicable. We should state, then, that a murderer of a *mukātab* has to be executed. Therefore, a ruling of the original case cannot be proved in such a case of disagreement.

Such a stance is named by *uṣūlīs* a complex analogy. If our fellows extracted the rationale for [the execution of a killer of] a *mukātab* through a textual evidence, analogy would be, then, sound.

3.1.2.2. The *ʿIlla* (Rationale)

Our discussion will focus on its prerequisites, its ways, that is, how to prove an attribute to be a [valid] rationale.

3.1.2.2.1. [Prerequisites of a Rationale]

We are going to elaborate its prerequisites in the following questions:
[Basing an affirmative ruling on a negative rationale.]

> It is legitimate, by consensus, to build an affirmative ruling on an affirmative rationale and a negative ruling on a negative rationale, such as basing the obligation of *zakat* on the possession of its minimum ratio and basing the execution [of a murderer] on deliberate and assailing murder.

Basing an affirmative ruling on a negative rationale is controversial among the *imams* of *uṣūl*. An example is our [Mālikī] fellows' conclusion that a physically sound non-traveler has to observe dry ablution [to offer obligatory prayer] by comparing him to the case of a traveler who does not find water. They argue that a resident has no water accessible so that dry ablution become incumbent on him like the case of a traveler who does not have water accessible. But others counter that non-existence of water is not a [valid] *ʿilla* for the obligation of dry ablution, because a negative attribute cannot be a cause for an affirmative ruling.

Similarly, [a negative attribute] cannot be a part of the effective cause as such basing the execution for murder on the absence of coercion. Ḥanafīs have not obligated the execution of a coerced [murderer] due to the lacking of the base for execution, that is, absence of voluntary will. Our [Mālikī] fellows argue that the absence of consent is a negative attribute, which cannot be a [valid] *ʿilla* or a part of *ʿilla*. Some of erudite among scholars tended to accept the opinion that negation should neither be [an appropriate] *ʿilla* nor a part of an *ʿilla*. They further stated that *an ʿilla* must contain by itself an interest which accrues on enacting a ruling. Nihility does not accommodate an interest.

As for basing a negative ruling on an affirmative attribute, it is tantamount to rationalization of a ruling by referring it to the existence of an impediment. The scholars of *uṣūl* are, however, in disagreement on whether rationalization of a ruling by endorsing its impediment does initially require, in addition to that, the existence of an effective cause for this ruling or not. The majority maintain that the existence of an *ʿilla* for the ruling is a prerequisite, because when a ruling is short of a rationale, it is regarded non-extant. The ruling cannot be regarded non-extant due to the existence of an impediment, but only when its respective rationale is absent.

[Rationalization of a ruling by basing it on impediment] often occurs in polemics. Many investigations are always conducted in cases where a negative ruling is extracted by reference to analogy which is based on affirmative rationales. For example, our [Mālikī] fellows state that gold ornaments are but a property held for possession and use so that they are not liable to *zakat* exactly like clothes and slaves. But a Ḥanafī may argue that the *ʿilla* you have assigned is an affirmative attribute, that is, the existence of common and frequent use [of ornaments] on which a negative ruling that is, the non-obligation of *zakat* is based. It is not valid unless you prove that such an [affirmative] attribute is the impediment of the obligation for *zakat* [on ornaments]. Claiming that it is an impediment is [an indication of] your approval that the *ʿilla* for the obligation of *zakat* initially exists. You have spared us the effort of proving the *ʿilla* of making *zakat* obligatory in such a polemical case and claimed that the *ʿlla* of its obligation is extant in *aṣl*, whose ruling has been extended. You have to take [the burden of] explaining it.

The answer of our [Mālikī] fellows is that wealth is a blessing and it entails praise giving while spending of it for a rightful duty of the bestower is a type of praise. *Zakat* is the spending of [wealth], so that it is an act of praise. Therefore, wealth by itself is suitable to be an *ʿilla* for the obligation of *zakat*.

The rationale must be evident.

The rationale that purports a ruling must be evident that is, it must not be obscure because a ruling is, by itself, imaginary. If an *ʿilla* is similarly invisible, it cannot be used for rationalization because a rationale has to be definite. An imaginary cannot clearly define the invisible. Such is the case of defining purely intentional homicide as the *ʿilla* for retaliation. An opponent argues that intentionality is an act of one's inner self; it is so invisible to be considered a rationale either as a whole or partially. It may be substituted by the identification of something that most probably occurs or exists when it happens. A rationale in this case is ostensible.

For example, if we rationalize the transfer of ownership of both merchandise and price by mutual consent of the purchasing parties due to Allah's saying, "but only [in lawful] business by mutual consent." (Q. 4: 29), consent is invisible because it is an act of self. It cannot be considered by itself but through a visible indication to suggest [the affirmation of] offer and acceptance. Therefore, a seller's saying, "I have sold you so and so" is a proof on his consent that he is dispossessed of a merchandise and price transfers to his possession. Such is the case of a purchaser's saying, 'I accept,' which is a proof that he is dispossessed of the price and he takes possession of a merchandise. This is the reason the Lawgiver based transfer of ownership on [verbal pronouncement of] offer and acceptance. The reason is that our consideration is for the indication which signified consent, which is the intent of the legal evidence. A [mere] act is, too, presumed to show consent such as *muʿāṭā*[19] occurring between the two purchasing parties [by giving price and taking merchandise without speaking]. Therefor, our [Mālikī] companions ruled out that such a sale transaction does not necessitate a spoken offer contrary to Shāfiʿīs who do not hold this type of sale as a valid transaction except when it is concluded with a formula that verbally indicates offer and consent. Ḥanafīs distinguish between precious and frivolous things. They stipulate a formulae in selling precious things and do not run it through *muʿāṭā*. Trivial items can sufficiently be sold by *muʿāṭah*. This is a juristic preference (*istiḥsān*) which is justified [by arguing] that a formulae of sale is more evident to prove consent than the act of *muʿāṭā*. It has to be required in selling precious items to safeguard sale against a lacuna resulting from an abjure of consent.

[*A rationale must be constant and consistent*]

A rationale has to be constant that is, not relative. It means that things, which relatively vary such as hardship which may [vary between] being mild or intense, have to be adjusted if the Lawgiver bases a ruling on them. For example, the Lawgiver grants a traveller the concession to shorten prayers and not fasting due to hardship, but hardship stipulated for shortening is not consistent. It varies in accordance with short and long distances of journeying and the amount of effort exerted, so that it is not preferable to base a ruling on it. The Lawgiver, hence, considered a standard for travelling by assigning a minimum distance of four *burud* (that is, 85 kilometres). Therefore, assiduous careers cannot be supplemented [to this concession].

They differed on the stipulation of consistency as a prerequisite for *ʿilla*. It means that when a rationale exists, a ruling exists [and when it does not exist, the ruling does not exist]. Those who stipulated this condition maintained that inconsistency nullifies the efficacy of a rationale. Inconsistency means that an attribute exists but its ruling does not. Verification demands giving details: when a ruling is absent at a case though it does contain an impediment that contradicts an *ʿilla*, inconsistency nullifies the validity of *ʿilla*. For example, basing a murder's impediment to inherit [of the estate of the relative he killed] on the [maxim that] whoever hastes to gain something [in an illegal means] before its due time is to be prevented from it, such as the case of a murderer of his legator. He has been treated according to the opposite of what he intended.

But Ḥanfīs and Shāfiʿīs maintain that this [legal] maxim has been vitiated by the case of *umm al-walad*.[20] If she kills her master to haste her emancipation, she becomes free. Furthermore, if a creditor kills a debtor to haste the payment of debt, it has to be paid off. In [those two examples,] the maxim has been vitiated.

But when the maxim does not apply in a case where the legal ruling is negative due to an impediment, the rationale cannot be, then, held void. For example, our [Mālikī] companions maintain that *zakat* is obligatory on a child's wealth because he owns a minimum ratio. They based this ruling on comparing his case to the wealth of a pubescent. But Ḥanafīs argue that this rationale is vitiated in the case of debt, where a debtor possesses a minimum ratio but *zakat* is not incumbent on him.

Our [Mālikī] companions counter that debt impedes the obligation of *zakat* because when two rights are due on a property, the more binding takes priority. The right of creditors is more binding. The reason is that a definite deserver takes priority to one who is not known for certain.

[*Inverse rationale.*]

They differed on whether an *ʿilla* should be an inverse. It means that when a rationale is absent the ruling is absent [and the opposite of a ruling exists]. Some scholars set it a condition and forbade giving two rationales for the same ruling. Others have not stipulated this condition and tolerated to base a ruling on two rationales such as basing the obligation of ablution on the execration of urine, defecation and passing wind and such as basing the prohibition of marriage [to certain categories of women] on consanguinity, marriage relation and nursing.

[*A ruling with multiple rationales.*]

They further differed on whether to relate a ruling to all rationales or to one of them and set aside the rest. Therefore, they disagreed on [who should conclude marriage] in case many guardians are available and they are all of equal grade. It is said that all should conclude the contract. It is also said that one of them can conclude marriage.

Shāfiʿīs differed on one who had two *ḥadaths* (states of ritual impurity) and intended to remove one of them and forgot to intend the removal of the other. Some of them said that it is not efficient [to remove the unintended one] because each state has a different rationale for the obligation of ablution. The removal of one of them cannot stand for the removal of another. Others said that both are removed because they overlap and are regarded like one *ḥadath.* Others said that if he intended [to remove] the first *ḥadath* both would be uplifted because it is the exigency of ablution while the other is not a subject for the ruling of obligation but if he intended to lift up the second alone, it would not be efficient since he intended to remove something which did not efface the obligation of ablution.

[*Transferability of an ʿilla*]

Scholars differed on making transitivity a condition for an *ʿilla,* that is, the *ʿilla* is transferable to cases other than what is mentioned in a legal text. Ḥanafis make it a condition but our companions and the companions of Shāfiʿī do not make it a prerequisite, but they see that if a text considers it, it becomes specifically a stable rationale for an original case regardless it is being transferable to other cases or not. For example, our [Mālikī] companions rationalize the prohibition of usury in gold and silver based on their being the main criterion of pricing. If they subject to [quantitative excess through] usury, they will need another thing to be a criterion for defining their prices.

Ḥanafis state that it is an intransitive rationale and is futile. The reason is that if the utility of a ruling is included in a legal text, the ruling must have been proved through that text not through the rationale. If it is not extant in the original case it is futile because it cannot, then, transfer to a new case. Our [Mālikī] companions counter that a ruling is proved in a text through its rationale that is, it is the incentive for enacting a ruling and the text only defines it. It does not prove the ruling.

Conclusion

They have differed on how the ruling of an original case is established. Our [Mālikī] fellows and the companions of al-Shāfiʿī maintain that the ruling of an original is usually established by an *ʿilla* while the companions of abū Ḥanīfa state that it is proved by the [legal] text not through *ʿilla.* Some *uṣūlī* claim that this difference is an equivocation fallacy which reveals no avail, while others refer to is as a reason for disagreement on some practical legal rulings and regard it a conflict among scholars which breeds a significant impact. Therefor, if our [Mālikī] fellows argue that little amounts of *nabīdh* are prohibited by extending the rule of wine to *nabīdh* through analogy, Ḥanfīs may argue that a little amount of wine is prohibited by scripture.

If the Ḥanafīs argue for the permissibility of *nabīdh* that does not cause intoxication by stating that the cause of prohibition is intoxication, it should be held absent in little amounts which do not intoxicate. Therefore, it is not prohibited [according to them] but this, however, conflicts with *ijmāʿ*. Ḥanfīs may, further, counter that large and little amounts of wine have not been rendered prohibited by means of *ʿilla* but they were prohibited by the text [of the Quran].

Similarly, Ḥanafīs maintain that the *ʿilla* for regarding gold and silver usurious is their saleability in weight. They extend [the ruling to] whatever is sold in weight such as copper, iron and lead, etc. Whatever is not sold by weight such as brass, iron or lead utensils are not usurious. They say that the *ʿilla* for prohibition is weight which does not exist in moulded minerals.

But our [Mālikī] fellows argue that it is binding on Ḥanafīs to regard moulded gold and silver usurious items. However, Ḥanafīs can counter that the ruling on usury is proved by text not through *an ʿilla*. Therefor, moulded [gold and silver] are not a part [of our argument].

3.1.2.2.2. [Methods of Extracting a Rationale]

The methods of extracting *ʿilla* are five. They are [defined as] signifiers which qualify an attribute to be a rationale for a [certain] ruling.

i. [Extraction from] a Scripture

This is of two categories; explicit and implicit.

1. An explicit textual [signifier] is the lawgiver's rendering of a [verbal] form which refers to an effective cause such as Allah's saying, "that it will not be a perpetual distribution among the rich from among you." (Q. 58: 7), and the Prophet's saying, "I have previously prohibited you to store meat of sacrificial animals because of the Bedouins who came to you,[21]" and his saying, "Marry to get offspring because I will boast of your great number among nations.[22]" He further said regarding the *muḥrim* whose neck was broken by his camel, "Do not cover his head, or bring any perfume near him because he will be resurrected reciting *talbiya*.[23]" and with respect to the martyrs of Uḥud he said, "Wrap them up in their wounds and blood

because they are resurrected on the Day of Resurrection with their wounds flowing with blood.[24]" These are examples of an explicit rationalization [extracted from scripture]. This is the reason Shāfiʿīs extended this ruling to every *muḥrim* and every martyr.

A similar example is also included in Allah's saying, "[As for] the thief, the male and the female, amputate their hands," (Q. 5: 38) and in Allah's saying, "The [unmarried] woman or [unmarried] man found guilty of sexual intercourse—lash each one of them," (Q. 24: 2) and in the Prophet's saying, "You have possessed [the right of divorce], so that you can choose.[25]"

2. Implicit [signifier of *ʿilla*] is however, of various degrees as follows:

The first category is when the Prophet (may God exalt his mention) provides, along with a ruling, an attribute which is hardly mentioned without referring to rationalization, such as his saying with respect to cat, "It is not unclean; it is one of those who intermingle with you.[26]" If a cat's mix [with people] is not the *ʿilla* for disproving its impurity, mentioning it in the text in connection with the ruling is futile. [But it is declared pure] because it is known that it mingles with people.

Similarly, The Prophet (may God exalt his mention) has been reported as saying, "May Allah curse the Jews, Allah made fat illegal for them but they sold it and ate its price.[27]" If there is no reason for curing them, there would be no significance for reporting their practice or invoking against them.

The second category is when [the Prophet] inquires on a specific uncontroversial matter, which is already known for him to make [his question] a base for an answer. If it is not intended to show the *ʿilla*, his inquisition on something he knows would be pointless. Such is the case when the Prophet (may God exalt his mention) has been asked about the ruling of selling dried dates for fresh dates, he inquired, "Does the dates diminish in size when they become dry?" He said, "Then, it is not [permissible].[28]"

Similarly, when the woman from Khathʿam asked him, "My father has passed away while the obligation of *hajj* is due on him. Should I offer *hajj* on his behalf?" He said, "Had there been a debt on your father, would you have paid it?" She said, "Yes." Then, he said, "The debt of Allah is most deserving to be paid off.[29]"

The third category is when the Prophet (may God exalt his mention) issues a legal determination subsequent to his acquaintance of the occurrence of an incident. It becomes known that such an incident is the cause of the ruling. A Bedouin said, "Messenger of Allah I have been ruined and made [my wife] ruined. I have had intercourse with my wife on a day of Ramaḍān" He said, "Emancipate a slave.[30]" It is like stating that if you have intercourse, you must expiate.

Shāfiʿīs maintained that sexual intercourse is the *ʿilla* for a penance so that they have not imposed it on one who intentionally eats or drinks during a day of Ramaḍān. The Ḥanfīs based penance on a reason included in sexual intercourse, that is, fulfillment of a desire which one has to abstain from, because fasting signifies refraining from the fulfillment of a stomach's need and sexual desire. Therefore, they imposed penance on one who intentionally eats or drinks during a day of Ramaḍān because he has fulfilled a desire which has to be refrained by fasting. They have not imposed it on the intake of an undesirable such as swallowing a pebble or the seed of a date.

Mālikīs disregarded sexual desire as the basis for an obligatory penance. According to them, the violation of fasting by intentionally invalidating it [requires a penance]. They obligated a penance by swallowing a pebble or a seed of a date. This is known for *uṣūlīs* as the *tanqūḥ al-manāṭ* (verification of a rationale) by excluding irrelevant attributes in a text and approving relevant contingencies. Ibn al-Qāsm quoted [Mālik] on the one who swallows a pebble. [Mālik] maintained that a penance is incumbent on him and he has not to make up the fasting of that day. But [this statement] goes beyond precepts we have previously proceeded.

The fourth category is when a narrator reports an action issued by the Prophet (may God exalt his mention) or any of his companions to construct a ruling based on that action. It entails a rationalization of this ruling by referring it to the legal ruling. For example, a narrator said, "The Messenger of Allah (may God exalt his mention) forgot [and made a mistake during prayer] so that he prostrated.[31]" It implies that forgetfulness is the *ʿilla* for prostration. This is the reason ibn al-Qāsim have not based *sujūd* on intentionally leaving a supererogatory act of prayer. This is contrary to Ashhab who made it obligatory to offer prostration before the final salutation because deficiency in prayer is the *ʿilla* for prostration of forgetfulness whether it is committed unintentionally or in advertence.

Such is the case when a narrator says, "Māʿidh committed adultery so that the Prophet (may God exalt his mention) stoned him to death." It indicates that adultery is the *ʿilla* for stoning. Therefore, ibn al-Qāsim stated that when four witnesses bear testimony that someone have committed adultery and then he has been stoned and later two of the four convicted that he has been chaste and the four have all disavowed their previous testimony, blood money is only due on those who confirmed he has committed adultery. Ashhab states that all have to share the payment of his blood money. These are the categories of implicit indications of an *ʿilla*.

ii. [Extraction from] *Ijmāʿ*

It means that consensus can approve that a certain attribute is valid to be an *ʿilla* for the legal ruling of an original case. For example, when a woman has two brothers;

one full brother and the other is an agnate brother, is the full brother more eligible to be her marriage guardian? This is the choice of ibn al-Qāsim [who stated that] the additional line of relationship through a mother [in the case of the full brother] is a reason for giving him precedence in inheritance. This is proved by consensus. It is extended by analogy to include marriage. His explanation of the view he related from Mālik is that a mother has a role in inheritance so that the additional line of relationship maintained through her became a means of preference. Since she cannot be [a guardian] in a marriage contract, an additional line of relationship through her is not effective in case of marriage.

iii. Extraction by Suitability

This is when a legal ruling includes an attribute which suites to provide a rational basis for the ruling. An example of this is the prohibition of wine. It has an attribute which suites to be a basis for its prohibition, that is, intoxication, which obscures mind. Reason is, however, a criterion for *taklīf* (responsibility) and is a basis for attaining wellbeing in both this life and the hereafter. Therefore, Abū Zayd al-Dabūsī says, "When a suitable reason [for a ruling] is exposed to [sound] minds it acquires credence." A proper *ʿilla* may be clearly stated by the Lawgiver or not. If it is suggested by indications in the text of the Lawgiver, it is further classified into effective and proper *ʿilla*.

An effective *ʿilla* is [defined as] a definite effective cause which is stated [to be a basis] for a definite ruling. An example of this is Allah's saying, "The [unmarried] woman or [unmarried] man found guilty of sexual intercourse—lash each one of them with a hundred lashes." (Q. 24: 2). According to this verse, fornication is definitely the cause of lashing. Examples of this type of *ʿilla* are numerous.

A proper *ʿilla* may be [one of the following] (1) a definite cause stated [in a scripture or *ijmāʿ*] to set the basis for a general ruling applied to a number of cases or (2) a general objective which is attainable in a definite case or (3) a general objective which is sought as the basis for a general ruling [applicable to many cases].

An example of the first type is the Ḥanafis' position regarding a previously married minor girl. They stated that she may be compelled to marry [by her father] because the minority of a child sets the basis for a guardian's authority over the property of his minors. It becomes a proper *ʿilla* for a father's guardianship over his minors regarding marriage. Therefore, the minority of a child has been definitely stated by consensus as an *ʿilla* for guardianships in general.

An example of the second type is the position of our [Mālikī] companions who assigned hardship and difficulty as the basis for combining two obligatory prayers at time of rain for a non-traveler. Therefore, hardship has been generally identified as the reason for combining prayers [in general].

An example of the third type is that according to *ijmā*ʿ, the rationale of enacting retaliation for a bodily injury is aggression [against human life,] which sets the basis for retaliation on homicide. Aggression is a general basis for all types of retaliation.

ʿ*Illas*, which have not been stated by the Lawgiver are of two categories: (1) an ʿ*Illa*, which proves to be the basis for one case only. It is called a *gharīb* (strange) attribute and (2) an ʿ*illa*, which can hardly be identified at any case. An example of the former is the position of our [Mālikī] companions who extended the ruling of a murder's deprivation of inheritance from his murdered relative to the case of depriving an irrevocably divorced woman of her right of inheritance when her husband divorces her during his death illness in order to exclude her from inheritance. In both cases, the evil intention of a murderer and that of a husband are identified, so that they have been treated contrary to their intentions. [Blocking] means for an evil end has not been evidently stated by the Lawgiver though it is a basis for the legal ruling in the case of homicide.

An example of the latter is al-Lakhmī's unique verdict that when riders of a boat are sure they will all be drawn in sea due to a boat's heavy load they are allowed to throw some of them by casting lots to secure lives of the rest. Though there is an appropriate objective of this ruling, the Lawgiver has not evidently stated it or made it the basis for any case.

iv. Extraction by Rotation

It means that when a certain attribute of a legal ruling exists, the law too exists along with it and if it does not exist the legal ruling does not exist either. Therefore, it becomes evident that such an attribute is the basis for such a specific ruling. An example of this is grape juice, which is not prohibited by consensus when it does not intoxicate. But if it intoxicates, it is rendered unlawful by consensus. When intoxication is removed, prohibition is uplifted. Therefore, when intoxication is annexed with prohibition in both cases, we made sure that intoxication is the basis for prohibition.

This is the position of our [Mālikī] fellows who maintained that both a dog and a swine are pure by essence. They based their view through analogy by comparing them to dead pregnant sheep. In both cases, life is the basis of purity. Therefore, when a pregnant sheep dies [without being legally slaughtered] but its baby is still alive, all parts of the sheep are impure but the living baby is pure. Life rotates with purity, that is, purity exists when life exists and it does not exist when life does not. Therefore, we could identify that life is the basis for the purity [of an animal].

v. Extraction by Resemblance

It is when a *far*ʿ (new case) vacillates between two distinct *aṣls* (original cases) and it resembles them in certain ways. For example, ablution may be compared to *tayamum* or to the act of removing impurities. It resembles the former in the sense that both uplift a state of ritual impurity. It resembles the act of impurity removal in the sense that both acts use water to get rid of physical filth. The latter is not applicable to *tayamum*. Therefore, Mālikī and Shāfiʿī scholars maintained that retaining intention is an obligatory act of ablution due to its strong resemblance for *tayamum* but Ḥanafī scholars have not made it obligatory due to its being similar to the removal of a physical impurity.

Similarly, our [Mālikī] companions maintain that a slave has the right to own properties because he resembles both humans and animals. Whoever compares him to humans [gives him right to possess] while those who held him like a [transferable] property compared him to an animal. One of the two resemblances that is, being human, grants him the right to own. He is strongly attached to humans due to two reasons:

1. He is a human being. Being a transferable property is a contingent attribute.
2. The Lawgiver gave weight to his humanity by granting him the right to marry. Therefore, he should have the right to keep slave girls under his authority due to strong similarity [with humans in respect of marriage].

3.1.2.3. *Farʿ* (New Case)

It must fulfill four conditions:

(a) The *ʿilla* must be applicable to the new case because establishing the legal ruling in a new case is subsequent to the application of its rationale. For example, our [Mālikī] companions compare bones of dead animals to its flesh by establishing both as impure.[32] Ḥanafīs disapprove qualifying bones to be dead, but our companions counter argue that life resides in bones based on Allah's saying, "Who will give life to bones while they are disintegrated?" (Q. 36: 78). Bones are susceptible to life and can therefore be described as dead.

(b) The rule of a new case should not have been enacted prior in time to the original case. Were a new case proved prior to its original case, the ruling would, thus, be established prior to the application of its *ʿilla*. For example, our [Mālikī] companions compare ablution to *tayamum* in their both wanting of an intention though ablution has been enacted prior to *tayamum*. It may be proved by syllogistic reasoning. Had not intention been obligatory for ablution, it would not have been proved obligatory in *tayamum*.

(c) The new case must not be covered by a text of either a general or a specific indication. An instance of a general indication is when the evidence covers the ruling of an *aṣl* and that of the *far*ʿ. For example, apple is proved to be as usurious as wheat by analogy [because both are edible]. Moreover, the ruling is further proved by the general indication of the Prophet's saying, "Do not exchange foodstuffs for foodstuffs [except in exact equivalence in amount, when the properties transacted be in the respective possession of buyer and seller before they part company and when the agreement does not mention any delay].[33]" This ruling includes both the original and the new cases. Therefore, the original case is not more worthy to be covered by the text.

An example of a specific indication of a text is the Ḥanafīs' view on the obligation of offering new ablution after vomiting or on having a nose bleeding by comparing these two cases to the rest of ablution invalidators. They further based their opinion on the Prophet's saying, "Whoever vomits or has a nose-bleed must perform ablution.[34]"

(d) The ʿ*Illa* must be applicable to the new case in the same way as it is applicable to original case without having any discrepancy. [An example of discrepancy is] like extending the ruling of marriage to sale or the ruling of a sale contract to marriage by means of analogy. Sale is based on contention while marriage is based on clemency and showing respect.

Therefore, Shafiʿīs extend the invalidity of a marriage contract which includes the giving of an undetermined slave as a dowry to the sale contract where the price is an undetermined salve. The invalidity of the latter is decided by consensus. But our [Mālikī] companions maintain that sale is based on contention while the affairs of marriage are based on showing leniency. Dowry is not intended to be an equivalent for a woman or paid in recompense for her. It is, however, called a gift by Allah. Therefore, it is like a gift which cannot be invalidated by just being undetermined.

3.1.2.4. *Ḥukm* (Legal Decision)

We will discuss it at the following issues:

(a) It must be a legal ruling because analogy is a sharia-based evidence. Therefore, analogy is not applicable to language-based rules. It is, however, a controversial issue, such as calling a *nabbāsh* (one who steals the shroud of the dead) a thief by analogy because both of them take away the property of another without his knowledge and calling *nabīdh* (date juice) wine by analogy since a grape juice is called wine when it [intoxicates and] obscures mind.

(b) A ruling based on a frequent habit cannot be proved through analogy. For example, our [Mālikī] companions maintain that a woman may have menses during her pregnancy since menstruation can be compared to vaginal discharge in the sense that both are usually discharged by the same woman. A young girl and an old woman who do not have menstruation cannot not usually have a vaginal discharge. This analogy is, however, procured through habit, which is not often consistent.

(c) A definitive ruling cannot be proved through analogy.[35] For example, Shāfiʿīs sought to prove that *basmala* as a verse of each chapter of the Quran [with the exception of *sura* 9] like other verses of the Quran because it was written in the *muṣḥafs* [copied at the time of the caliph ʿUthmān] like other verses.[36]

(d) *Uṣūlīs* differed on a negative ruling whether it is established through analogical deduction or by means of *istiṣḥāb*.[37] Whoever based it on a *sharia* proof attempted to prove it through analogy. Whoever regarded it a ruling proved through a rational proof did not use analogy. The erudite among *uṣūlīs* establish [a negative ruling] through *qiyās al-dalāla* (analogy by inference)[38] but they do not prove it through *qiyās al-ʿilla* (analogy where an effective cause is explicitly provided). For example, our [Mālikī] companions maintain that *zakat* is not obligatory for golden ornaments like slave taken for home serving and clothes taken for personal use. But the opponents of this view maintain that the rule proposed is not *sharia* based and therefore, analogy cannot be applicable.

3.1.3. Types of *Qiyās Al-Ṭard*

In a coextensive analogy, the common attribute between an *aṣl* and its respective *farʿ* may be (1) an overall attribute which is identical in both the original and the new cases. This is called *lā fāriq* (analogy where there is no trace of a discrepancy between *aṣl* and *farʿ*) or is also called *qiyās fī maʿna al-aṣl* [where the *aṣl* and *farʿ* are of the same meaning]. (2) Where *aṣl* and *farʿ* have a partial commonality. It is further classified into (a) *qiyās al-ʿilla,* where both have the same [exact] rationale and (b) *qiyās al-Dalāla* where both have an indication that refers to a rationale.

3.1.3.1. Analogy of No Discrepancy

It is when there is equality between the original and the new case. The *ʿilla* exists in the *aṣl* because its ruling is proved for it. It becomes common between *aṣl* and *farʿ* whether it expounds commonality in whole or partially. For example, Ḥanafīs maintained that a creditor has to pay *zakat.* They reached this conclusion by comparing accreditor to one who is free from debts, that is, there is no difference between *aṣl* and *far*ʿ except debt which is only found in the new case. If it does not exist in the new case, both *aṣl* and *far*ʿ should be identical. Debt, [according to them] is not an impediment for the obligation of *zakat.* It is not held as an impediment for *zakat* on crops or cattle. Since debt is not an impediment of *zakat* and no other differences can be traced between *aṣl* and *far*ʿ, commonality is identified in all other phases including the ʿ*illa,* which is found in the *aṣl.* Therefore, both cases must have something in common.

Another example is the case of non-Muslim warriors usurping Muslims' properties. Shāfiʿīs maintain that ownership is not transferred [by the act of usurp], but Ḥanafīs hold that it is transferred. According to our [Mālikī] companions, usurp constitutes a probable unreal ownership.

Shāfiʿīs argue that the majority of scholars and Ḥanafīs had consensus on the fact that a usurper does not own what he takes illegally. A non-Muslim must not own what he usurps. There should be no difference between them except that the *aṣl* is a Muslim and the *far*ʿ is a non-Muslim. Being a Muslim, however, is not an impediment of ownership and being a non-Muslim is not an ʿ*illa* for ownership. Therefore, there is no reason for a Muslim or a non-Muslim usurpers to own what they have taken illegally.

3.1.3.2. *Qiyās Al-ʿIlla* (Analogy Whose Rationale Is Indicated in the Text)

It is also called *qiyās al-ma*ʿ*na* (analogy based on a common meaning between the *aṣl* and the *far*ʿ) and *qiyās al-shabah* (analogy of resemblance). We have presented their examples when we discussed the ways of extracting ʿ*illa.*

3.1.3.3. Analogy by Allusion

Qiyās al-Dalala (analogy by inference or allusion) is a type of analogy where an *aṣl* is not compared to a *far*ʿ by a definite ʿ*illa* but through an indication which refers ʿ*illa.* According to some *uṣūlīs,* it is a type of reasoning which will be discussed later.

3.1.4. Conclusion

Objection is raised [against the application of] *qiyās* [in certain cases] either due to the absence of the ruling in the original case, the absence of an ʿ*illa* at the *aṣl,* its unsuitability to be a valid effective cause, its being opposed by another attribute which may be better suited to be the ʿ*illa,* the inapplicability of an effective cause to the *far*ʿ or the *far*ʿ having an ʿ*illa* contrary to that existing in the *aṣl.* These are six objections.

The reason that objections are confined to those six is that when a ruling is established in the *aṣl*, the *aṣl* has an attribute which suits to be a valid *ʿilla* it stands as a rationale by itself, the *ʿilla* is applicable to the new case and the new case is free of conflict with that *ʿilla,* [therefore, by the fulfillment of those requirements,] an analogy is valid. However, objections are only raised based on one of the following reasons:

3.1.4.1. When the Ruling Does Not Exist in the Original Case

For example, Shāfiʿī scholars and some of our [Mālikī] companions maintain that a vessel licked by a swine has to be washed seven times because it is a filthy animal. They extended the ruling of a dog to swine. But Ḥanafīs do not apply this ruling to the original case, that is, washing a vessel licked by a dog seven times. Shāfiʿīs, however, established the ruling of the original case by reference to the Prophet's saying, "If a dog licks the vessel of any one of you, let him wash it seven times.[39]"

3.1.4.2. When the *ʿIlla* Does Not Exist in the *Aṣl*

For example, Shāfiʿī scholars and those who followed them of our [Mālikī] companions maintain that it is obligatory to offer ablution in a sequential order. They argue that it is an act of worship which may be invalidated by the occurrence of *a ḥadath* (ritual impurity) so that a sequential order is obligatory by comparing it to *salat* through analogy. Ḥanfīs and those who followed them among the Mālikīs do not admit that the effective cause exists in the *aṣl* that is, *salat.* They maintain that *ḥadath* does not [directly] affect the validity of *salat.* It only affects one's state of purity. When purity is invalidated, *ṣalat* [subsequently] becomes void

The first group counter argue that *salat* is invalidated by *ḥadath*, since the one who offers *salat* [without ablution or *tayammum*] due to the inaccessibility of both water and dust has his prayer invalid upon the occurrence of a *hadath* though he is not in a state of ritual purity. Moreover, according to Ḥanafī scholars, when *ḥadath* occurs involuntarily during *salat,* one has to offer ablution and carry on his prayers. This is identical to our view regarding one whose nose bleeds during prayers. But if one voluntarily passes a wind upon voluntarily losing his ritual purity, he has to offer ablution in addition to resuming his prayer. It proves that *ḥadath* directly affects the validity of *ṣalat.*

3.1.4.3. When an Attribute is Not Fitting to Be a Proper *ʿIlla*

For example, Ḥanafī scholars maintain that when a slave girl becomes free while being married to a free man, she has the choice to either continue a marriage contract or dissolute it. But our [Mālikī] companions do not admit that her emancipation is the *ʿilla* for giving her option to either continue or dissolute marriage. Ḥanafī scholars maintain that the text of the Prophet's *hadith* provided this *ʿilla* [when he said to Barīra], "You [have been emancipated and] became in possession of yourself so that you may choose.[40]" The text of a *hadith* is source for deriving an effective cause. Generally speaking, this is one of the most intricate objections on which many questions arise. They are ten in number but are mostly elaborated in large compendiums [of *fiqh*].

3.1.4.4. When an *Aṣl* Contains Conflicting Attributes Each is Valid to Be an *ʿIlla*

However, it has two major types:

(A) The original case may contain another attribute which fits to be a fully independent *ʿilla*.
(B) The original case may contain an attribute which fits to be a part of the *ʿilla*.

An example of the first [type] is the Shāfiʿīs' view that apple is an edible staff so it is considered one of the items where usurious gain is prohibited like grain. But our [Mālikī] companions argue that edibility is not the effective cause but [it is that] grain has been one of the items where usurious gain is prohibited due to its being a nutritious substance which maintains life and growth. It does not exist in apples. The answer of Shāfiʿī scholars is to maintain that edibility is the effective cause by basing their view on the Prophet's saying, "Do not sell food for food [except equivalent in weight or amount].[41]" They have to show that the text tacitly implies the *ʿilla*.

An example for the second type is the view of our [Mālikī] companions who maintained that retaliation is due on one who kills another by use of something heavy [such as a rock] as being classified a purely intentional homicide. Retaliation is effective by extending the ruling applied to the type of murder where a sharp instrument [such as a knife] is used. Our companions maintain that intentional homicide is the effective cause of retaliation and leads to the attainment of its objective, that is, deterrence. Therefore, this [attribute] must be considered an independent [*ʿilla*].

3.1.4.5. When an *ʿIlla* Cannot Be Identified in the New Case

For example, our [Mālikī] companions maintain that hiring someone to offer *hajj* on behalf of another is permissible since *hajj* is an act of worship that may be offered by proxy so that it may be offered by hiring someone to do it. It is extended by means of analogy by comparing it to the act of hiring someone to tailor a dress.

But the companions of Abū Ḥanīfa argue that they do not admit the permissibility of offering *hajj* by proxy. Our [Mālikī] companions counter argue that it has been proved through the report of the man who was heard by the Prophet as offering *hajj* on behalf of Shubrumah. The Prophet asked him, "Have you offered *hajj* on yourself?" He said, "No." Then the Prophet commanded him to offer hajj for himself first before offering it on behalf of Shubrumah.[42]

3.1.4.6. When the New Case Includes an Attribute That Conflicts with the Ruling Reached through Analogy

For example, the Shāfiʿīs maintain that a creditor has to pay *zakat* by comparing him to the one who does not have debts since both possess the minimum *zakattable* amount. Our Mālikī companions and the fellows of Abū Ḥanīfa state that the new case includes an attribute that conflicts with the ruling reached through analogy. that is, the debt due on a creditor. *Zakat* cannot be due on him since debtors has due rights on wealth. But Shāfiʿīs counter argue that debt does not conflict with the ruling we have reached through analogy since debt has not to be paid from a creditor's property but it is his responsibility to pay it. Therefore, if such a property is exposed to damage by the creditor through other causes, debt is still due on the creditor [not specifically contingent to the wealth]. But *zakat* has to be paid from wealth itself. It is not due on the debtor's credit. Therefore, if a *zaktable* wealth destroys without any intervention of the owner, it is waivered.

3.2. *Qiyās al-ʿAks* (Analogy by Coexclusiveness)

Qiyās al-ʿAks is to extend the opposite rule of the original case to the new case due to discrepancy in their respective effective causes. We will give examples to make it clear.

The first example is the view of our [Mālikī] companions who maintain that ablution has not to be offered again upon having excessive vomiting as it not due upon [execration of] a little vomiting. The opposite of this is urination. Little execration of urine invalidates ablution exactly as much amounts thereof. Our [Mālikī] companions hold that excessive vomiting does not invalidate ablution but Ḥanafīs regard it as an invalidator of ablution. Our companions extend the opposite rule of urine to vomiting. They base the discrepancy between urine and vomiting on their discrepant effective causes.[43] Despite of their dispute on the discrepancy of *ʿillas* in both cases, both groups [of Ḥanafīs and Mālikīs] agree that ablution is not obligatory after little vomiting but it is due on little urine.

Ḥanafīs may argue by using the same method of analogical deduction to maintain that sleeping does not require ablution though Shāfiʿīs regarded it an invalidator of ablution since it is a direct cause of *ḥadath* according to some scholars amongst them while it is a probable cause of *ḥadath* according to others. Ḥanafīs state that when ablution is not due on much or little sleeping its ruling should be opposite to urine which necessitates renewing ablution either when it is much or little.

The second example is the view of our [Mālikī] companions and the fellows of Abū Ḥanīfa who maintain that fasting is a prerequisite for the validity of *iʿtikāf* (spiritual retreat in a mosque). They said that when a person vows to fast during the period of his *iʿtikāf*, it becomes incumbent on him to enjoin fasting then. When he does include fasting in his intention, it still becomes incumbent on him when he vows to make *iʿtikāf*. This is proved in contradiction to prayer. When one vows to offer prayers during his *iʿtikāf* it does not become incumbent on him to do so during the period of his *iʿtikāf*. He is not, therefor, obliged to do prayers if he does not stipulate it as a part of his *iʿtikfāf*.

The third example is the Ḥanfī's position that retaliation is not due on murder by use of a heavy object [such as by throwing a person with a heavy rock or hitting him by a car]. They claim that retaliation is not due on murder by use of a small or big heavy instruments because it is, by opposite, due on killing by small and big piercing instruments [such as a knife or a gun].

3.3. *Istidlāl* (Reasoning)[44]

Reasoning may be attained by [a relationship of] consequence between two practical legal decisions or by determining a state of incongruity between them. In case [the relation is that] of a consequence, it is of three types:

1. A practical legal decision (*ḥukm*) attained as a consequence of [the existence of] a rationale (*ʿilla*).
2. A rationale attained in consequence of a legal decision.
3. A legal decision is elicited in consequence of another legal ruling.

In case it is deduced through incongruities, it is further sub-divided into three types:

1. Contradiction traced between two legal decisions either positive or privative
2. Contradiction between two positive legal decisions.
3. Contradiction between two privative legal decisions.

3.3.1. Rationale Deduced from a Legal Decision

For example, our [Mālikī] fellows argue that *witr* can be offered on a ride. Prayers that can only be offered on a ride are supererogatory prayers. As a consequence, *witr* is a supererogatory prayer. The possibility of being observed on a ride is a consequence of being *nafl* (supererogatory) and one of its rationales. Therefore, obligatory ordinances cannot be performed while riding. In case we extend this ruling to the two supererogatory *rak'as* of *fajr*, it should be then termed as *qiyās al-dalāla* (analogy by reasoning).[45]

Similarly, our [Mālikī] fellows and Shāfiʿīs argue that manumission of a *mukātab* (a slave who pays his master off to get emancipated) cannot be legally efficient to be a penance for a vow because he is emancipated by other means. Any emancipation that occurs through other means cannot stand as a penance. We confirmed that he is not qualified for a penance because he is free by the contract he signed with his master and he has the right to get married and to possess his earnings. This is a consequence of the contract he abides by. In case he is set free [as a penance of a vow], he still owes to pay off his master.

We prove that something exists because its consequences exist and we prove that something does not exist because of the absence of its consequences. For example, Shāfiʿī scholars maintain that *fuḍūlī* sale (selling a property which belongs to another) is invalid since it does not entail a transfer of ownership and it has not consequently been effective initially. A consequence of a [valid] contract is the transfer of ownership. Conceptual rationales are not intended for themselves but they are meant for their consequences.

3.3.2. Allusion Reached by Correlating a Rationale to a Legal Decision

For example, our [Mālikī] fellows maintain the validity of selling merchandise not present at the place of a sale contract because it is lawful. They based their view on the saying of Allah, "Allah has permitted trade and has forbidden interest." (Q. 2: 275). Since it is lawful it must [consequently] be legally valid. Being lawful is, therefore, the *'illa* of its validity.

Similarly, Shāfiʿī scholars and some of our [Mālikī] companions hold that profits procured from a usurped property must be given to the owner because the property [itself] is legally his by consensus of all scholars. If the profit is the right of the one from whom it has been taken wrongfully, it must consequently go to him.

The existence of a legal decision (*ḥukm*) is an indication for the existence of its rationale. Similarly, the absence of a rationale indicates the non-existence of a *ḥukm*. For example, Shāfʿī scholars maintain that if A admits that he owes a property for B but B fails to prove his right, he does not deserve to take anything. This is based on the fact that when one fails to attribute someone to his wedlock, he does not consequently have the right to claim [a share of his estate].

3.3.3. Allusion Reached by Identifying an Identical Rationale for Two Rulings

A conclusion has to be a legal decision while the premise can be a legal or an empirical ruling. [An example for] the empirical, is the position of Shāfiʿīs and our [Mālikī] companions that bones of dead animals are impure because they hurt when being amputated. Any part that hurts when being cut off a living animal turns impure after death. Therefore, bones of a dead animal are impure. To explain this, life is the cause of a pain feeling and [its lacking] is the cause of impurity after death.

An example for a legal ruling which sets as a premise for a reasoning is the Shāfiʿīs' position that *zakat* is obligatory for a creditor. He has to extract it from the property liable to *zakat* as it has to paid for cattle and crops. Both cases are the result of the same *ʿilla*, that is, possessing the minimum *zakattable* ratio. Both rules [of obligation with regard to *zakat* on property and on cattle and crops] are legal decisions.

Similarly, our [Mālikī] fellows maintain that one who is coerced to murder another has to be retaliated because killing under coercion is prohibited and incurs a sin by *ijmāʿ*. Being a sin and retaliation are both two legal decisions effected by the same rationale, that is, the responsibility of a murderer addressed by the law.

3.3.4. Allusion Reached by Identifying a Contradiction between Two Legal Decisions in Both Positive and Privative Cases

For example, our [Mālikī] fellows hold that it is not obligatory for a creditor to pay zakat because in this case he has to pay it and is contradictorily presumed to receive it. To explain, he is either affluent or poor. In case he is affluent, he has to give zakat and it is prohibited to receive it from others. In case he is poor he is allowed to receive a part of zakat and it is not due on him. When contradiction occurs between two legal decisions in both positive and privative cases and one of these two decisions has been proved that is,that is, it is permissible by consensus for him to receive zakath, the other decision that is, his obligation to pay it, cannot be proved.

3.3.5. Allusion Reached by Identifying a Contradiction between Two Positive Legal Decisions

For example, Shāfiʿīs maintain that sperm is not impure because there is a contradiction between holding it impure and the permissibility of offering prayer [in a cloth] smeared with it. As the observance of prayer is permissible when one is smeared with sperm, it is [consequently] not impure. Offering prayer in this case is permissible based on the report of ʿAisha who said, "The Prophet (may God exalt his mention) used to wipe sperm from his clothes by the stem of juncus, then he offered prayer therein.[46]"

3.3.6. Allusion Reached by Identifying a Contradiction between Two Privative Legal Decisions

For example, our [Mālikī] companions maintained that dead animals of a sea are pure because they permitted to eat. Purity and prohibition to eat are not congruous, since every impure is prohibited to eat and whatever is permissible to eat is pure. The dead animal of a sea is lawful to eat. This is based on the Prophet's saying, "Its water is pure and its 'dead meat' is permissible [to eat].[47]" Therefore, the dead animal of sea is pure. This is the conclusion of our discussion on reasoning. This is further the completion of our discussion on the first category [of independent legislative source].

Notes

1. *Aṣl* refers to the original case of analogy. It signifies a ruling sought by direct recourse to a text of the Quran or the Sunna and is extendable to be applicable to further new cases.
2. *Dawrān* (rotation) is an *uṣūlī* concept which means that if a certain quality of the legal ruling exists, the law too exists along with it and if it does not exist, the law should not exist (Salamī, 1999, 75). Rotation may be coextensive (*ṭardī*) or coexclusive (*ʿaksī*). The former is an extension of the legal ruling of an original case to a new case due to the existence of a common effective cause. The latter is the nonexistence of a ruling due to its nonexistence. Both means of rotation are applicable to one and the same case or to two different objects. An example of the former is grape juice which turns into prohibited by the existence of the cause, that is intoxication. It turns permissible when intoxication is not extant. Rotation applicable to two different objects is illustrated by the Ḥanafīs who identified the cause of regarding a commodity as usurious if it is sold in measurement. Therefore, they regarded plaster like wheat by confirming that both have the same effective cause, that is being sole in measurement. It is coextensive rotation. If we compare cars to wheat, the nonexistence of the effective cause in cars confirms that it does not have the same ruling, that is being usurious.
3. It is defined as the extension from an original case to a new case because both are equal in containing the same common effective cause (Sulamī, 2005, 143).

4. *Aṣl* is an issue or case which a ruling is given in the text and which analogy seeks to extend to a new case.
5. It is the rationale common between the original case which is provided in the text and the new case on which the text is silent.
6. The new case on which a ruling is wanting.
7. The tenth day of Muḥarram; the first month of lunar calendar.
8. It is a husband's foreswearing he will not have sexual intercourse with his wife, either for an unrestricted period or for more than four months (Miṣrī, 1982, 219).
9. Bukhārī, 2001, 7, 101; Muslim, n.d., 2, 1525.
10. This is an error from the author. The correct name is Sahla bint Suhayl.
11. Bukhārī, 2001, 2, 75; Muslim, n.d., 2, 865.
12. Aḥmad, 2001, 39, 64; Nasā'ī, 1986, 4, 78.
13. Where a person is found slain in any district, and it is not known who was the murderer, and his heir demands a satisfaction for his blood from the inhabitants of the district, or from any number of them not spccificdl1y named, fifty of the inhabitants, selected, by the heir, must be put to their oaths, and depose to this effect, "by God I did not kill him nor do I know his murderer." (Mirghinānī, n.d., 4, 655).
14. In both cases a wife gets divorced promptly by the issuance of both phrases. As long as menstruation will certainly occur, delaying effectiveness of divorce will make it similar to contemporary marriage where both parties consent to remain in *marriage* for a limited period of time.
15. For example, we can extend the ruling of wheat to apple by considering both as usurious. This is based on the identification of common effective cause between them, that is edibility. Wheat is an *aṣl* while apple is a *far'* and edibility is the *'illah*. In case we need to extend the rule of apple to quince, we should regard apple, which used to be a *far'* in the first case, as the *aṣl* of the second (here called intermediary). The *'illa* sought between apple and quince in this case is that both are weighed. Therefore, the *'illa* which related quince to apple that is weight does not exist between apple and wheat. This is the reason such an example of analogy is futile.
16. The word used here has to be added because Mālikī scholars regard water which has been used for ritual purification can be used again. It may be one of their arguments for the validity of reusing water for ritual purification.
17. We should note that the *'illa* between analogy A which related a change by algae and a change by a change caused by dust is not identical to the rationale that relates the change by dust to the change by a pure water. The former's *'illa* is emergency while the latter's is purity of an additive.
18. *Mukatab* is a slave who consents with his master to free him upon the full redemption of himself by installments.
19. Give and take sale wihout verbally expressing offer and consent.
20. A concubine who gives a birth to a child and is attributed by her master and becomes free upon his death.
21. Muslim, n.d., 3, 1561; abū Dāwūd, n.d., 3, 99; ibn Ḥibbān, 1988, 3, 250.
22. Aḥmad, 2001, 21, 91; abū Dāwūd, n.d., 2, 220.
23. Bukhārī, 2001 2, 75; Muslim, n.d., 2, 865.
24. Aḥmad, 2001, 39, 64; Nasā'ī, 1986, 4, 78.
25. The wording of this report does not exist in any of Hadith compilations. The closest text of it is 'A'ishah's report related by Bukhārī, 2001, 7, 43; Muslim, n.d., 2, 1103. The text of hadith is as follows: "The Prophet gave us our choice and we chose him so that was not reckoned anything [i.e., divorce]."

26. Aḥmad, 2001, 37, 211; abū Dāwūd, n.d., 1, 19; Trimidhī, 1998, 1, 151; ibn Māja, n.d., 1, 239; Nasāʾī, 1986, 1, 187.
27. Bukhārī, 2001, 4, 170; Muslim, n.d., 2, 1207.
28. Aḥmad, 2001, 3, 100; Muslim, n.d., 2, 1020; abū Dāwūd, n.d., 2, 251; ibn Māja, n.d., 3, 371; Trimidhī, 1998, 2, 519.
29. Bukhārī, 2001, 3, 35; Muslim, n.d., 2, 804.
30. Muslim, 2, 781.
31. Abū Dāwūd, n.d., 1, 273; Trimidhī, 1998, 1, 509; Nasāʾī, 1986, 3, 26.
32. Effective cause in this example is death without legal slaughtering. It rendered both bones and meat of dead animals impure according to the view of the majority of scholars.
33. Aḥmad, 2001, 45, 223; Muslim, n.d., 3, 1214; ibn Ḥibbān, 1988, 11, 385; Dāraquṭnī, 2004, 3, 420.
34. It is related by ibn Māja (n.d., 2, 281, but it has been graded as *ḍaʿīf.* The exact wording of the hadith reads as follows: "Whoever vomits, bleeds through the nose, or released *Madhiy* (urethral discharge) should go, perform ablution and then complete his prayer [by continuing from where he had stopped at] on condition that he does not speak in the process."
35. The author refers to *qiyās* as a legal evidence he does not refer to analogy in the field of logic.
36. Proving that a specific phrase or a sentence is a part of the Quran cannot be proved through a speculative evidence or evidence based on reasoning. It is only proved through a definitive evidence.
37. A legal ruling may be positive such as stating that washing a vessel polluted by a dog's saliva is obligatory or drinking *nabīdh* is prohibited or it may negative such as marinating that the payment of *zakat* on golden ornaments is not obligatory. For the former, it can be proved by means of analogy. Scholars differed on the latter. Some of them maintained that it can be proved by analogy which is a *sharʿī* proof or by *istiṣḥāb* through a presumption of continuity of its *status quo ante,* which is a rational proof of *sharia*. In the case of golden ornaments, they further say that as long as no proof is found to prove that they are *zakatable*, they are presumed to remain free from any obligations.
38. The correlation between an original case and the new case accoridng to *qiyās al-dalāl*a is based on on an inference to the existence of an effective cause. For example, comparing *nabīdh* to wine because both of them have common smell which necessarily correlated with intoxication.
39. Bukhārī, 2001, 1, 45; Muslim, n.d., 1, 234.
40. Aḥmad, 2001, 40, 58; Bukhārī, 2001, 3, 71; Tirmidhī, 1998, 2, 452.
41. Muslim, n.d. 3, 1210.
42. Abū Dāwūd, n.d., 2, 162; ibn Māja, n.d., 4, 147; ibn Khuzayma, n.d., 4, 345; ibn Ḥibbān, 1988, 9, 299.
43. The effective cause of the impurity of urine is different from that of vomiting. Urine invalidates ablution while vomiting does not.
44. *Istidlāl* which is meant by the author is a reasoning by consequence. It is defined by *uṣūlīs as* a relationship between two rulings without discerning a rationale (al-Sarīrī, 2012, 582).
45. It is possible to make it an example of *qiyās al-dalāla* by making *witr* an original case and the two *rakʿas* of *fajr* as a new case. The common attribute is the permissibility of being offered on a ride. There is not rationale between the *aṣl* and the *farʿ*, but their relationship has been based on a legal determination.
46. Aḥmad, 2001, 43, 179.
47. Abū Dāwūd, n.d. 1, 21; Tirmidhī, 1998, 1, 125; Nasāʾī, 1986, 1, 50. Ibn Ḥibbān, 1988, 4, 49.

CHAPTER FOUR

Evidence Which Is Comprehensive of a Proof

4.1. Ijmaʿ

The first type includes a preface and four questions:

4.1.1. Preface

Ijmāʿ is an authoritative legal evidence according to the view of the majority[1] of scholars. They based their view on Allah's saying, "And whoever opposes the Messenger after guidance has become clear to him and follows other than the way of the believers—We will give him what he has taken and drive him into Hell, and evil it is as a destination." (Q. 4: 115). So, whoever violates consensus and follows other than the way of the believers he is liable to this punishment. Moreover, the Messenger of Allah (may God exalt his mention) said, "My community shall never agree on an error.[2]" There are many *mutwātir* reports,[3] which confirm the infallibility of Muslim community to unanimously agree on an error.

4.1.2. [Questions Which Raised Disagreement among Scholars]

4.1.2.1. [Tacit Consensus]

When a Companion or a Follower of the Prophet passes a legal decision in the presence of a congregation without being contradicted or opposed [by anyone of his time], though it spread and became known for all, can we regard it an authoritative consensus? The majority of scholars deemed it a type of a speculative evidence, not a definitive consensus. For example, a woman who has been given in marriage to two men through two consecutive contracts concluded by two different guardians and second marriage is consumed without knowing that she is already married, she has to remain with the second man based on the judgment of ʿUmar who passed a legal decision in the presence of the Prophet's Companions without receiving opposition from one of them. Similarly, Muʿāwiya passed the same decision for al-Ḥasan ibn ʿAlī against his son Yazīd ibn Muʿawiya at the presence of the Prophet's Companions without receiving any opposition from them. Contrary to this view, Ibn ʿAbdul-Ḥakam maintained that the first one to conclude marriage deserves to be the husband.

4.1.2.2 Consensus Breached by a *Ṣaḥābī*

When all the Companions of the Prophet agreed on a legal decision but only one of them showed opposition, could their view be authoritative?

The most preponderant view [of scholars] is that their opinion is authoritative because it can be hardly presumed that a single person's view overweigh the opinion held by a massive majority. For example, our [Mālikī] fellows maintain that adjustment (*ʿawl*[4]) is employed in cases where the estate is not enough to give everyone their full shares. They based their view on the consensus of the Prophet's Companions, but Ibn ʿAbbās has been reported as opposing them in this issue. They further maintained that a deep sleep invalidates ablution. They based their view on the consensus of the Prophet's Companions with the exception of Abū Mūsa al-Ashʿarī.

4.1.2.3. [Consensus Past Discord]

When scholars of a specific generation differ on a legal decision [into two groups] but their succeeding generation unanimously agree on a view one group, can we regard it a type of authoritative consensus? The most preponderant view among scholars is that it is an authoritative consensus.

For example, our [Mālikī] fellows maintain that a concubine who became pregnant due to having a sexual relation with her master is not permissible to be sold. They based their view on the consensus of the *tābiʿūn* though the Prophet's Companions differed on that.

4.1.2.4. Consensus of the *Medinese*

The consensus of the people of Medina is authoritative according to the view of Mālik, but others differed with him. For example, our [Mālikī] fellows maintain that the phrases of *adhān* are fifteen and those of Iqāma are eleven and exact amount of *mudd*[5] and *ṣā*ʿ and other transmitted decisions [related through generations of Madani scholars]. This is the conclusion of our discussion on the topic of consensus.

4.2. Uncorroborated Opinion of a *Ṣaḥābī*

The second type of evidence that is comprehensive of a proof is the saying of a Companion. Scholars differed on whether to regard it an evidence or not. Those who maintain that it is an authoritative evidence based their view on the Prophet's saying, "My Companions are like stars. Whomsoever of them that you follow will guide you to the right path.[6]"

One of its examples is the position of our [Mālikī] fellows who maintain that if a husband addresses his four wives by saying that they are all prohibited to him like his mother, he is to pay one expiation. They based their view on the statement of ʿUmar who is reported as saying, "Whoever swears an oath of *ẓihār* to four wives is to pay one single expiation.[7]"

The view of Abū Ḥanīfa is that when the view of a Companion conflicts with default norms, it becomes authoritative because it is an indication that his view is based on a text. If his view is based on default norms, his view cannot be authoritative because there is a possibility that he reached it through his own personal reasoning. For example, ʿĀʾisha stated that the maximum period a fetus can remain in his mother's abdomen is two years. Such a determination cannot be reached through personal experience. An example of a Companion's statement, which is based on analogy is Ibn ʿAbbās' saying, "two brothers cannot be called *brothers.*[8]" This is based on language standards. This the conclusion of our discussion on the second type and the end of our book.

Praise is due to Allah the One Who bestows of His support and guidance and all prayers are upon our Prophet Mohammad and upon his family, prayers, which will continue [up to the Day of Judgment].

Notes

1. The author used the word *jumhūr* which is translated as 'the majority', but it is not accurate. It is well known that *ijmā*ʿ is an authoritative proof according to the view of the unanimous agreement of all Muslim scholars except al-Naẓẓām, the well-known Muʿtazilī scholar. His disagreement with other scholars does not affect the validity of *ijmā*ʿ since his discord came later after recording the unanimous agreement of all Muslim scholars. Moreover, there is much disagreement on whether he disagreed with Muslim scholars or not.

2. The wording of this hadith as quoted by the author does not exist in major Hadith compilations. The closest report is Anas ibn Mālik's where the Prophet is reported as saying, " My nation will not unite on misguidance, so if you see them differing, follow the great majority." It is related by ibn Māja, n.d., 5, 96; ibn abi ʿAṣim, 1991, 1, 103.
3. A report is classified as *mutāwatir* if it was reported by a significant number of narrators at each level, in the chain of transmission, thus reaching the succeeding generation through multiple paths of transmission leading back to its source.
4. It is when shares of all heirs exceed the estate. In this case, the estate has to be readjusted through redistribution of shares.
5. *Mud* and *ṣāʿ* are volume measurements. The former is estimated to be almost 0.51 liters and the latter is almost 2.03 liters.
6. Ibn ʿAbdul-Barr, *Jāmiʿ*, 1994, 4, 1166; ibn Ḥazm, *n.d.*, 5, 64.
7. ʿAbdur-Razzāq, *Muṣannaf*, 1983, 6, 438; Bayhaqī: 2003, 7, 630.
8. He means that the number two cannot be called plural. He refers to (Q. 4: 11).

Glossary of Terms

ʾAdāʾ: Prompt performance.

Adhān: *Call to prayer.*

Aḥād: *Solitary* hadith. A report which does not fulfill the requirements of a *mutawātir*.

ʿĀmm: A word which applies to many things, not limited in number, and includes everything to which it is applicable.

Aṣl: *Original case. It is* an issue or case which a ruling is given in the text and which analogy seeks to extend to a new case.

ʿAṣr: *Afternoon prayer.*

ʿAwl: It is when shares of all heirs exceed the estate. In this case, the estate has to be readjusted through redistribution of shares.

ʿAwra: *Parts of a Muslim male of female's body which must be covered.*

Bayʿ al-gharar: Sales on which there is a chance or risk.

Bayʿ wa salaf: '*Selling and lending*,' sale transaction in which a seller says: 'I shall sell you this product for such and such price if you lend me so much money.

Dalīl al-khiṭāib: *See mafhūm al-mukhālafa*

Dhimmi: a non-Muslim living under the auspice of a Muslim state.

Dirham: Silver coin used in pre and early Islam. It weighs 3.15 g. according to Ḥanafī scholars and 2.975 according to the majority of Muslim scholars.

Faḥwā al-khiṭāb: See *Mafhūm al-mwāfaqa*
Farʿ: The new case on which a ruling is wanting.
Fiqh: Islamic law.
Fitna: T*rial or civil war.*
Fuḍūlī sale: Selling a property which belongs to another.
Ghāya: A grammatical structure used to indicate the end of something or a period of time (*intihā' al-ghāyah*) such as the example, 'he purchased the land extending from the mosque *ilā* (to) the canal'.
Ḥadath: S*tate of ritual impurity.*
Ḥaqīqa: To use of a word in in its primary meaning such as using the word 'lion' to refer to the ferocious beast.
Ḥukm: L*egal determination, decision or ruling.*
Ibāḥa: P*ermissibility.*
Ighlāq: *Straitness.*
Iḥrām: State of consecration to perform major or minor pilgrimage.
Īlāʾ: a husband's foreswearing he will not have sexual intercourse with his wife, either for an unrestricted period or for more than four months (Miṣrī, 1982, 219).
ʿIlla: It is the rationale common between the original case which is provided in the text and the new case on which the text is silent.
Inqiṭāʿ: Interruption occurring in the chain of transmission because of a missing link between two narrators.
Intibādh: Adding raisins and dates to water to better change its taste.
Irsāl: R*elating a report to the Prophet without mentioning the name of the Companion who received it.*
Isnād: C*hain of transmission.*
Istidlāl: Reasoning may be attained by [a relationship of] consequence between two practical legal decisions or by determining a state of incongruity between them.
Istiṣḥāb: A *rule of law and reason, whose existence or non-existence had been proven in the past, and which are presumed to remain so for lack of evidence to establish any change.* (Kamali, 1991, 259).
Iʿtikāf: S*piritual retreat in a mosque.*
Janāba: State of major ritual impurity.
Jizya: Tribute.
Kaffāra: *Penance.*

Khāṣṣ: A word or a phrase, which is applied to a limited number of things.

Khiyār al-majlis: The right to nullify sale agreement at any time before purchasing parties physically part company, or both waive the right to cancel, or until one of them cancels the sale (Miṣrī, 1982, 380).

Li'ān: Public imprecation. It consists of the Islamic magistrate (or his equivalent) telling the husband to repeat four times, "I testify by Allah that I am truthful in charging her with adultery.

Madhhab: S*chool of law.*

Mafhūm al-mukhālafa: Inference based on the assumption that a case whose judgment was not mentioned in a text must be decided in a manner opposite to the one mentioned in the text (Ahmad, 2006, 41). It is also called *dalīl al-khiṭāb.*

Mafhūm al-mwāfaqa: The implicit meaning on which the text may be silent but it is more worthy of the stated ruling than the meaning explicitly conveyed. It is also called *faḥwā al-khiṭāb.*

Mafhūm: I*mplied meaning of a text.*

Mafūm al-mukhālafa: 'D*ivergent meaning,*' a meaning which is derived from the words of the text in such a way that it diverges from the explicit meaning thereof

Maghrib: Sunset prayer.

Maḥfūẓ: An authentic and accepted *hadith* related by reliable narrators versus the anomalous, which is related by less accurate or less retentive transmitters.

Maḥram: Husband or any other relative to whom she is prohibited to marry.

Majāzī: M*etaphorical meaning.*

Majhūl al-'ayn: A narrator whose report was received by only one student and is not known in the literary circles.

Majhūl al-'adālah: A *narrator of unproven integrity.*

Majhūl al-ḥāl: A narrator whose integrity is not verified.

Makrūh: R*eprehensible or offensive.*

Mandūb: R*ecommended or liked.*

Mandūb: R*ecommended.*

Manṭūq: P*ronounced meaning of* a *text.*

Mu'adhin: P*rayer caller.*

Muʿāṭāh: *Give and take sale without verbally expressing offer and consent.*

Muʾawwal: Secondary meaning of a word or a phrase which predominates other connotations due to an external proof.

Mu ʾawwal: 'Amenable to interpretation,' a term with multiple meanings, one of which can be said to be preponderant based on non-textual evidence.

Muḥrim: *see iḥrām.*

Mujmal: E*quivocal or ambiguous word or phrase.*

Mujtahidūn: pl. of *mujtahid,* jurist with high qualifications.

Mukallaf: H*uman agent.*

Munqaṭiʿ: S*ee inqiṭāʿ.*

Mursal: *see irsāl.*

muṣarrāh: C*amel with retained milk; see taṣriya.*

Mutʿa: C*ompensation upon divorce.*

Mutabāyiʿān: P*urchasing parties.*

Muṭlaq: I*t* denotes a word which is neither qualified nor limited in its application (Kamali, 1991, 110).

Mutwātir: A report is classified as *mutāwatir* if it was reported by a significant number of narrators at each level, in the chain of transmission, thus reaching the succeeding generation through multiple paths of transmission leading back to its source.

Nabbāsh: One who steals the shroud of the dead.

Nabīdh: Beverage made of dates, and of raisins; that is, must; and of honey, that is, mead; and of wheat and of barely; that is, wort or made of dates or of raisins which one throws whence its appellation into a vessel or skin of water and leaves until it ferments and becomes intoxicating.

Nabīdh: Soaking raisins or dates in water.

Nafl: S*upererogatory act of worship.*

Nahy: P*rohibition.*

Naṣṣ: U*nivocal*

Qaḍāʾ: B*elated observance of a religious duty.*

Qasāmah: When a person is found slain in any district, and it is not known who was the murderer, and his heir demands a satisfaction for his blood from the inhabitants of the district, or from any number of them not spccificdl1y named, fifty of the inhabitants, selected, by the heir, must be put to their oaths, and depose to this effect, "by God I did not kill him nor do I know his murder." (Mirghinānī, n.d., 4, 655).

Qibla: Prayer direction.

Qīrāṭ: Proportionate reward.

Qiyās al-ʿaks: 'Analogy by Coexclusiveness.' To extend the opposite rule of the original case to the new case due to discrepancy in their respective effective causes.

Qiyās al-dalāla: Analogy by inference or allusion. It is a type of analogy where an *aṣl* is not compared to a *farʿ* by a definite *ʿilla* but through an indication which refers *ʿilla*.

Qiyās al-ʿilla: analogy where an effective cause is explicitly provided.

Qiyās fī maʿna al-aṣl: Analogy in which the *aṣl* and *farʿ* are of the same meaning.

Qiyās lā fāriq: Analogy where there is no trace of a discrepancy between *aṣl* and *farʿ*.

Qulla: Volume measurement which equals 108 liters. Two *qullas* equal 216 liters.

Qunūt: Special supplication made either in *witr* or in other prayers as the Muslims are overtaken by a calamity.

Rakʿa: M*inimal unit of Muslim prayers.*

Ṣāʿ: Volume measurement estimated to be almost 2.03 liters.

Ṣaḥāba: Those who witnessed the Prophet Moḥammad and believed in him before his death.

Salat*:* Muslim prayer.

Shighār: To marry by trading daughters or sisters. It means a man gives his daughter in marriage on the condition that the other gives his daughter to him in marriage without any dower being paid by either.

Shufʿa: preemption.'

Siwāk*:* tooth brushing stick.

Sujūd: P*rostration.*

Sunna: P*rophetic normative precedent. If it is used an adjective it means 'recommended'.*

Sunna ghayr tashrīʿiyya: 'Non-legal Sunna,' natural and instinctive activities of the Prophet

Tabiʾūn: Those who witnessed the Companions of the Prophet Moḥammad.

Takbīr: *pronouncement of 'Allahu Akbar (Allah is the most great)'.*

Takhṣīṣ: Specifying the scope of a general text.

Talbiya: C*ertain invocations pronounced by a performer of hajj or ʿumra.*

Tanqīḥ al-manāṭ: Verification of a rationale in a given text by excluding irrelevant attributes in a text and approving relevant contingencies.
Taqyīd: Limiting the scope of an absolute text.
Taslīm: S*alutation marking the conclusion of prayer.*
Taṣriya: Retaining milk in an animal's utters to impress the buyer.
Ṭawāf: Circumambulation around the *kaʿba*
Tayammum: R*itual purification with clean earth.*
Thayyib: A woman who has been previously married.
Umm al-walad: A concubine who gives a birth to a child and is attributed by her master and becomes free upon his death.
Uṣūl: Islamic legal theory.
Uṣūlīs: *Islamic legal theorists.*
Walī: G*uardian.*
Waqf: Attributing a report to a Companion of the Prophet.
Yamīn ghamūs: 'F*alse oath.*' It is literally translated as 'a dipping oath' because, according to a report from the Prophet, it dips one who pronounces is in the fire of hell.
Ẓāhir: A locution that while it may be used to indicate two meanings is preponderantly used for one as opposed to the other with respect to its primary meaning.
Ẓāhir: P*rimary meaning of a word which has two or more connotations.*
Zakat: C*ertain proportions of wealth paid for particular categories of people.*
Ẓihār: Injurious dissimulation expressed by a spouse when he compares his wife to his mother or one to whom marriage is prohibited.
Zuhr: N*oon prayer.*

References

ʿAbd ibn Ḥumayd, Abū Moḥammad ʿAbdul-Ḥamīd b. Ḥumayd b. Naṣr (1988). *Al-Muntakhab min Musnad ʿAbd b. Ḥumayd*. Ed. Ṣubḥī al-Badrī al-Samirrāʾī and Maḥmūd Moḥammad Khalīl. Cairo: Maktabat al-Sunna.

ʿAbdur-Razzāq b. Hammām Al-Ṣanʿānī (1983). *Muṣannaf ʿAbdur-Razzāq*. India: Al-Majlis al-ʿIlmī.

Abū al-Ḥusayn al-Baṣrī, Muḥammad b. ʿAlī al-Ṭayyib (1983). *Al-Muʿtamad*. Ed. Khalīl al-Mīs. Beirut: Dār al-Kutub al-ʿIlmiyya.

Abū Dāwūd, Sulaymān b. al-Ashʿath b. Isḥāq b. Bashīr b. Shaddād b. ʿAmr al-Azdī al-Sijistānī (n. d.). *Sunan Abī Dāwūd*. Ed. Moḥammad Muḥiy al-Dīn ʿAbdul-Ḥamīd. Beirut: Al-Maktaba al-ʿAṣriyya.

Abū Dāwūd, Sulaymān b. al-Ashʿath b. Isḥāq b. Bashīr b. Shaddād b. ʿAmr al-Azdī al-Sijistānī (1988). *Al-Marāsīl*. Ed. Shuʿayb al-Arnāʾūṭ, Beirut: Muʾassasat al-Risāla.

Abū Dāwūd, Sulaymān b. Dāwūd b. al-Jārūd al-Ṭayālisī (1999). *Musnad Abī Dāwūd*. Ed. Moḥammad b. ʿAbdul-Muḥsin al-Turkī. Egypt: Dār Hajar.

Abū Yaʿla, al-Qāḍī Moḥammad b. al-Ḥusayn b. Moḥmmad b. Kalaf al-Farrāʾ (1990). *Al-ʿUdda*. Ed. Aḥmad b. ʿAlī b. Sayr al-Mubārakī. Riyadh: Imam Moḥammad b. Suʿūd University.

Aḥmad, Abū ʿAbdullah Aḥmad b. Moḥammad b. Ḥanbal b. Hilā b. Asad Al-Shaybānī (2001). *Musnad Aḥmad*. Ed. ʿAbdullah b. ʿAbdul-Muḥsin Al-Turkī. Riyadh: Muʾassasat Al-Risāla.

Ahmad, Atif Ahmad (2006). *Structural Interrelations of Theory and Practice in Islamic Law. A Study of Six Works of Medieval Islamic Jurisprudence*. Studies in Islamic Law and Society, ed. Rudd Peters and Bernard Weis, vol. 27. Leiden: Brill.

ʿAlā' al-Dīn al-Bukhārī, ʿAbdul-ʿAzīz b. Aḥmad b. Muḥammad al-Ḥanafī (n. d.). *Kashf al-Asrār Sharḥ Uṣūl al-Bazdawī*. Beirut: Dār al-Kitāb al-Islāmī.

ʿAlāʾī al, Ṣalāḥ al-Dīn al-Dimashqī (1996). *Tafṣīl al-Ijmāl fī Taʿāruḍ al-Aqwāl wa al-Afʿāl*. Ed. Moḥammad Ibrāhīm al-Ḥifnāwī. Cairo: Dār al-Ḥadīth.

Albānī, abū ʿAbdur-Raḥmān Muḥammad Nāṣir al-Dīn al- (1992). *Silsilat al-Aḥādīth al-Ḍaʿīfa wa Athrahua al-Sayyiʾ fī al-Umma*. Riyadh: Dār al-Maʿārif.

Albānī, Muḥammad Nāṣir al-Dīn al- (1985). *Irwāʾ al-Ghalīl fī Takhrīj Aḥādīth Manār al-Sabīl*. Beruit: al-Maktab al-Islāmī.

Albānī, Muḥammad Nāṣir al-Dīn al- (n. d.). *Ḍaʿīf al-Jāmiʿ al-Ṣaghīr wa Ziyādatuh*. Ed. Zuhayr al-Shāwīsh, Beirut: Al-Maktab al-Islāmī.

Āmidī, Abū al-Ḥasan Sayyid Al-Dīn ʿAlī b. Moḥammad al-Thaʿālibī al- (n. d.). *Al-Iḥkām fī Uṣūl al-Aḥkām*. Ed. ʿAbdul-Rāziq ʿAfīfī. Beirut: Al-Maktab Al-Islāmī.

Ar-Rahawān, Moḥammad Saeed (2014). *Hadith Terminology and Classification: A Handbook*. Riyadh: IIPH.

ʿAṭṭār, Ḥasan b. Muḥammad b. Maḥmūd al- (n. d.). *Ḥāshiyāt al-ʿAṭṭār ʿala Sharḥ al-Jālāl al-Maḥlī ʿala Jamʿ al-Jawāmiʿ*. Beirut: Dār al-Kutub al-ʿIlmiyya.

ʿAṭṭār, Ḥasan b. Muḥammad b. Maḥmūd al- (n. d.). *Ḥāshiyāt al-ʿAṭṭār ʿla Sharḥ al-Jalāl al-Maḥallī ʿla Jamʿ al-Jawāmiʿ*. Beiruit: Dār al-Kutub al-ʿIlmiyya.

ʿAynī, Badr Al-Dīn Abū Moḥammad Maḥmūd b. Aḥmad b. Mūsa b. Aḥmad b. Ḥusayn Al-Ghaytābī al- (2000). *Al-Bināya Sharḥ Al-Hidāya*. Beirut: Dār al-Kutub al-ʿIlmiyya.

ʿAynī, Badr al-Dīn Maḥmūd b. Aḥmad b. Mūsa al- (1429). *Nukhabt al-Afkār fī Tanqīḥ Mabānī al-Akhbār fī Sharḥ Maʿānī al-Athār*. Ed. Yāsir b. Ibrāhīm, Qatar: Ministry of Waqfs.

Bābartī, Muḥammad b. Muḥammad b. Maḥmūd b. Akmal al-Dīn abū ʿAbdullah al- (n. d.). *Al-ʿInāya Sharḥ al-Hidāya*. Beirut: Dār al-Fikr.

Baghawī, abū Muḥammad al-Ḥusayn b. Masʿūd b. Muḥammad b. al-Farrāʾ al-Baghawī al- (1983). *Sharḥ al-Sunna*. Ed. Shuʿayb al-Arnāʾūṭ and Muḥammad Zuhayr al-Shāwīsh. Beirut: al-Maktab al-Islāmī.

Baghdādī, ʿAbdul-Qāhir b. Ṭāhir b. Moḥammad b. ʿAbdullah (1977). *Al-Farq bayna Al-Firaq*. Beirut: Dār al-Afāq.

Baghdādī, Abū Bakr Aḥmad b. ʿAlī b. Thābit b. Aḥmad b. Mahdī al-Khaṭīb al- (n. d.). *Al-Kifāya fī ʿIlm al-Riwāya*. Ed. Abū ʿAbdullah al-Sawraqī and Ibrāhīm Ḥamdī al-Madanī. Medina: Al-Maktaba al-ʿIlmiyya.

Bahūtī, Mansūr b. Yūnus b. Ṣalāḥ add-Dīn b. Ḥasan b. Idrīs (1993). *Daqāʾiq Ulī al-Nuha li Sharḥ al-Muntaha*, Beirut: ʿĀlam al-Kutub.

Bājī, abū al-Walīd Sulaymān b. Khalaf b. Saʿd b. Ayyūb b. Wārith al-Tajībī al- (n. d.). *Al-Muntaqa Sharḥ al-Muwaṭṭaʾ*. Cairo: Maṭbaʿat al-Saʿāda.

Baldaḥī, ʿAbdullah b. Maḥmūd b. Mawdūd Al-Mūṣilī al- (1937). *Al-Ikhtiyār li Taʿlīl al-Mukhtār*. Cairo: Al-Ḥalabī.

Bayhaqī, Aḥmad b. al-Ḥusayn b. ʿAlī b. Mūsa al-Khusrawjirdī al- (1989). *Al-Sunan al-Ṣaghīr*. Ed. ʿAbdul-Muʿṭī Qalʿajī. Karachi: Islamic Studies University.

Bayhaqī, Aḥmad b. al-Ḥusayn b. ʿAlī b. Mūsa al-Khusrawjirdī al- (1991). *Maʿrifa al-Sunan wa al-Athār*. Ed. ʿAbdul-Muʿṭī Amīn Qalʿajī. Damascus: Dar Qutayba and Karachi: Islamic Studies University.

Bayhaqī, Aḥmad b. al-Ḥusayn b. ʿAlī b. Mūsa al-Khusrawjirdī al- (2003). *Al-Suan al-Kubra*. Ed. Moḥammad ʿAbdul-Qādir ʿAṭa. Beirut: Dār al-Kutub al-ʿIlmiyya.

Bazdawī, ʿAbdul-ʿAzīz b. Aḥmad b. Muḥammad ʿAlā' al-Dīn al-Bukhārī al- (n. d.). *Kashf al-Asrār Sharḥ Uṣūl al-Bazdawī*. Beirut: Dār al-Kitāb al-Islāmī.

Belewy, Aishah (1998). *A Glossary of Islamic Terms*. London: TaHa Publications.

Brown, Jonathan A.C. (2007). *The Canonization of al-Bukhārī and Muslim: The Formation and Function of the Sunnī Ḥadīth Canon*. Leiden: Brill.

Bukhārī, Moḥammad b. ʿIsmāʿīl Abū ʿAbdullah Al-Bukhārī al-Juʿfī al- (2001). *Ṣaḥīḥ al-Bukhārī*. Ed. Moḥammad Zuhayr b. Nāṣīr Al-Nāṣir._Cairo: Dār Ṭawq al-Najāh.

Bukhārī, Moḥammad b. ʿIsmāʿīl Abū ʿAbdullah Al-Bukhārī al-Juʿfī al- (2005). *Al-Ḍuʿafā' al-Ṣaghīr*. Ed. Abū ʿAbdullah Aḥmad b. Ibrāhīm b. Abī al-ʿUnayn. Cairo: Maktabat Ibn ʿAbbās.

Bukhārī, Moḥammad b. ʿIsmāʿīl Abū ʿAbdullah Al-Bukhārī al-Juʿfī al- (n. d.). *Al-Tārīkh al-Kabīr*. Ed. Moḥammad ʿAbdul-Muʿīd Khān. India: Dāʾirat al-Maʿārif al-ʿUthmāniyya.

Daraqūṭnī, abū al-Ḥasan ʿAlī b. ʿUmar b. Aḥmad b. Mahdy b. Masʿūd al- (2004). Al-*Sunan*. Ed. Shuʿayb al-Arnāʾūṭ, *et al.* Beirut: Muʾassasat Al-Risāla.

Dardīr, Aḥmad b. Aḥmad b. abī Ḥāmid al-ʿAdawī al- (n. d.). *Al-Sharḥ al-Kabīr*. Beirut: Dār al-Fikr.

Dārimī, Abū Moḥammad ʿAbdullah b. ʿAbdur-Raḥmān b. al-Faḍl b. Bahrām b. ʿAbduṣ-Ṣamad al- (2000). *Sunan Al-Dārimī*. Ed. Ḥusayn Salīm Asad Al-Dārānī. Saudi Arabia: Dār al-Mughnī.

Dhahbī, Shams al-Dīn Abū ʿAbdullah Moḥammad b. Aḥmad b. ʿUthmān b. Qāymāz al- (1963). *Mīzān al-Iʿtidāl fī Naqd al-Rijāl*. Ed. ʿAlī Moḥammad Al-Bajāwī. Beirut: Dār al-Maʿrifa.

Ḍuwayḥī, ʿAlī b. Saʿd (2010). Al-Qirāʾa al-Shādha wa Atharuha ʿInd Al-Uṣūliyyīn. In *Majallat al-Buḥūth Al-Islāmiyya*, vol. 49.

Farkūs, Abū ʿAbdul-Muʿiz Muḥammad ʿAlī (2013). ed. Introduction. In *Miftāḥ al-Wuṣūl ila Binā' al-Furūʿ ʿala al-Uṣūl*. Algeria: Dār al-Mawqiʿ and Dār al-ʿAwāṣim.

Fawzān, Ṣāliḥ b. Fawzān al- (1999). *Al-Irshād ilā Ṣaḥīḥ al-Iʿtiqād*. Riyadh: Dār Ibn al-Jawzī.

Fayyūmī, Aḥmad b. Muḥammad b. ʿAlī al-Ḥamawī al- (n. d.). *Miṣbāḥ al-Lugha*. Beirtu: al-Maktaba al-ʿIlmiyya.

Ghāzalī, Abū Ḥāmid Moḥammad b. Moḥammad al-Ghazālī al-Ṭūṣī al- (1993). *Al-Muṣtaṣfā*. Beirut: Dār al-Kutub al-ʿIlmiyya.

Ḥākim, Abū ʿAbdullah Moḥammad b. ʿAbdullah b. Ḥamdawayh b. Nuʿaym b. al-Ḥakam al- (1990). *Al-Mustadrak ʿla al-Ṣaḥīḥayn*. Ed. Muṣtafa ʿAbdul-Qādir ʿAṭa. Beirut: Dār al-Kutub.

Ḥaṭṭāb, Shams al-Dīn abū ʿAbdullah Muḥammad b. Muḥammad b. ʿAbdur-Raḥmān Al-Ṭrābulṣī al- (1992). *Mwāhib al-Jalīl Sharḥ Mukhṭaṣar Khalīl*, Beirut: Dār al-Fikr.

Haytamī, Aḥmad b. Muḥammad b. ʿAli b. Ḥajar al- (n. d.). *Al-Fatāwā al-Ḥadīthiyya*. Beirut: Dār al-Fikr.

Haythamī, Abū al-Ḥasan Nūr al-Dīn ʿAlī b. Abū Bakr b. Sulaymān al- (n. d.). *Mawārid al-Dham'ān ilā Zawā'id ibn Ḥibbān*. Ed. Moḥammad ʿAbdur-Rāziq Ḥamza. Beirut: Dār al-Kutub al-ʿIlmiyya.

Ḥumaydī, Abū Bakr ʿAbdullah b. Al-Zubayr b. ʿIsā b. ʿUbaydullah al-Qurashī al- (1996). *Musnad al-Ḥumaydī*. Ed. Ḥasan Sulaym al-Asdī al-Dārānī. Damascus: Dār al-Saqqā.

Ibn ʿAbdul-Barr, Abū ʿAmr Yūsuf b. ʿAbdullah b. Moḥammad b. ʿAbdul-Barr b. ʿAṣim Al-Namrī (1980). *Al-Kāfī fī Fiqh Ahl al-Madīna*. Ed. Moḥammad Aḥmad Aḥīd Wild Mādīk. Riyadh: Maktabat Al-Riyāḍ al-Ḥadītha.

Ibn ʿAbdul-Barr, Abū ʿUmar Yūsuf b. ʿAbdullah b. Moḥammad b. ʿAbdul-Barr (1967). *Al-Tamhīd li-ma fī al-Muwaṭṭa' mina al-Maʿanī wa al-Asānīd*. Ed. Muṣṭafa b. Aḥmad Al-ʿAlawī. Morocco: Minstry of Waqfs.

Ibn ʿAbdul-Barr, Abū ʿUmar Yūsuf b. ʿAbdullah b. Moḥammad b. ʿAbdul-Barr (1994). *Jāmiʿ Bayan al-ʿIlm wa Faḍlih*. Ed. Abū al-Ashbāl al-Zuhayrī. Saudi Arabia: Dār ibn al-Jawzī.

Ibn abi ʿAṣim, Aḥmad b. ʿAmr b. al-Ḍaḥḥāk (1991). *Al-Aḥād wa al-Mathānī*. Ed. Bāsim Fayṣal Aḥmad al-Jawābra. Riyadh: Dār al-Rāya.

Ibn abī Ḥātim, Abū Moḥammad ʿAbdullah b. Moḥammad b. Idrīs b. al-Mundhir al-Tamīmī (1952). *Al-Jarḥ wa al-Taʿdīl*. India: Dāʾirat al-Maʿārif al-ʿUthmāniyya.

Ibn Abī Shayba, Abū Bakr ʿAbdullah b. Moḥammad al-Kūfī (1989). Ed. Kamāl Yūsuf al-Ḥūt. Riyadh: Maktabat al-Rushd.

Ibn ʿĀbidīn, Moḥammad Amīn b. ʿUmar b. ʿAbdul-ʿAzīz al-Dimashqī al-Ḥanafī (1992). *Radd al-Muḥtār ʿala al-Durr al-Mukhtār*. Beirut: Dār al-Fikr.

ibn ʿAdiy, Abū Aḥmad al-Jurjānī (1997). *Al-Kāmil fī Ḍuʿafā' al-Rijāl*. Ed. ʿAdil Aḥmad ʿAbdul-Mawjūd and ʿAlī Moḥammad Moʿawwaḍ. Beirut: Dār al-Kutub al-ʿIlmiyya.

Ibn al-ʿArabī, Moḥmmad b. ʿAbdullah Abū Bakr al-Muʿāfirī al-Ishbīlī (1999). *Al-Maḥṣūl fī al-Uṣūl*. Ed. Ḥusayn ʿAlī al-Yadarī and Saʿīd Fūda. Ammān: Dār al-Bayāriq.

Ibn al-Ḥājib, Abū ʿAmr b. ʿUmar b. Abī Bakr (2006). *Mukhtaṣar Muntahā al-Suʾl wa al-Amal fī ʿIlmay al-Uṣūl wa al-Jadal*. Ed. Nadhīr Ḥamadū. Riyadh: Ibn Ḥazm.

Ibn al-Humām, Kamāl al-Dīn Moḥammad b. ʿAbdul-Wāḥid al-Sīwāsī (n. d.). *Fatḥ al-Qadīr*. Beirut: Dār al-Fikr.

Ibn al-Mulaqqin, abū Ḥafṣ ʿUmar b. ʿAlī b. Aḥmad al-Anṣārī al-Shāfiʿī (n. d.). *Al-Iʿlām bi Fawā'id ʿUmdat al-Aḥkām*. Ed. ʿAbdul-ʿAzīz b. Aḥmad b. Muḥammad al-Mushayqiḥ. Riyadh: Dār al-ʿĀṣima.

Ibn al-Najjār Taqiy al-Dīn abū al-Baqāʾ Muḥammad b. Aḥmad b. ʿAbdul-ʿAzīz al-Fatūḥī (1997). *Sharḥ al-Kawkab al-Munīr*, ed. Muḥammad al-Zuḥaylī and Nazīh Ḥammad. Riyadh: al-Ubaykān.

Ibn al-Ṣalāḥ, ʿUthmān b. ʿAbdur-Raḥmān Abū ʿAmr Taqiyy al-Dīn. *Maʿrifat Anwāʿ al-Ḥadīth* (1986). Ed. Nūr al-Dīn ʿItr. Beruit: Dār al-Fikr.

Ibn al-Ṣamʿānī, abū al-Muẓaffar Manṣūr b. Muḥammad b. ʿAbdul-Jabbār b. Aḥmad al-Marwazī (1999), *Qawāṭiʿ al-Adilla*. Ed. Muḥammad Ḥasan Muḥammad Ḥasan Ismāʿīl. Beirut: Dār al-Kutub al-ʿIlmiyya.

Ibn al-Turkumānī, ʿAlā al-Dīn ʿAlī b. ʿUthmān b. Ibrāhīm b. Muṣṭafa al-Mārdīnī (n. d.). *Al-Jawhar al-Naqiyy ʿala Sunan al-Bayhaqī.* Beirut: Dār al-Fikr.

Ibn Farḥūn, Ibrāhīm b. ʿAlī b. Moḥammad Burhān Al-Dīn Al-Yaʿmūrī (n. d.) *Al-Dībāj Al-Mudhahhab fī Aʿyān Al-Madhhab.* Cairo: Dār Al-Turāth.

Ibn Fāris, Aḥmad b. Fāris b. Zakariyyā al-Qazwīnī abū al-Ḥasan (1979). *Muʿjam Maqāyiyīs al-Lugha.* Ed. ʿAbdus-Salam M. Hārūn. Damascus: Dār al-Fikr.

Ibn Ḥajar b. ʿAlī (1989). *Talkhīṣ al-Ḥabīr fī Takhrīj Aḥādīth al-Rāfiʿī al-Kabīr.* Beirut: Dār al-Kutub al-ʿIlmiyya.

Ibn Ḥajar, Abū al-Faḍl Aḥmad b. ʿAlī b. Moḥammad b. Aḥmad b. Ḥajar al-ʿAsqalānī (1908). *Tahdhī al-Tahdhīb.* India: Maṭbaʿat Dāʾirat al-Maʿārif al-Niẓāmiyya.

Ibn Ḥajar, Aḥmad b. ʿAlī, *al-Maṭālib al-ʿĀliya bi Zawāʾid al-Masānīd al-Thamāniya* (1418). Riyadh: Dār al-Waṭan.

Ibn Ḥajar, Aḥmad b. ʿAlī, *al-Maṭālib al-ʿĀliya bi Zawāʾid al-Masānīd al-Thamāniya* (1998). Ed. Saʿd al-Shithrī. Saudi Arabia: Dār al-Ghayth and Dār al-ʿAṣima

Ibn Ḥazm, Abū Moḥammad ʿAlī b. Aḥmad b. Saʿīd b. Ḥazm al-Andalusī (n. d.). *Al-Muḥallā bi al-Athār.* Beirut: Dār al-Fikr.

Ibn Ḥazm, abū Muḥammad ʿAli b. Aḥmad b. Saʿīd b. Ḥazm al-Andalusī al-Qurṭubī (n. d.). *Al-Iḥkām fī Uṣūl al-Aḥkām.* Ed. Aḥmad Muḥammad Shākir. Beirut: Dār al-Afāq al-Jadīda.

Ibn Ḥibbān, Muḥammad b. Ḥibbān b. Muʿādh b. Maʿbid al-Bustī (1976). *Al-Majrūḥīn mina al-Muḥaddithīn wa al-Ḍuʿafā' wa al-Matrūkīn.* Ed. Maḥmūd Ibrāhīm Zāyid. Aleppo: Dār al-Waʿiy.

Ibn Ḥibbān, Muḥammad b. Ḥibbān b. Muʿādh b. Maʿbid al-Bustī (1988). *Al-Iḥsān fī Taqrīb Ṣāḥīḥ b. Ḥibbān.* Ed. Shuʿayb al-Arnā'ūṭ. Beirut: Dār al-Risāla.

Ibn Khaldūn ʿAbdur-Raḥmān bin Moḥammad bin Moḥammad Abū Zayd al-Ishbilī. *Al-Taʿrīf bi Ibn Khaldūn wa Riḥlatih Sharqan wa Gharba* (1979). Beirut: Dār al-Kitāb al-Libnānī.

Ibn Khuzayma, Abū Bakr Moḥammad b. Isḥāq b. Khuzayma b. al-Mughīra b. Ṣāliḥ b. Bakr al-Sulamī (n. d.). *Ṣaḥīḥ ibn Khuzayma.* Beirut: Al-Maktab al-Islāmī.

Ibn Māja, Abū ʿAbdullah Moḥammad b. Yazīd (2009) *Sunan Ibn Māja.* Ed. Shuʿayb al-Arnāʾūṭ. Beirut: Dār Al-Risāla

Ibn Maryam, Abū ʿAbdullah Moḥammad b. Moḥammad b. Aḥmad al-Tilmisānī (n. d.). *Al-Bustān fī Dhikr al-ʿUlmāʾ wa al-Awlyāʾ bi Tilmisān.* Algeria: Dār al-Maṭbūʿāt al-Jāmiʿiyya.

Ibn Mujāhid, Aḥmad b. Mūsa b. Al-ʿAbbās Al-Tamīmī (1979). *Kitāb al-Sabʿa fī al-Qirā'āt.* Ed. Shawqī Ḍayf. Egypt: Dār al-Maʿārif.

Ibn Naṣr, al-Qāḍī abū Muḥammad ʿAbdul-Wahhāb b. ʿAlī (1999). *Al-Ishrāf ʿla Masāʾil al-Khilāf.* Riyadh: Ibn Ḥazm.

Ibn Nujaym, Zayn al-Dīn b. Ibrāhīm b. Muḥammad (n. d.). *Al-Baḥr al-Rāʾiq Sharḥ Kanz al-Daqāʾiq.* Beirut: Dār al-Kitāb al-Islāmī.

Ibn Qudāma, Abū Moḥammad Muwaffaq al-Dīn b. ʿAbdullah b. Aḥmad b. Moḥammad al-Jamāʿīlī (1968). *Al-Mughnī.* Cairo: Maktabat al-Qāhira.

Ibn Qudāma, abū Muḥammad Muwaffaq al-Dīn ʿAbdullah b. Aḥmad b. Muḥammad b. Qudāma al-Jamāʿīlī (1968). *Al-Mughnī*. Cairo: Maktabat al-Qāhira.

Ibn Qudāma, abū Muḥammad Muwaffaq al-Dīn ʿAbdullah b. Aḥmad b. Muḥammad b. Qudāma al-Jamāʿīlī (1994). *Al-Kāfī fī Fiqh al-Imām Aḥmad*. Beirut: Dār al-Kutub al-ʿIlmiyya.

ibn Qutayba in his *Tafsīr Gharīb al-Quran*

Ibn Quṭlūbagha, abū al-Fidāʾ Zayn al-Dīn Qāsim al-Ḥanafī (2003). *Khulāṣat al-Afkār Sharḥ Mukhtaṣar al-Manār*. Ed. Ḥāfiẓ Thanāʾ Allah al-Zāhidī. Riyadh: Dār ibn Ḥazm.

Ibn Rushd, Abū al-Walīd Moḥammad b. Aḥmad b. Moḥammad b. Aḥmad b. Rushd Al-Qurṭubī (2004). *Bidāyat al-Mujtahid wa Nihāyat al-Muqtaṣid*. Cairo: Dār al-Ḥadīth.

Ibn Saʿd ʿAbdullah bin Moḥammad bin Manīʿ. *Al-Ṭabaqāt al-Kubrā* (1968). Beirut: Dār Ṣādir.

Ibn Taymiya, Taqy al-Dīn Abū al-ʿAbbās Aḥmad b. ʿAbdul-Ḥalīm b. ʿAbdus-Salālam b. Taymiya (1987). *Al-Fatāwā al-Kubrā*. Beirut: Dār al-Kutub al-ʿIlmiyya.

Ibn Zanjāwayh, Abū Aḥmad Ḥumayd b. Makhlad b. Qutayba b. ʿAbdullah al-Khurasānī (1986). *Al-Amwāl*. Ed. Shākir Dhīb Fayyāḍ. Saudi Arabia. King Faisal Centre for Research and Islamic Studies.

Jaṣāṣ, Aḥmad b. ʿAlī abū Bakr al-Rāzī al-Ḥanfī al- (1405). *Aḥkām al-Quran*. Ed. Muḥammad Ṣādiq Qamḥāwī. Beirut: Dār Iḥyā' al-Turāth al-ʿArabī.

Jaṣāṣ, Aḥmad b. ʿAli Abū Bakr al-Rāzī al-Ḥanfī al- (1994). *Al-Fuṣūl fī al-Uṣūl*. Kuwait: Ministry of Waqfs.

Jīzānī, Muḥammad b. Ḥusayn al- (1431). *Sunnat al-Tark wa Dalalatuha ʿla al-Aḥkām al-Sharʿiyya*. Riyadh: Ibn Ḥazm 1431.

Judayʿ, ʿAbdullah b. Yūsuf b. ʿIsa al-ʿAnzī al- (1997). *Taysīr Uṣūl al-Fiqh*, Beirut: Al-Rayyān.

Juwaynī, ʿAbdul-Malik b. ʿAbdullah b. Yūsuf b. Muḥammad al- (1997). *Al-Burhān*. Ed. Ṣalāḥ b. Moḥammad b. ʿUwayḍa. Beirut: Dār al-Kutub al-ʿIlmiyya.

Juwaynī, ʿAbdul-Malik b. ʿAbdullah b. Yūsuf b. Muḥammad al- (2007). *Nihāyat al-Maṭlab fī Dirāyat al-Madhhab*. Ed. ʿAbdul-ʿAẓīm al-Dīb. Jeddah: Dār al-Minhāj.

Kamali, Muḥammad Hashim (1991). *Principles of Islamic Jurisprudence*. Cambridge: Islamic Texts Society.

Kāsānī, ʿAlāʾ Al-Dīn Abū Bakr b. Masʿūd b. Aḥmad al-Kāsānī al-Ḥanafī al- (1986). *Badāʾiʿ al-Ṣanāʾiʿ fī Tartīb al-Sharāʾiʿ*. Beirut: Dār al-Kutub al-ʿIlmiyya.

Khalīl, abū ʿAbdur-Raḥmān al-Khalīl b. Aḥmad b. ʿAmr b. Tamīm al-Farāhīdī al- (n. d.). *Al-ʿAyn*. Ed. Mahdī al-Makhzūmī and Ibāhīm al-Sāmirrā'ī. Cairo: Dār al-Hilāl.

Khallāf, ʿAbdul-Wahhāb (n. d.). *ʿIlm Uṣūl al-Fiqh*. Cairo: Shabāb al-Daʿwa.

Khan, Muhammad Akram (1990). *Islamic Economics and Finance: A Glossary*. London and New York: Routledge.

Kharqī, abū al-Qāsim ʿUmar b. al-Ḥusayn b. ʿAbdullah al- (1993). *Muktaṣar al-Kharqī*. Egypt: Dār al-Ṣaḥaba.

Khāṭṭābī, Abū Sulaymān Ḥamad b. Moḥammad b. Ibrāhīm b. al-Khaṭṭāb al-Bustī al- (1932). *Maʿālim al-Sunan*. Aleppo: Al-Maṭbaʿa al-ʿIlmiyya.

Khustrū, Muḥammad b. Frāmurz (n. d.). *Durar al-Ḥukkām Sharḥ Ghurar al-Aḥkām*. Beirut: Dār Iḥiyāʾ al-Kutub al-ʿArabiyya.

Lane, E. W. (1984). *Lane's Lexicon*. Cambridge: Islamic Texts Society.

Mālik (1994). *Al-Mudawwana*. Beirut: Dār al-Kutub al-ʿIlmiya.

Mālik b. Anas b. Mālik b. ʿĀmir al-Aṣbaḥī (1992). *Al-Muwaṭṭaʾ through the Transmission of Abū Muṣʿab al-Zuhrī*. Ed. Bashshār ʿAwwād and Maḥmūd Khālīl. Beirut: Muʾasasat al-Risāla.

Mālik, b. Anas b. Mālik b. ʿAmir Al-Aṣbuḥī (2004). *Al-Muwaṭṭaʾ*. Ed. Moḥammad Muṣṭafa al-Aʿẓamī. Abu Dhabi: Muʾassasat Zāyid.

Manbajī, Jamāl al-Dīn abū Muḥammad ʿAlī b. abī Yaḥya Zakariyya b. Masʿūd al-Anṣārī al-(1994). *Al-Lubāb fī al-Jamʿ bayna al-Sunna wa al-Kitaāb*. Ed. Muḥammad Faḍl ʿAbdul-ʿAzīz al-Murād. Syria: Dār al-Qalam.

Manīʿ, Moḥammad Sulaymān al- (1999). "Baḥth fī Taḥwīl al-Mawāzīn wa al-Makāyīl al-Sharʿiyya ila Al-Maqādīr al-Muʿāṣira." In *Majallat Al-Buḥūth Al-Islāmiyya*, vol. 59.

Māwardī, abū al-Ḥasan ʿAlī b. Muḥammad b. Muḥammad b. Ḥabīb al-Baṣrī al-Baghdadī al-(1999). *Al-Ḥāwī al-Kabīr*. ed. ʿAlī Muḥammad Muʿawwaḍ and ʿAdil Aḥmad ʿAbdul-Mawjūd, Beirut: Dār al-Kutub al-ʿIlmiyya.

Mirghinānī, ʿAlī b. abū Bakr b. ʿAbdul-Jalīl al-Farghānī al-Marghinānī Burhān al-Dīn al-(n. d.). *Al-Hidāya fī Sharḥ Bidāyat al-Mubtadī*. Ed. Ṭalāl Yūsuf. Beirut: Dār Iḥyāʾ al-Turāth.

Miṣrī, ibn al-Naqīb al- (1982). *ʿUmdat al-Sālik wa ʿUddat al-Nāsik*. Ed. ʿAbdullah bin Nadīm al-Anṣārī. Jeddah: Dār Al-Minhāj.

Miṣrī, ibn al-Naqīb al- (1997). *ʿUmdat al-Sālik wa ʿUddat al-Nāsik*. Translated by Nuh Ha Meem Keller. US: Amana Publications.

Moḥammad b. ʿAbdul-Wahhāb b. Sulaymān Al-Tamīmī (n. d.). *Risāla fī al-Radd ʿala Al-Rāfiḍa*. Riyadh: Imām Moḥammad b. Suʿūd Islamic University.

Muslim, b. Al-Ḥajjāj Abū al-Ḥasan al-Qushayrī (n. d.). *Al-Musnad al-Ṣaḥīḥ al-Mukhtaṣar bi Naqli al-ʿAdl ʿan al-ʿAdl ʿan Rasūl Allah*. Ed. Moḥammad Fuad ʿAbdul-Bāqī. Beirut: Dār Iḥiyāʾ al-Turāth.

Muzanī, Ismāʿīl b. Yaḥya b. Ismāʿīl al- (1990). *Mukhtaṣar al-Muzanī*, Beirut: Dār al-Maʿrifa.

Nasāʾī, abū ʿAbdur-Raḥmān Aḥmad b. Shuʿayb b. ʿAlī al-Khurasānī al- (1986). *Al-Sunan al-Kubrā*. Ed. ʿAbdul-Fattāḥ Abū Ghudda. Aleppo: Maktabat al-Maṭbūʿāt al-Islāmiya.

Nawawī, Abū Zakariyyā Muḥiy al-Dīn Yaḥya b. Sharaf al- (2011). *Minhāj al-Ṭālibīn wa ʿUmdat al-Muftīn*. Jeddah: Dār al-Minhāj.

Nawawī, abū Zakariyyā Muḥiyy al-Dīn b. Sharaf al-Nawawī al- (n. d.). *Al-Majmūʿ Sharḥ al-Muhadhab*. Beirut: Dār al-Fikr.

Qāḍī ʿIyāḍ al-Yaṣubī. *Nasīm Al-Riyāḍ fī Sharḥ al-Shifā* (2001). E. Moḥammad ʿAbdul-Qādir ʿAṭa. Beirtut: Dār al-Kutub al-ʿIlmiyya.

Qarāfī, Abū al-ʿAbbās Shihāb Addīn Aḥmad b. Idrīs b. ʿAbdur-Raḥmān Al-Mālikī al- (n. d.). *Al-Dhakhīra*. Ed. Moḥammad Ḥijjī and Saʿīd Aʿrāb. Beirut: Dār al-Gharb.

Qarāfī, abū al-ʿAbbās Shihāb al-Dīn Aḥmad b. Idrīs b. ʿAbdur-Raḥmān al- (2000). *Juzʾ min Sharḥ Tanqīḥ al-Fuṣūl fi ʿIlm al-Uṣūl*. Ed. Nāṣir b. ʿAli b. Nāṣir al-Ghāmidī. Mecca: Umm al-Qura University.

Qarāfī, abū al-ʿAbbās Shihāb al-Dīn Aḥmad b. Idrīs b. ʿAbdur-Raḥmān al-Mālikī al- (n. d.). *Anwār al-Burūq fī Anwāʾ al-Furūq*. ʿAlām al-Kutub.

Qudūrī, Aḥmad b. Moḥammad b. Ja'far b. Ḥimdān Abū al-Ḥusayn al- (1997). *Mukhtaṣar al-Qaddūrī fī al-Fiqh al-Ḥanafī*. Beirut: Dār al-Kutub al-'Ilmiyya.

Qurṭubī, Abū 'Abdullah Moḥammad b. Aḥmad b. Abī Bakr al- (1964). *Al-Jāmi' li Aḥkām al-Qurān*. Cairo: Dār al-Kutub al-Miṣriyya.

Rāghib, abū al-Qāsim al-Ḥusayn b. Moḥammad al-Asfahānī al- (1992). *Mufradāt al-Qur'ān*. Ed. Ṣafwān 'Adnān al-Dāwūdī. Beirut: Dār al-Qalam al-Shāmiyya.

Ramlī, Shiḥāb al-Dīn Aḥmad b. Aḥmad b. Ḥamza al- (2005). *Ghāyat al-Ma'mūl Sharḥ Warqāt al-Uṣūl*. Ed. 'Uthmān Yūsuf Ḥājjī Aḥmad. Beirut: Al-Risāla.

Rāzī, abū 'Abdullah Muḥammad b. 'Umar b. al-Ḥasan b. al-Ḥusayn al-Taymī al-Rāzī al- (1997). *Al-Maḥṣūl*. Ed. Tāha Jābir al-'Ilwānī. Beirtu: Mu'asasat al-Risāla.

Robert Gleave and Eugenia Kermeli (ed.) (2001). *Islamic Law: Theory and Practice*. London: I.B. Tauris.

Safārīnī, Shams Al-Dīn Abū Al-'Awn Moḥammad b. Aḥmad b. Sālim Al-Safārīnī al- (1982). *Lawāmi' Al-Anwār Al-Bahiyya wa Ṣawāṭi' Al-Asrār Al-Athariyya li Sharḥ Al-Durra Al-Muḍiyya fī 'Aqd Al-Firqa Al-Marḍiyya*. Damascus: Mu'assasat Al-Khāfiqayn.

Sa'īd b. Mansūr, Abū 'Uthmān Sa'īd b. Manṣūr b. Shu'ba Al-Khursānī al-Jawzajānī (1982). *Sunan Sa'īd b. Manṣūr*. India: Al-Dār al-Salafiyya.

Sa'īd ibn Mansūr, Abū 'Uthmān b. Shu'ba al-Khurāsānī (1997). *Tafsīr* Sa'īd b. Manṣūr. Ed. Sa'd b. 'Abdullah b. Ḥumayd. Riyadh: Dār Al-'Uṣaymī.

Salamī, Muḥammad al-Mukhtār (1999). *Al-Qiyās (Analogy) and Its Modern Applications*. Translated by Mohammad Hashim Kamali. Eminent Scholars Series, Vol. 15. Islamic Development Bank: Islamic Research and Training Institute.

Salisbury, Edward E. (1862) "Contributions from Original Sources to our Knowledge of the Sciences of Muslim Tradition." *Journal of the American Oriental Society*, 7.

Samarqandī, Moḥammad b. Aḥmad b. Abī Aḥmad al- (1994). *Tuḥfat al-Fuqahā'*. Beirut: Dār al-Kutub al-'Ilmiyya.

Sarakhasī, Moḥammad b. Aḥmad b. Abī Sahl Sahms Al-A'imma al- (n. d.). *Uṣūl Al-Sarakhsī*. Beirut: Dār al-Ma'rifa.

Sarīrī, abū al-Ṭaiyyb Mawlūd al-Sūsī al- (2012). *Sharḥ Miftāḥ al-Wuṣūl ila Binā' al-Furū' 'ala al-Uṣūl*. Beirtu: Dār al-Kutub al-'Ilmiyya.

Shāfi'ī, Abū 'Abdullah Moḥammad b. Idrīs b. al-'Abbās b. 'Uthmān al- (1940). *Al-Risāla*. Ed. Aḥmad Shākir. Egypt: Al-Ḥalabī.

Shāf'i'ī, abū 'Abdullah Muḥammad b. Idrīs al-Shāfi'ī b. al-'Abbās b. 'Uthmān b. Shāfi' b. 'Abdul-Muṭṭalib b. 'Abd Manāf al-Muṭṭalibī al- (1990). *Al-Umm*. Beiruit: Dār al-Ma'rifa.

Shāf'i'ī, abū 'Abdullah Muḥammad b. Idrīs al-Shāfi'ī b. al-'Abbās b. 'Uthmān b. Shāfi' b. 'Abdul-Muṭṭalib b. 'Abd Manāf al-Muṭṭalibī al- (1940). *Al-Risāla*. Ed. Aḥmad Moḥammad Shākir. Egypt: Maktabat al-Ḥalabī.

Shaltūt, Maḥmūd (2001). *Al-Islām 'Aqīda wa Sharī'a*. Cairo: Dār al-Sharūq.

Sharnablālī, Ḥasan b. 'Ammār b. 'Alī al-Miṣrī al- (2005). *Marāqī al-Falāḥ Sharḥ Matn Nūr al-Īḍāḥ*. Ed. Na'īm Zarzūr. Beirut: Al-Maktabh al-'Aṣriyya.

Shawkānī, Moḥammad b. ʿAlī b. Moḥammad b. ʿAbdullah (1999). *Irshād al-Fuḥūl ilā Taḥqīq al-Ḥaqqi min ʿIlm al-Uṣūl*. Ed. Aḥmad ʿIzzo ʿInāya. Beirut: Dār al-Kitāb al-ʿArabī.

Shawkānī, Moḥammad b. ʿAlī b. Moḥammad b. ʿAbdullah al- (1993). *Nayl al-Awṭār*. Ed. ʿIṣām al-Dīn al-Ṣabābṭī. Egypt: Dār al-Ḥadīth.

Shinqīṭī, Muḥammad al-Amīn al- (2001). *Al-Mudhakirra fi Uṣūl al-Fiqh*, Medina: Maktaabt al-ʿUlūm wa al-Ḥikam.

Shīrāzī, Abū Isḥāq b. Ibrāhīm b. ʿAlī b. Yūsuf (n.d.). *Al-Muhadhdhāb fi Fiqh al-Imām al-Shāfiʿī*. Beirut: Dār al-Kutub al-ʿIlmiyya.

Shīrāzī, abū Isḥāq Ibrāhīm b. ʿAlī b. Yūsuf (1983). *Al-Tabṣira fi Uṣūl al-Fiqh*. Ed. Muḥammad Ḥasan Hītū. Damascus: Dār al-Fikr.

Shīrāzī, Abū Isḥāq Ibrāhīm b. ʿAlī b. Yūsuf (2003). *Sharḥ al-Lumaʿ*. Beirut: Dār al-Kutub al-ʿIlmiyya.

Shirbīnī, Shams al-Dīn Moḥammad b. Aḥmad al-Khaṭīb al-Shirbīnī (1994). *Mughnī al-Muḥtāj ila Maʿrifat Maʿānī al-Minhāj*. Beirut: Dār al-Kutub al-ʿIlmiyya.

Sindī, Muḥammad b. ʿAbdul-Hādī al-Tatawī abū al-Ḥasan Nūr al-Dīn al- (1986). *Ḥāshiyāt al-Sindī ʿalā Sunan al-Nasāʾī*. Aleppo: Maktab al-Maṭbūʿāt al-Islāmiyya.

Smyth, Herbert Weir (1920). *Greek Grammar*. Cambridge MA: Harvard University Press..

Subkī, ʿAlī b. ʿAbdul-Kāfī al- (2003). *Jamʿ al-Jawāmiʿ*. Ed. ʿAbdul-Munʿim Khalīl Ibrāhīm. Beirut: Dār al-Kutub al-ʿIlmiyya.

Subkī, ʿAlī b. ʿAbdul-Kāfī al- (2004). *Ibhāj Sharḥ al-Minhāj*. Ed. Aḥmad Jamāl al-Zamzamī and Nūr al-Dīn ʿAbdul-Jabbār Ṣaghīrī. Saudi Arabia: Dār al-Buḥūth li al-Dirāsāt al-Islāmiyya.

Sulamī, ʿIyāḍ b. Nāmī, *Uṣūl al-Fiqh al-Ladhī lā yasʿu al-Faqīh Jahluh* al- (2005). Riyadh: Dār al-Tadmuriyya.

Ṭabarānī, Sulaymān b. Aḥmad b. Ayyūb b. Muṭayr al-Lakhmī abū al-Qāsim (1994). *Al-Muʿjam Al-Kabīr*. Ed. Ḥamdī b. ʿAbdul-Ḥamīd al-Salafī. Cairo: Maktabat ibn Taymiya.

Ṭabarānī, Sulaymān b. Aḥmad b. Ayyūb b. Muṭayr al-Lakhmī abū al-Qāsim al- (1984). *Musnad al-Shāmiyyīn*. Ed. Ḥamdī ʿAbdul-Majīd al-Salafī. Beirut: Muʾassasat Al-Risāla.

Ṭabarānī, Sulaymān b. Aḥmad b. Ayyūb b. Muṭayr al-Lakhmī abū al-Qāsim al-. *Al-Muʿjam al-Awṣaṭ*. Ed. Ṭāriq ʿAwaḍullah and ʿAbdul-Muḥsin Ibrāhīm. Cairo: Dār al-Ḥaramyn.

Ṭaḥāwī, Abū Jaʿfar Aḥmad b. Moḥammad b. Salāma b. ʿAbdul-Malik b. Salama al-Azdī (1994). *Sharḥ Maʿānī al-Athār*. Ed. Moḥammad Zuhrī al-Najjār and Moḥammad Sayyid Jād al-Ḥaqq. Caior: ʿAlam al-Kutub.

Ṭaḥāwī, Abū Jaʿfar Aḥmad b. Moḥammad b. Salāma b. ʿAbdul-Malik b. Salama al-Azdī (n.d.). *Mukhtaṣar al-Ṭaḥāwī*. Ed. Abū al-Wafa al-Afghānī. India: Lajnat Iḥiyāʾ al-Maʿārif al-Nuʿmāniyya.

Ṭaḥāwī, Abū Jaʿfar Aḥmad b. Moḥammad b. Salāma b. ʿAbdul-Malik b. Salama al-Azdī (1994). *Sharḥ Mushkil al-Athār*. Ed. Shuʿayb al-Arnāʾūṭ. Beirut: Muʾassasat al-Risāla

Tilmisānī, al-Sharīf abū ʿAbdullah Muḥammad b. Aḥmad al-Ḥasanī al-Tilmisānī al- (2013). *Miftāḥ al-Wuṣūl ila Bināʾ al-Furūʿ ʿala al-Uṣūl*. Ed. Abū ʿAbdul-Muʿiz Muḥammad ʿAlī Farkūs. Algeria: Dār al-Mawqiʿ and Dār al-ʿAwāṣim.

Tirmidhī, Muḥammad b. ʿĪsā b. Sawra b. Mūsā b. al-Ḍaḥḥāk al- (1998). *Al-Sunan*. Ed. Bahshār ʿAwwād. Beirut: Dā al-Gharb al-Islāmī.

Tunbaktī, Aḥmad Baba b. Aḥmad b. al-Faqīh al-Ḥajj b. ʿUmar b. Moḥammad (2000). *Nayl al-Ibtihāj bi Taṭrīz al-Dībāj*. Ed. ʿAbdul-Ḥamīd ʿAbdullah al-Harāma. Lybia: Dār al-Kitāb.

Wanshrīsī, Aḥmad b. Yaḥya al- (1981). *Al-Miʿiyār al-Muʿrib wa al-Jāmiʿ al-Mughrib ʿan Fatāwa ʿUlmāʾ Ifriqiyya wa al-Andalus wa al-Maghrib*. Ed. Moḥammad Ḥijji *et al.* Beirut: Dār al-Gharb al-Islāmī.

Zabīdī, Muḥammad b. Muḥammad b. ʿAbdur-Razzāq al-Ḥusaynī al- (n.d.). *Tāj al-ʿArūs min Jawāhir al-Qāmūs*. Dār al-Hidāya.

Zarkashī, Abū ʿAbdullah Badr al-Dīn Moḥammad b. ʿAbdullah b. Bahadir al- (1994). *Al-Baḥr Al-Muḥīṭ fī Uṣūl al-Fiqh*. Cairo: Dār Al-Katbī.

Zaylaʿī, Jamāl al-Dīn Abū Moḥammad ʿAbdullah b. Yūsuf b. Moḥammad al- (1997). *Naṣb Al-Rāya li Aḥādīth al-Hidāya*. Ed. Moḥammad Yūsuf al-Banūrī. Ed. Moḥammad ʿAwwāma. Beirut: Moʾassasat Al-Rāya.

Zinjānī, Maḥmūd b. Aḥmad b. Maḥmūd b. Bikhtiyār abū al-Manāqib Shihāb al-Dīn al- (1398). *Takhrīj al-Furūʿ ʿla al-Uṣūl*. Ed. Muḥammad Adīb Ṣāliḥ. Beirut: Al-Risāla.

Index

D

E

F

G

H

I

J

K

L

M

N

O

P

P

Q

R

S

T

U

V

W

Y

Z